WHERE THE WAGON LED

A cowboy's saddle

WHERE THE WAGON LED

*One Man's Memories of
the Cowboy's Life in
the Old West*

R. D. SYMONS

FIFTH
HOUSE
PUBLISHERS

Front cover photograph courtesy Glenbow Archives/NA–1508–5
Cover design by John Luckhurst/GDL
Series and logo design by Sandra Hastie/GDL

The publisher gratefully acknowledges the support received from
The Canada Council and the Department of Canadian Heritage.

Printed in Canada by Best Book Manufacturers
97 98 99 00 01 / 5 4 3 2 1

CANADIAN CATALOGUING IN PUBLICATION DATA
Symons, R.D. (Robert David), 1898–1973

Where the wagon led
2nd ed. —

(Western Canadian classics)
ISBN 1–895618–84–3

1. Symons, R.D. (Robert David), 1898–1973.
2. Cowboys – Prairie Provinces – Biography.
3. Cowboys – West (U.S.) – Biography. 4. Ranch
life – Prairie Provinces. 5. Ranch life – West (U.S.)
I. Title. II. Series.

FC3239.C68S95 1997   971.2'02'092   C97–920002–4
F596.S95 1997

FIFTH HOUSE LTD.
#9 – 6125 – 11th Street SE
Calgary AB Canada T2H 2L6

To the horses and men of the range.
May they never be parted.

ACKNOWLEDGMENTS

I wish to give thanks to the memory of the late Mr. Alexander ("Scotty") Gow of Grayburn, Alberta, a good boss, a loyal friend, and a fine gentleman who taught me so much of men, horses, and ranching. And since this book was written under difficulties and proofread in a hospital, I wish to thank the staff of the Grey Nun's Hospital in Regina; Dr. Jack Bailey of the Cancer Clinic, whose gruff manner covers such a wealth of skill and understanding; Mr. Cliff Blight who gave me hospitality in convalescence; Mr. Cooper Coles who reminded me of certain events of the '30s; Dr. Jack McClinton of the Health of Animals Branch of the Saskatchewan Department of Agriculture who checked my notes on horse disease epidemics; the Fort Worth (Texas) *Cattleman* and the Saskatchewan *Centennial Magazine* (1967) who first published the accounts of the "die-off" of 1906-7; Messrs. Riley and McCormick of Calgary who checked my references on early saddling; Señor E. Esquirios of the Mexican Cattlemen's Association; Mrs. Beth Favel who typed the manuscript; Mr. Terry Fenton of the Mackenzie Art Gallery of Regina who helped choose the illustrations; the Rev. D. Apivor, chaplain who kept me in spiritual health; my wife, Hope, daughter of a British horseman, whose ministrations and understanding helped so much; and, finally, my publishers, especially Mr. Douglas Gibson, editor, and his staff, who spared no effort on behalf of the book.

To all these my thanks, and to the many forgotten, my apologies.

R. D. Symons
Silton, Saskatchewan
August 27, 1971

CONTENTS

THE CODE OF THE RANGE

(1) Be independent, but always ready to help your neighbor.

(2) Ask nothing of the government boys, or you'll find yourself in the rat race.

(3) Feed the stranger and his hoss; and ask no questions.

(4) Say little, talk soft, and keep your eyes skinned.

(5) Don't argue with the wagon boss. If he's wrong, he'll find out.

(6) Don't stare at the brand on a stranger's hoss. But make a note.

(7) Deal with the other fellow's stock as you would your own. Feed the stray, help the bogged. He's doing the same for you.

(8) If paper and pen aren't handy, back up your word as you would your signature.

(9) Don't stick a plow in the land. It's catching.

(10) Women come in two breeds; the ones like your mother, and the one behind the lace curtains. And you don't talk about neither kind.

Dragging out the bogged

FOREWORD

To begin reading R.D. Symons more than two decades after his death is to face questions about how we in western Canada regard our nonfiction writers. *Why have I never heard anyone mention this writer? Why is it that I know the literature of distant writer-naturalists from Massachusetts, California, or Ontario, but have never encountered the wisdom of a man who wrote eight books about his life in nature amidst the plains, forests, and valleys of western Canada?* Bob Symons would have had answers to such questions. Like all naturalist-malcontents, from H.D. Thoreau to Edward Abbey, he did not hesitate to respond to the questions of his day. Anyone who reads this book, then sets out to find Symons's other works, will discover his thinking on everything from modern education to supermarket food. Symons's voice, a cowboy prophet's cry in the erstwhile prairie wilderness, can be inspiring one moment and exasperating the next, but it remains a voice to be reckoned with.

Among the reasons R.D. Symons's work deserves more attention within the gallery of western Canadian literature is its rooted-in-the-landscape legitimacy as a source of social critique. By condemning the private greed and public arrogance that continue to undermine the cultural and ecological health of the northern Great Plains, Symons helps us to see that the "good" in the good old days did not disappear suddenly or simply, or without the participation of the pioneers themselves. To be sure, a book such as *Where the Wagon Led* would have initially appealed as a compendium of horse and cowboy stories. What sets it apart from the literature of settler nostalgia, however, is its consistent and radical assertion that most of the prairie should never have been ploughed, that the Homestead Act set the stage for the environmental and social trauma we see today in western Canada's farm country.

Where the Wagon Led is more than an indictment of the way this land was settled; it is an eloquent lament for the passing of the prairie's horse-powered economy. From the opening narrative depicting the disastrous winter of 1906–07 to the epilogue denouncing today's motorized farms, Symons speaks of the grace, wisdom, and satisfaction that can be a part of working with horses. Now that Wendell Berry and other critics of modern agriculture have taken the bold step of calling for a return to draft animals as part of the resettlement and renewal of rural North America, Symons's insights are more valuable than ever.

Still, it is the characters, not the social protest, that stay with you after reading *Where the Wagon Led*. Characters such as the saddle tramp who has to range his fifty mares on railway easements and scraps of unfenced land, and who is found frozen in his bedroll one November morning. Characters in good prairie stories set in places familiar to prairie people: Medicine Lodge Coulee, Old-Man-on-His-Back, Blackstrap Lake, Eagle Hills. Between the covers of this book you will come across tipi rings, buffalo-rubbing stones, Chinook winds, cactuses, juniper, meadowlarks, bunkhouses, ornery steers, and ferocious snowstorms. Some stories describe the transition from open-range cattle ranching to homesteads and barbed-wire fences; others show the life of a greenhorn; many tell of the intelligence and quiet dignity of horses, or rangy brood mares that know the country better than any cowboy, of faithful saddle ponies that herd cattle with gentle nudges and spurn the oat pail, of day-old foals swimming Battle Creek at spring flood.

The man who wrote these stories enjoyed telling who he was, and so included several brief autobiographies in his books. From his desk at Meadowlark Cottage, overlooking Last Mountain Lake, a sixty-seven-year-old Symons wrote these opening lines to *Silton Seasons*, recalling a life as varied as the landscape he had lived in: "I am a countryman, descended from many centuries of Cornish countrymen. All my life has been spent in the country, at country pursuits."

Robert David Symons was born in 1898 in rural Sussex, the seventh son of an artist and illustrator, William Christian Symons, and a composer, Cecilia Davenport Symons. Schooled at home by their parents, the Symons children grew up in a modest but lively household, where everyone learned to draw and paint, to appreciate music and literature, and to understand and apply ethics, horticulture, and natural history as a part of everyday life and chores. According to the introduction to *Many Trails*, in which Symons describes his father and childhood with great affection, he spent much of his early years either painting birds in a corner of his father's studio or roaming the Sussex countryside in the company of gamekeepers, shepherds, and poachers.

When Symons was twelve, he met an English naturalist who had returned to England for a visit after emigrating and setting up a homestead near Lloydminster. This man showed Symons several bird specimens he had collected in the Saskatchewan country. These study skins, as well as several books, including W.F. Butler's *The Great Lone Land* and R.M. Ballantyne's *The Young Fur Traders*, fired Symons's imagination with dreams of adventure in a wilder land, leading four years later to his arrival at Maple Creek.

From 1914 to 1960, Symons made his living as a cowboy, game guardian, and rancher. During this period, he chased the receding prairie frontier from the Cypress Hills to the Eagle Hills near North Battleford, then to the secluded river valleys of Fort St. John, British Columbia. Along the way, he picked up the open-range cowboy's disdain for the homesteader's plough and anything else—barbed wire, tractors, bureaucracy—that threatened the integrity of the prairie world. He also acquired an admiration for the Métis and First Nations of the northern Plains, and learned enough Cree and Saulteaux to get by when visiting friends on the reserves. Perhaps most remarkable, at least to those who knew Symons personally, was his intimate and detailed knowledge of Saskatchewan landscapes. There are Regina naturalists who remember well Symons's uncanny ability to look at photographs of undistinguished landscapes and identify precisely where the photographer had stood to take each picture.

Symons's early cowboy years in the Cypress Hills were interrupted by service overseas in the First World War. He returned to Canada after the war, living briefly in BC's Chilcotin country, then in the Arm River Valley, north of Davidson, Saskatchewan, where he began a small cattle operation in the 1920s. When the homesteaders and Herd Law moved in, Symons took a job as a game guardian with the department of Natural Resources, working for over a decade in Saskatchewan's parkland and boreal forest. In 1939, he transferred to his beloved Cypress Hills, where he policed the fescue range on horseback for three years. In 1942, he left for the wilder country northwest of Fort St. John, BC, finally settling at the age of forty-seven with his wife, Hope, on a remote stump ranch in the Peace River country, where he believed he would be shed of mechanized humankind.

During the winters of the 1950s, Symons came to Regina to paint large mural backgrounds for the new Saskatchewan Museum of Natural History. By 1960, his health was failing and the oil industry was gaining inroads into his valley in northern BC, so he and Hope decided to retire to a small cottage at Pelican Point overlooking Last Mountain Lake, near Regina. From this tiny studio at the end of the road, Symons wrote seven books, two of which became Book-of-the-Month-Club selections. Eventually, as Symons's health worsened, he and Hope moved into a small house in the nearby village of Silton, where he continued to write. On 1 February 1973, R.D. Symons died after a long and painful struggle with cancer.

Artist, writer, naturalist, cowboy, rancher, game guardian—Symons tried his hand at any wholesome task that allowed him space within the wild country of his affections and kept him in touch with the honest rural people who shared his regard for the prairie and its creatures. Despite his many careers and apparent restlessness, though, R.D. Symons was never a dilettante. He did not research the lives he wrote about. He never set out to live as a cowboy or a game guardian for a year with an eye to gathering material for his imagination or his writing. When Symons finally sat down and wrote his books, he was reflecting on five decades of living and working in Canada's West: fifty years that paralleled the transition from horse-powered frontier to the machine-powered resource extraction we call agribusiness.

Within the tradition of writing about prairie landscapes and history, R.D. Symons helps us bridge elements that, without his kind of testimony, we could only link in theory. His tales span the divisions we have created between memoir and fiction, history and story. Symons shared tobacco and campfires with the real characters our novelists write about—people such as Rusty or Spurlock in Wallace Stegner's "Genesis," or Shorty McAdoo in Guy Vanderhaeghe's *The Englishman's Boy*. The remittance men, soldiers, wolfers, saddle tramps, ranch bosses, and stud grooms of *Where the Wagon Led* hover in that nether region between fiction and nonfiction because, while Symons has called them up from memory, they have not made it to the page unembellished by the storyteller's craft.

In the uncompromising ethics he applies to every question of human agency in the world, Symons is also a bridge between the common person and the lofty aspirations and egocentricity of North American naturalist-philosophers. In this sense, Symons was not "like" Thoreau; he was Thoreau in application. (Symons knew and quoted Thoreau's writing but would have had little patience for the New England writer's self-absorbed ways.) On the other hand, while he has much in common with American conservationist Aldo Leopold, it is Symons's life and convictions rather than the depth of his philosophizing that sustains the parallel.

In other ways, Symons is comparable to Grey Owl (Archie Belaney) or Ernest Thompson Seton. Like these two writer-naturalists who spent time in Saskatchewan, Symons came to the West as an English boy inspired by the romance literature of the frontier, and later wrote books expressing devotion and respect for its natural world and first peoples. Thrown off balance by the sheer weight of their own immodesty, however, both Grey Owl and Seton faltered from time to time as they walked this line between the factual truth and the philosophical truth of their "true" nature stories. Although Symons walked this line as well, and cultivated something of a persona for himself as the last-of-a-dying-breed cowboy, he never allowed his ego to usurp his stories and the messages they conveyed.

Therefore, while Symons lends his voice to the literary tradition that has long called for ecological sanity, it is his honesty and authenticity as a rural man that finally bears his words into our hearts. When he speaks of the tragedy of rural life, of how oil and mechanization turned "the farm into the firm"; when he rails against the "modern Babylon . . . where football and beer took the place of the meadowlark's whistle, and potato chips replace the crusty farm loaf"; when he laments the passing of the horse-powered culture and the accompanying exodus of a once landed and self-reliant people into cities where they become landless labourers; when he puts forward each of these tenets within his critique of modernity, we are compelled to listen because his thoughts carry the conviction of fifty years in the country.

It is this legitimacy that allows Symons to create some much-needed common ground between, for example, urban activists promoting prairie conservation and the rural people who live and work in prairie landscapes every day. And it provides, as well, a connection to more recent western

Canadian writing about ecology, culture, and place. While Symons may not be the father of this literature, which has in some regards been fostered by more distant relatives, he is certainly an unacknowledged kinsman—a local elder all but forgotten, but worth getting to know. This second edition of *Where the Wagon Led* introduces the voice of this important prairie writer-naturalist to a new generation of readers, in a time when it has become easy to dismiss the experience and vision of our own forebears.

With R.D. Symons on our side, the conversation we have been holding with the hills, plains, and coulees of this region regains some of the integrity and vigour it needs. In his moral and unwavering testimony, there is hope that we might yet come to dwell wisely in this sometimes fair, sometimes forbidding, land.

TREVOR HERRIOT

INTRODUCTION

No hour of the life is lost that is spent
in the saddle. (*Sir Winston Churchill*)

A good man and a good horse are a working team in which loyalty,
forbearance, trust, and affection all work together for good; be that
man or horse of any color.

I think of working cowboys and broke cow-horses as I have known
them. And I know, too, that to separate a good man from a good horse
of his breaking is like parting man and wife.

I myself have known horses—and horsemen—since I was a child. As
a boy I studied skeletons in Cassells' *Natural History,* and could give
the Latin names for the bones common to men and horses. But it was
on the plains of the Canadian west that I learned the cowboy's names,
and could speak of pinbones and stifles and croups; as well as of such
ills as swamp fever and what the vets call equine encephalomyelitis—
(but we call it sleeping sickness) for I saw the 1919 plague of the first
and the scourge of the second in the '30s, just as I saw the 1918–19
"flu" which took so many horsemen and for which the only help was
brandy.

I have broken horses, I have flayed them, disarticulated them,
branded them, and unsexed them. The smell of them is in my mind
like a nostalgic memory.

There are as many and varied opinions of the worth of a horse
according to its color, as there are opinions as regard color and race
in humans. But as with men, so with horses, and I can only say that
a bad horse is made, not foaled. Careless handling, lack of proper
discipline, lessons too prolonged, and above all, brutal treatment have
spoiled many a man and animal. A man who cannot put a snub on
his temper had better leave horses alone.

It is in such areas as the high plains of the Canadian west that these

things are plainly seen, for men's actions are not shrouded by ano-
nymity or by drawn curtains.

In the chapters to follow I shall tell something of the lives of men
and horses from sixty years ago to the present, as well as of my own
introduction to those scented plains which roll south from the Saskatchewan River to the breaks of the Missouri; where the buttes squat
ice-blue in the distance. Where the creeks may be six or sixty feet wide,
as the whim of the storm godlings direct. Where the air is clean, the
earth new-born, the sky like the gate of heaven. Where the heart of
man rides high, and his horse is his best friend.

Here my heart and hand have been bound for almost a lifetime.
Here live my friends of many years. And here the vague shadows of
horses of many colors run and buck and play as we talk,

> There ain't a hoss that can't be rode,
> Nor there ain't a man that can't be throwed
> (Old range saying)

WHERE THE WAGON LED

When I was young my pride was centred 'round about a horse and gear,
Buckskin, pinto, dapple-gray,
Or fiddleheaded short-backed bay—
No matter, so he held his feet a-roping of a dogie steer.

When I was young I cared not for the desk or pen—I had a horse
To ride among the cattle red
To follow where the wagon led,
Beyond the tawny uplands where the buckbrush shone like gorse.

To ride 'til night, and sleep, and ride again another day,
Where the gumbo roses growed,
Where the sweet crick waters flowed,
Across the leagues of sage-gray plains to the blue horizons far away.

If I were young once more I know I'd choose to ride again,
To hear the creak of saddle leather,
To smell the cattle all together,
Branding fug and campfire smoke, greasewood—and a wagon in the rain.

I'm chair bound now . . . But memory leaps, spooky as a spotted fawn,
An outlaw breeze from Cypress Gap
A sprig of sage or winter fat
Turns back the years. Again I ride the wind-swept range to meet the dawn.

R.D.S.

PROLOGUE

A lone cowhand

A lone cowhand checked his pony in the shelter of a hill and looked to the northwest. The sky was overcast, the wind chilly, flattening the yellowed grass and the gray sage.

On the northwest horizon a faint gleam of duck-egg green showed momentarily, then the clouds shut down, and snow began to fall.

It was November the fifth in the year 1906.

The place was the wide prairie of Southwest Saskatchewan.

"Blizzard comin'," the man said, half aloud, and taking his neckerchief tied his battered Stetson down over his ears.

xviiiWHERE THE WAGON LED

"Come on, hoss," he said, and touched spur to flank.

Long before he pulled into the shelter of the 76 line camp darkness had fallen and the snow had turned sharp and brittle, stinging the back of his neck.

The cowboy felt little concern. He had been out in many such storms and knew that "Bunco," his pinto pony, would take him to safety. Shucks—just a little ole early flurry. Freeze-up wasn't due yet. This skiff would go, and there'd be open weather again.

What he did not know was that this skiff would stay; that it was the first breath of a "die-up" winter that would gradually alter the concept of cattle ranching on the Canadian ranges. Sure, the short-grass plains—the high plains—had seen the "Blue Northers" before. Any of the older cattlemen could talk for hours of the "die-up" of 1886— cattlemen from the States especially. Not that the infant cattle industry of Canada hadn't suffered, too—the big outfits the worst—the Quorn, the Cochrane, to name a couple only.

Nothing that has been said or written of '86 could give the picture as well as young Charlie Russell's famous drawing of the bonerack steer, standing with its tail frozen off, "Waiting for the chinook" while the lobos, too, waited to get their teeth into "The Last of 5,000."

But the cattle business had recovered, as it had recovered from the years of low prices, rustlers, "sheeping off," and (in the States) the hated Kincaid Act which gave a new impulse to settlement by farmers.

It had recovered because the bankers, too, had faith in the sacred cow. It would not recover so well from the overstocked, overgrazed conditions of the Wyoming and Montana ranges.

So more and more herds were pushed north to Canada, where miles of good grass still lay unclaimed, the lines of marching cattle nosing aside for any scraps of grass left by the herds of yesterday, grass soured by trampling. But "on to Canada" was the cry. Once you got the stock on those cool northern prairies, you had it made. "Push them, boys," they said, and horn clicked horn in the dry Montana dust, as they headed for the new Eldorado where a bag of bones would soon be a twelve-hundred-pound steer.

In this way had come seven-thousand head carrying Moreton Frewen's 76 brand from Powder River, Wyoming, across the Missouri breaks and up to Canada. But Frewen was finished, as the Cheyenne

Club was finished. His new company didn't back him, and the cattle were purchased after their arrival by Sir John Lister Kaye, to form the nucleus of The Canada Land and Ranch Company herds. Finally the 76 cattle were purchased in 1906 by Gordon, Ironside and Fares of the Canada Stock and Cattle Company with ranch headquarters at Crane Lake, Saskatchewan, and half an empire under lease.

I knew Frewen back in England when I was a boy, and I have heard him tell of the winter of '86–87. Even as late as 1963 I found that his memory was fresh in the mind of the Cheyenne folks.

Many more outfits followed the 76—the Circle Diamond, the Turkey Track, the Matador with the Flying U—and men from the Old Country and the East, too; for the free-grass bonanza was a siren whose dulcet voice charmed the ears of investors in Glasgow and London and Ontario—men who would never themselves know a "Blue Norther," would never hear the whine of a blizzard, never push a tired horse through a five-foot snowdrift, never see cattle frozen to death on their feet.

So the trains came in from Manitoba to unload the scraggy barnyard "dogies" on the brittle, unfenced prairies where they could wander at will. They would fatten on the grama grass and perhaps meet and stare at the native stock. But later they would mingle with those rawboned, long-horned steers that had coughed in the alkali dust as they flinched from the rawhide ropes of the Circle Diamond Texans who had nagged them on, pushing them ever north from the Canadian River of Texas to the Canadian range.

By 1906 the North West Territories Brand Book looked like a page of heraldic devices. Old brands from the United States took on a new lease of life—Uncle Tony Day's Turkey Track, the Bloom Cattle Company's T Down, to name two—while new brands filled many pages cheek by jowl with the older timers. There was Gilchrist's N 4, Armstrong's I D, Douglas's Bar B, Treffle Bonneau's 2 L Bar, Conrad Price's F G monogram. Many identified the owners at once and more personally. Robert Pollock's looked like a poleax, Bottleley's had a bottle followed by E, Broadfoot's looked like a grizzly bear's track, and Fysh Brothers of Moose Jaw branded a fish head on the left ribs of their bawling calves. There were hundreds more, and these knights of the range, as they pressed their irons on the fat and sassy spring crop of

1906 calling the brands crisply to the tallymen, little knew that within
six to eight months, they would throw those tally books away.

2

The summer of 1906 saw the Canadian short-grass ranges stocked
to capacity. It was a wet summer and the grass made a green carpet
from Moose Jaw Creek to the Milk River. Even the sheepmen were
forgiven that year, for the grass sprang up behind the cropping bands
as if the prairies were a watered lawn.

The creeks were full, and the sloughs and potholes noisy with
waterfowl.

True, the trails were soft, and the roundup crews cursed the soggy
ground when the spread their damp tarps. Chuck wagons got bogged
in some of the creek crossings, and as they groaned and the horses
strained, the cowboys had to snub their ropes to the wagon poles to
help. But the cowmen were happy. Grass was what they lived by, grass
which they put into beef that could walk to market on four legs. Nothing
mattered but grass, and the Texans who had trailed into neighboring
Alberta forbade their women folk to cultivate a garden. "This is grass-
country," they said. "You plant a garden and someone'll see it an'
we'll have nesters. Let the farmers by the railway grow the garden-sass
an' the hogs—sure, one steer'll buy what we need for winter." And
they'd mount and ride across the swelling grasslands to see the steers
"larding-up," and they'd turn their cuds, too, in time with the beasts'
jaws. Only the haying crews really cursed the rain. They worked by
the day, so no work, no pay. Not that much hay was put up by today's
standards—not that (in a normal year) there was much to put up,
anyway.

But the lesson of '87 had been partly learned. Big George Lane of
the Bar U, over west in the foothills, McMullen of the C.P. R. Livestock
Branch, A. E. Cross, and Pat Burns had all said: "Best put up plenty
hay, boys, we've seen what she can do!" The short-grass ranchers said,
"Shucks! These aren't the foothills. The chinook is bound to come
a-rarin', and anyways the wind'll sweep the sidehills bare." They
weren't going to run no cow-hospital! Enough hay to feed the

weanling calves, that made sense, because that would give the cows a chance to lard-up before the real cold of January. And some for the bulls and the saddle stock—not that there wouldn't be plenty feed on the range, but the herd sires and the men's mounts had to be corralled or stabled anyway.

"You let a bull run all year and you'll just naturally have calves mixed with snowballs," they said. "And anyways them bulls—big Herefords and such—cost foldin' money, and the more sassy they are by turn-out time the better."

As for she-stuff and steers, what was a little snow and wind to them? At best they'd have plenty grass to rustle. At worst they'd have salt-sage and winter fat; if things got really bad they'd drift into the brush-breaks or the Cypress Hills and could wait her out with a belly full of brouse. So the hay crews sweated it out to put up the minimum requirements. Some of the hay was stacked too damp—"tough" they called it—and turned musty; some of it was left in big "coils" to be hauled later—they reckoned.

It didn't, as it turned out, make much odds. Even the best quality hay isn't worth a damn when the deep snow and drifted hollows won't allow a team and hayrack within a mile!

But the cow country faced the future with high hopes that fall. Those range yearlings and two-year-olds, no less than those off-colored dogies only had to keep their cud-cheeks full for another year—mebbe two—and Pat Burns would pay "cash on the hoof" to keep his beef contracts with the railroad companies. Not that the ranchers wanted any iron roads in *their* domain. The C.P.R. main line, anything up to a hundred miles away, was plenty close enough—or they could ship on the Great Northern in Montana.

3

The puff from the northwest that sent the 76 cowboy loping into camp was nothing to what followed. On November 11, the wind shrieked again. This time the blizzard lasted three days and the thermometer hit the below-zero mark—and kept going. When it blew itself out the range was deep in snow. Cattle- the luckier ones—had drifted into the Cypress Hills; others had gone into the valley of Frenchman River—the Whitemud, as the ranchers called it. But the riders, weary from the saddle, shucking off their sheepskin coats and woolly chaps in the warmth of the bunkhouses, could still laugh and chaff. The chinook would come, they said, looking at the inscrutable skies.

But the chinook didn't come. It was held back west of the mountains, and now storm followed storm. The cattle were plunging knee-deep, their muzzles snow-wreathed to their eyelashes, their legs weary. Riding became limited to a few hard-won miles. Even fed saddle horses couldn't go on, plug-plug, all day. Fetlocks began to bleed and the gaunted ponies began to leave red tracks.

"Uncle" Tony Day, who'd brought the Turkey Track outfit up from Dakota, was beginning to think that maybe the homesteaders he'd left behind weren't the only enemy he and his fifteen-thousand cattle would ever face. He was an old-timer—one of the cow-hospital haters, and he didn't wean his calves—"Range weanin'," he'd say—"nature's way is good enough."

O Mama

North, across the South Saskatchewan, the boys of the Matador—the Flying U—told of what they'd seen in the sand hills. Antelope drifting into the breaks—perhaps across the river. Cattle dying. Too many wolf tracks. Perhaps those "loafers" smelled something in the frosty air—something the little pronghorns knew about, that they'd shared with the buffalo. But the hump-backed Indian cattle had already fallen prey to a worse enemy than Old Keewadin.

The T Down wolfer, Jack Brown, saw the wolf-sign, too; saw it as he squinted across the white glare of the high plains, his weathered and whiskered face crinkled into a thousand lines. No chance for his hounds here; they'd soon play out. No chance to make a circle with his poison bait either. In this weather, that would be sowing a harvest he couldn't reap. He spat and turned back to the bunkhouse. The boys dropped their dog-eared books, their out-of-date papers, and their "Hambly Saddle Catalogues," as above the lash of the wind those mournful wolf howls told them that another critter had given up the fight out there in the cold and dark.

The boys looked at each other. One ran his mouth organ softly across his lips, another stoked the stove noisily, still another reached for the thumbmarked pack of cards at his bunk-head. "Laugh Kills Lonesome" said the print tacked on the log wall—it was Charlie Russell who had said that, for sure—yes, and he'd painted the picture. *He* knew!

Well, Harry Otterson, the T Down foreman had said, "We'll make 'er till March. They's enough hay at Stone Pile for the bulls and calves." *He* knew, too. This outfit—the Bloom Cattle Company—were running ten-thousand head, but on a big range. But a lot of 76 cattle and stock from the smaller ranches had drifted onto their range, and these extras sorely taxed the resources of the brush coulees and other sheltered spots. And March was a long way off.

Christmas dinner on the far-flung ranches of Southwest Saskatchewan was the best the owners could provide. But many a cowboy as he sucked on a drumstick or heaped his tin plate with pudding could not keep his thoughts from the critters who wandered and plunged aimlessly in the white fury that was beating them down, blinding their eyes with ice, and stripping their ribs to washboards till they could only stand and dully watch their companions go down.

Tom Carr, at the Forks of the Red Deer, could not sleep nights for the click of cattle hooves which rang like castanets above their bawling as they tramped round and round his barnyard, keeping the snow packed, probably thinking they were going some place where they could eat. They did go some place, into the ground in time, starved to death. And Tom had to vacate his premises when the hot weather came at last, for that stench of death was more than any man could put up with.

New Year's Day of 1907 was cold, real cold, with the thermometer at sixty below zero. Harry Otterson remembered how, on January 10, it took him fifteen hours to ride thirty miles to Stone Pile. He wrote: "I noticed a few dead ones all the way. The boys at Stone Pile . . . were riding all the time, picking up the weakest cattle and trying to get them to the ranch, probing the coulees looking for bunches that were snowed in."

And so it went, riders coming and riders going, tramping the snow with their saddle horses to make a way out for drift-bound cattle which would mostly die by spring anyway. But cowboys aren't spawned by accident. They are born that way. Men who love freedom, who stand up to a challenge, who love nature and animals and wind-swept places. Not for them the ease of the armchair, the boredom of the office. They worked from an inner compulsion and even if, like the Matador boys, they did not personally know the owners of their spread, they were loyal to "the outfit," to the range boss, to each other, and to the sacred cows that had walked by the side of man since the dawn of history.

Theirs was not "unskilled labor"; theirs was a craft that Jacob knew, that the Scottish beef breeders understood, that had come to America with the Spanish language; theirs was a freemasonry of dedication that still operates from the Chihuahua Desert north to the Peace River. Not one of these men, despite the grumbling around the bunkhouse stove, would have chosen to be elsewhere during the bitter months of that epic winter.

4

Toward the end of February 1907, a rooster crowed loud and clear in the pale dawn, to be followed by another, and another, and the cowboys, choring in the barn, felt a change of air. One of them looked out the barn door to the west and—"Chinook!" he shouted, throwing high his greasy rat-skin cap. Sure enough, an arch hung in the west.

Far out on the range a cow bawled. A coyote, belly-deep in the drifts, raised its sharp muzzle and pricked its frozen ears. From behind the weathered pole corral, in the willows, a grouse clucked and was answered by another. The smell of the barn hung strong on the air.

"A chinook!" The boys crowded outside and stared, turning a cheek to the soft wind. One of them spat his tobacco juice against the barn door and as they watched, wide-eyed, the mahogany liquid flowed slowly, unfreezing, down the warped boards.

The short-lived hope died almost as soon as it was born. That night the wind switched to the north again and the snow froze to steel. The cattle cut their feet and couldn't move. The rich grass below was now really sealed in, and only the top of scraggy sage and creek-side willows were left to gnaw on. Now the range horses began to suffer, too, although they were of sterner stuff than cattle. While the snow was loose they could paw down fairly easily to feed on the grass beneath and keep their flesh. But now they had to work harder to break the icy crust, and some began to fail.

Many a small bunch of cattle owed their lives to the horses. Led by some cranky old cow, the critters would fall in behind the broncs, and the ponies had to work double time, for as soon as one opened up a patch of grass, the old cow would hook it away, and the cattle would jostle and crowd for half a mouthful apiece.

The ranchers—some of them—took their cue from this and built big snowplows to which they hitched team after team of horses; but the beasts plunged and flinched, the snow was too deep, and they had to be unhitched, leaving the plows to be buried under the drifts till spring. I remember one old plow slowly rotting just south of Battle Creek on the Badger ranch, a grim reminder of 1907.

March came at last. A few mild days offered relief, and again the riders belted on their heavy chaps, shrugged themselves into their canvas-covered sheepskins, and rode their circles.

They found a few cattle alive, they tailed some up, but it was heartbreaking work, and their saddle Winchesters could be heard barking in the draws as the worst cases were put out of further suffering.

Then, again, the storms broke.

By now everything that a cow could eat was gone; old musty hay and sticks from the shed roofs, cleanings from the horse mangers, buckbrush, and moldy lumps of chaff. Some of the smaller ranchers in the hills cut brush, poplar, and willow, anything, but now it was too little and too late. A pile of manure hauled from the barn would be eaten up like alfalfa by any range cattle that came to it. They'd even learn to wait at the dumping ground. Curiously, some of these lived!

Those ranchers who still had some hay stocked on the prairie couldn't get at it. It might as well have been in China.

Over in Alberta a rancher took off one mitt to claw the ice from his eyelashes. The mitt slipped from his lap into the snow, and before he could dismount to retrieve it a cow had seized and eaten it—a serious business at thirty-five below!

Only the Indians allowed the ghost of a smile to run across their saddle-colored faces. They had beef again. It was lean, but it was beef. Meat from dead animals filled their stew pots, and perhaps it was the Manito, they said in soft Cree, the Manito who was punishing the white men for what they had done to the Manito's cattle, the hump-backed buffalo which had been made for the high plains.

And the wolves: *they* fattened! So did the coyotes, and the little kit foxes that slipped among the drifts like wraiths, those that hadn't succumbed to wolfer Brown's poison the year before, for they are less suspecting than the gray lobos. Eagles gorged, for "where the carcass is, the eagles will gather," and the robed and sandaled man who wrote that didn't mean vultures either, for eagles, too, are carrion lovers.

April came, and the storms began to let up, for the sun had long passed across the equator, and slowly the cold moderated and the snow settled, gradually thawing in the shallower, wind-swept spots.

Now the riders could begin to get about and assess the damage: here a bunch of cattle, legs still encased in ice, staring with white frozen eyeballs, all dead on their feet. Here a horn, here a foreleg, sticking out of a drift. Looking more closely the cowboys could see where the wolves had worked through the snow and eaten into the carass till it was a mere shell. Yet, by a merciful Providence, here also was the odd steer grazing unconcernedly on a patch of soggy, thawed-off grass; or perhaps a heifer proudly nuzzling a new born calf, a heifer who, despite her frozen ears and shortened tail made quick, angry charges on her wobbly legs, warning off the intruding riders. And the cowboys' stern, angry faces relaxed, and they laughed and said, "Sho', now, old girl, we don't aim to hurt your baby!" and they laughed as they rode on; for it was, after all, spring, and laugh kills lonesome.

And the men of the lariat soon became men of the skinning knife, flaying the dead for the few dollars that the hides would contribute to their winter wages. They had to skin the upper side as the beasts thawed, then turn them over to thaw and skin the underside.

5

In May, the "Big Smell" came.

Scotty Gow, the rancher for whom I worked seven years later, said it was still in his nostrils, that sweet, sickly odor of carrion.

He said, too, that as late as the end of June there were snow drifts among the pines at the edge of the Cypress Hills bench, for that was a cold and backward spring and a cool summer, in the year 1907.

The antelope herds were nearly wiped out north of the C.P.R. The animals seen moving south by the 76 men had piled up against the railway fence and all perished except a few latecomers who were able to get over on the backs of their kind, imbedded and frozen in the snow. An old C.P.R. conductor told me that when the wind blew from the north that summer, even his engine flinched.

The ranchers' herds were almost wiped out.

Out of fifteen-thousand head turned out in 1906 by the Turkey Track, not enough were left to run a wagon for spring roundup. This was between Swift Current and the Whitemud.

The Smith and Musson Cattle Company, north of the South Saskatchewan River, had only 250 Manitoba dogies left out of three-thousand imported in 1906.

At the end of what Harry Otterson called "the grim fight," the T Down had lost over 50 per cent of their cattle. And they got off lucky, as well they might, for the Whitemud Valley is the best winter range north of the Missouri.

The Flying U—the Matador outfit—also lost 40–50 per cent. The river breaks and the sand hills, well spotted with brush, saved many; that, and the fact that their policy was to run, principally, a "dry herd"—mostly steers.

Some said it was a death-blow to ranching. To some men it was. "Uncle" Tony Day decided to call it quits. The following summer, in a hotel lobby in Medicine Hat, he addressed himself to some farmers in these words: "You fellows, of your profession, have chased me from the land of Old Mexico north across the Canadian border, and now you can have it all!" He said good-by with moist eyes, and died in 1928 in California. I used to own a little Turkey Track mare years ago. Her ears were frozen short, and that was another reminder of 1907.

Brown, the T Down wolfer, packed his turkey and left for the States that spring. He died while attempting to swim his horse across the Milk River.

Most of the range horses had wintered, however, and with the coming of more settlers the demand was growing, so many ranchers turned to raising them. Like Ad Day with his famous Q, a brand that got to be known all over the west. A few years later it was known in France and Flanders and Palestine, too, for animals carrying that brand on the right shoulder were tops for cavalry chargers.

Gradually the big smell died down, for 1907 was dry, and the carcasses withered in their piles and in their singles. Dead cows hanging in the tops of trees gave a clue to the depth of snow in the coulees; but these gradually disintegrated and fell, bone by bone and rib by rib, as the maggots rustled and dropped also, like grains of wheat.

Some said the cattle died of "hollow-gut," like it was a disease. They didn't want to say they "winter-killed"—that would have let down their dedication to the high plains that could do no wrong, and they still spat in the dust at the mention of fences and wells and irrigation and all the trimmings of a cow-hospital.

And men died, too. A police patrol on the Sounding Lake trail found, beside their broken wagon, the remains of a father and son who had started north early in November 1906 to stake out a ranch—men who had been warned. But they were from Oklahoma and did not see danger ahead on the yellow-grass prairie that looked like home.

So nature had revenged herself against the men who had dared to try and cheat her. For nature plans that production shall be cyclical, not running a steady course. There shall be lean years, as well as fat ones, lest we and our beasts and the wild rabbits and the wolves and the birds become too numerous and destroy our environment. We plan for so many cows, so much crop, so much yearly increase, year by year, steady and unalterable, only to find that drouth, blizzard, grasshoppers, hail, and a thousand other things have the laugh on our tally books. The results of 1907 were many. One was that the range improved tremendously with the easing of pressure from grazing. Another was that outfits realized that they must control their herds, have them where they could get at them to feed them. So more and more leases were fenced. Most of the holdings were smaller now, in spite of the ninety miles of fence put up by Wallace and Ross in the southwest corner.

And now the haying crews came into their own. More men worked now with pitchforks than with lariats, as the herds were once more coaxed into production. Everybody weaned their calves, and only the steers and heifers and dry cows were expected to winter out completely.

Many small irrigation projects were started, to save the waters of Battle Creek and Swift Current Creek and the Whitemud River, to turn these waters on the flats to nourish the lush alfalfa that the calves and the herd bulls would munch. Homesteaders came, it is true, but many didn't stay, and the others could sell their poorer crops and their straw to cattlemen, and some got into cattle themselves.

Cattle ranching didn't die, as was predicted; it simply changed its ways. Today it is on a fairly even keel, with the hay crew gone, it is true, but from a different reason: mechanization. For that same reason the horse ranch, as such, is gone; and that has left more grass to turn into beef, for any old cowman will tell you that he can raise three beef steers to one horse on the range.

So the man who hitched up a team of "broncs" to the mower and let them run full bat through the tough prairie grass till they "gentled themselves" now rides a tractor or a pick-up baler.

Few wagons have their wheels greased for the spring gather today, but cowboys still ride good horses, still throw their ropes, and still do an artistic job with the branding iron.

And the older men, the retired—or, as they would say "broken down"—cowboys, still sit and talk of "nineteen and seven," disregarding the fact that we younger men, too, saw cattle ice-blinded and frozen in subsequent winters, even as late as 1938. As one old cowboy said to me in Maple Creek, "If it hadn't been for them new-fangled fences and feeding hay, them cattle in thirty-eight would of made it. They'd been free to drift like the old days, they'd all of got down to Milk River and lived, 'stead of a few hundred that hit the Havre trail. Why, I mind in nineteen and seven"—and he'd tell of some steers that made it *that* year, for we forget the bad and remember the good, and the good is always long ago.

Which is why old cowmen are happy, because "long ago" is but yesterday, and the sweet savor of dedication and comradeship is stronger than the smell of death, to men who have "made it" themselves, through seventy, eighty winters.

6

That was the land to which I came in early 1914.

A harsh land, at times. A land that challenges you. But she can be also a land of scented grasses, of soft breezes, of bird song, and rippling water.

She is a land you sometimes feel you hate, yet deep down you know she is a land you cannot leave for long; for she will call you back—back to the hiss of the ground-blizzard, back to the star-lit nights, back to the scent of wolf-willow and sage, back to the uplands of yellow grass where the horses gallop, back to the ranch folk and the call, "Come in and eat!"

That hard winter of 1907 was fresh in the minds of range men when I arrived in Saskatchewan a few years later. All the men I worked with had been through it, and they all talked of it.

But it wouldn't happen again, said the optimists—or, if it did, the big haystacks would save the cattle.

That it could happen again I was soon to see. And the hay was not always forthcoming in the dry years, nor was it always possible to take it to the cattle; for there is a limit to depth of snowdrifts that even horses can get through.

So the storms of the 'teens took their toll, as did the big March storm of 1938 that came out of the northwest on the eve of a mild, sunny day at the end of that month, to catch the ranchers unaware, and the cattle scattered far and wide over the spring range.

The dry years would later persuade some ranchers to fold up and trek north in search of lusher pastures, but most of them stayed in spite of drouth, bad winters, and the low price of beef, upheld by their faith in their land and their cows.

Their descendants are still in the Cypress Hills, down on the White-mud River, over west at Wild Horse and Chin Coulee, north in the Great Sand Hills and the breaks of the Saskatchewan River.

Names like Parsonage, Reesor, Nuttal, Small, Naismith, Ramsey, Gaff, Faulkner, Gilchrist, Lindner, Ross, Perrin, Mitchell, and many others are still heard at the annual meetings of the Western Stock Growers' Association. And these people still need horses as their fathers did before them.

Part I: GREEN HAND

Snow on the cow camp

CHAPTER ONE

The saddle bunch

1

The first job I had in the Canadian West was with a rancher called Alex Gow, a grizzled Orkneyman who had once been a cook with the North West Mounted Police at Fort Walsh in what had then been the District of Assiniboia. He had left the Force in the 1890s and had taken up ranching just north of the Cypress Hills in what became the province of Saskatchewan.

He was called "Scotty" for short.

Actually, what brought me to Canada at the age of sixteen has been told in another book, but suffice it to say that I did have my people's permission to come, and that I had some knowledge of what I was coming to because a friend of the family had been one of the original Barr Colonists of 1903. My father having died in 1911, this friend,

Rex Holmes, stood more or less in *loco parentis* to me, and it was he who had promised to back me up in my ambition to come to the prairies, on condition that I did well in my studies. I studied hard under the tutorship of an ex-master of Shrewsbury, for I never saw the inside of a school.

I had read and reread Butler's "Great Lone Land." I had read and reread copies of the *Farm and Ranch Review* (which my friend took) and I had studied both the history and geography of Canada until I was to find that I knew a good deal more (academically) than most of the Westerners I first met and worked with.

I had arrived by train at Maple Creek, direct from England, having been told by this friend that this town was the main supply point for the stock ranchers, with the added information that the best place to ask for a job would be at one of the livery and sales stables which were then one of the main features of any prairie town.

I had traveled by way of New York, so that I could visit a brother who was in business there.

After six days at sea, I found myself being taken all over that city to see the sights, but bricks and mortar didn't seem too interesting to one intent on seeing the prairies. The vision from the top of the Singer Building is no doubt wonderful, but I was wishing to see the real mountains.

What I had enjoyed most was a dispute as to right-of-way between an Italian garbage man and an Irish brewery driver. It took place on the "East Side," and after the first exchanges of bottles and dead cats, the crowd had begun to take sides on a national scale, and the uproar was terrific. All the while a city policeman chewed gum and gently twirled his nightstick as he supported the corner of a tall building. Most New York policemen can claim descent from the Old Sod, but here at least was a neutral.

As a parting gift my brother had given me a most splendid pair of boots from a Fifth Avenue store. They were knee high, laced, and of a glossy tan—very superior "surveyor boots," of the kind worn by the upper stratum of oilmen and "hunters." These were considered (by owner of the store) "Vurry appropriate wear for Canada."

My journey from New York to Chicago had been lightened by the interest of two yellow-faced Americans of that uncertain age so commonly observed in the United States. They were from Arizona, and I now suspect they had something to do with real estate. Like so many of their countrymen, they were both inquisitive and kind. They usually occupied the window seats in the glossy smoking room, with its polished brass cuspidors.

They obviously spotted me as English by my clothes, which included a pair of good country-style boots and tweed jacket and pants. I had started off with a tweed cap, but at St. Paul I had seen a more Western-style hat which I had bought, for I saw no caps in the States. I was not, of course, wearing my new boots on the train.

So there I was, sitting in a Pullman (I had no need to travel colonist) all done up in Victorian plush, and I suppose looking like a young English Gentleman, yet perhaps not quite a dude, for I was, after all, a country boy and well sunburned, although this was early March.

My companions, by contrast, were dressed alike in panama hats and seersucker suits without waistcoats. Their jowls were shaved to a gloss, and so were the backs of their necks. They both wore rings. One smoked Pittsburgh stogies from a tall tin. The other chewed from a plug of Pieper Hiedsick, which he extended to me. My refusal did not disturb him. He had broken the ice.

"Where was you raised, bub?" he asked.

I told him.

"Where are you headin' for?"

I told him that, too.

The gentlemen exchanged glances.

"You're makin' a mistake, bub," said the first. "That there country won't never amount to a hill er beans. It's all snow." I said I didn't think I was going to the Arctic part, but to a part where they raised cattle. "Well, bub, if it's cattle you want, you go to Arizony—Arizony with a big A, and it's the ranchinist country on this yere universe. Ain't that right, Tex?"

Tex said he was Godamn right.

"A young feller like you," he added, "don't want to go to Canady. It's mostly wheat farmers, and they're a triflin' lot. I know. I been to Winnipeg. Nice little town Winnipeg—but why freeze up there when you could be a "baskin" in Phoenix—or Yuma. Say, bub—I'm going to tell you something. Yuma in the state of Arizony is the hottest place this side er hell—*that's statistics.* You turn your ticket around, bub, an' head for Arizony."

About this time a white-clad Negro announced, "*Fust* call for dinnah in the dining car."

We adjourned.

The C.P.R. train from Moose Jaw had got into Maple Creek at midnight. All across the North Dakota plains my eyes had been glued to the great spreading scene outside. It was mostly vast wheat farms, but I had expected that. It was getting dark as I changed from the Soo line to the Main line at Moose Jaw, but I could still dimly see the flatness and sense the distance to the horizon that lay under the twinkling stars.

I had been the only passenger for Maple Creek that night. The only other person on the platform was a tall man in boots and spurs with a broad-brimmed hat. I guessed he was a Mounted Policeman, and later learned that a member of the Force met every train. I asked him where I could get a room and he said, "I'll show you." With my heavy suitcase banging against my leg, I tried to keep step with his jingling stride, but when he saw my predicament he eased up. We crossed a dusty street, and he pointed with his riding crop to a building with a light over the door, and the sign "Cypress Hotel."

"You'll be all right there, boy—good night." And he jingled away.

2

Next morning I enquired about breakfast. "Try the B. C. Café down the street," I was told. "We don't serve meals here."

So I found the little restaurant with the false front. I had only once met a Chinese in my life, and he was a young university student who came to our vicarage for his summer holidays.

The proprietor of the B.C.—Mah Lee—was a smiling and friendly personality; middle-aged, and as serene as any of the lovely Chinese calendars on his wall. "What you want—bleakfast?" he asked.

"Yes, please," I answered, "can I have bacon and eggs?"

"Allight," he said, and communicated with the kitchen in a high singsong. "You new here?" he asked. I said I was. "Velly good place—Maple Click," he said, "velly good people—you like."

Later I got to know Mah much better, and kinder men never plunked down a bowl of soup than he and his various male relatives who came and went in their mysterious oriental way. There seemed to be always a young one coming and an old one going back to China. For ways that are dark, the "heathen Chinese" may be "peculiar," but he is certainly not sinister.

I went next to the station to ask about my trunk. The only person there was sitting on a swivel chair with his back to me and his feet on a desk where a telegraph key was ticking away. He wore gray pants, box-toed yellow shoes, a green eye shade, and black silk sleeve-protectors. In short, he was the dead spit of every "Station Agent" from Winnipeg to Vancouver.

I coughed at the wicket. No response. I finally said, "Excuse me, could you . . . ?" The Presence wheeled slowly, chair and all. He looked at me very hard, took a cigar from his shirt pocket, looked at it, put it in his mouth, and rolled it several times.

"I think I have a trunk . . ." I began again. He swiveled his chair abruptly, showing me his coatless back criss-crossed with gay suspenders.

"Express opens ten o'clock," he said.

I tried once more—"Is there any way I can get my trunk up to the Cypress Hotel?"

Silence for a bit, then—"Ask them." I was dismissed.

At that time, trained Canadian telegraphists were hard to get. Almost all on the main line came from the land of our Friendly Neighbors, and they did not care for Englishmen—or English boys. On the whole, it was a mistake to be too polite to them.

Back at the Cypress Hotel I was admiring a mounted buffalo head—a big bull. I was observed by a lean, pale man with the inevitable box-toed shoes and panama hat. "Yep," he said, and spat. "That there's a genuwine Amurrican Bisson."

I thought to myself that except for the Mounted Policeman, everyone in Canada was an American. I felt forlorn.

After the affair of the trunk was settled—the hotel porter brought it on his go-cart for fifty cents—I went to look around the livery barns, which my friend Rex had told me was the best place to look for a job.

At the bottom of the main street was an enormous hip-roofed building painted red, with the name "A. Gow Livery and Sales Stable" painted in foot-high letters across the front.

I went into its cool shady interior with the rows of horses munching, and the sweet smell of hay and grain. A short, thickset man was watering a team at a big trough in the alleyway. He looked at me and grinned. I said, "Hello."

He said—"Hello, young fellow, you don't belong 'round here, do you?" I said no, I'd come here looking for a job—on a ranch. He looked me up and down—"You're light, and you're young—know anything about ranch work?"

"Not a thing," I said.

"Good," he said—why he said "good" I couldn't imagine. "There's Scotty," he went on, "as owns this barn—I'm looking after it for him, you'll understand—there's Scotty out on Box Elder Ranch"—he jerked a thumb to the southwest. "He told me to look out for a young fellow that'd learn. You might be that—but mind you, he won't pay much to start."

"Where is he?" I asked.

"I told you—out at the ranch—but he'll be in tomorrow. You be here before noon." I thanked him and helped him fork down some hay. I found his name was Geordie Griffin.

Just before noon the next day I went to the barn. Geordie said, "I didn't think you'd come—well, that's him—there in the office. Tell him I sent you."

In the office sat a heavy, aging man with blue eyes, the complexion of a boy, and a heavy down-curled moustache. He was looking over some papers at a cluttered desk; and a broad-brimmed hat was pushed to the back of his head.

"Are you Mr. Gow?" I asked.

"Oh, aye, that's me." He looked up and smiled. "Forbye they call me Scotty," he added, "and ye'll be the laddie as Geordie here was speaking aboot—the laddie that's for a job?"

I said, "Yes, I'm looking for a job."

"Weel," said Mr. Gow, "I'm not wishing to pry, ye'll understand,

but you look but a wean and it's a rough way we have oot here . . .
I doot ye'll suit the job or the job suit ye, for it looks to me that fair
spoke as ye are you'd be better in a store like—a counter jumper. Could
ye no find a better place to come to? And besides, laddie, ye wouldna
be in trouble would ye? Did ye run away and leave a mither grieve
for ye?"

"Oh, no," I stammered, "my mother and my brothers let me come.
You see, I like horses and, well, everything about the country, and
actually I've done a lot of gardening and I'm stronger than you may
think; and I like horses and I've ridden a bit, and then I met a fellow
in England who'd been here and he told me I wouldn't get much wages,
but he said the ranch people were awfully nice, and . . ." I came to
a lame halt and felt very confused beneath Mr. Gow's steady gaze.

"So ye like horses?" he said finally. "And ye're willing to take small

Scotty Gow

wages and learn to work?" I nodded. "Weel, I'll take ye on. It'll be but twenty dollars a month and board, an' ye'll understand, if ye think better o' it, ye can give a month's notice, an' if ye'r nae good, I'll do the same. I'm that short o' gear I'll have to get ye a saddle and ye can pay me back oot o' your wages."

I said, "Oh, I've got enough money—I think—for a saddle, and perhaps if you'd be good enough to show me what to get. . . ?"

My employer asked my name. I told him. "But I'll just call ye Charlie . . . for we call young lads wi' schooling 'Charlies,' and ye look and talk like one," he said. And that was my introduction to a man who has long since passed on, but whose memory will always be green with me.

Scotty gave me five dollars to "seal the bargain"—as he said—and took me to the saddlers and then to Dixon's store for blue denim pants and one of the short jackets we called a smock. We were to be ready to leave by noon. It was thirty-five miles to the ranch.

The winding, rutted trail seemed endless, but some time after dark I stumbled sleepily to a table and stuffed myself with hot biscuits, syrup, and bacon. I was shown a bed and in seconds was asleep, dreaming of the sway and rattle of the buggy and the soft clip-clop of the ponies' hooves.

3

The following day Scotty called me early, and while we had breakfast he explained that two of the three men in his employ were out in the south country with the roundup wagon. The one remaining, Jake, was away looking for horses. Jake, my boss explained, was definitely in charge of the horses, and acted in between times as a sort of foreman, or in western parlance, "ramrod" of the outfit.

Scotty himself was growing old, and his wife was far from well, and often unable to attend to the housework. Female help was difficult to get, and therefore Scotty himself undertook more and more of the cooking. He had got breakfast that morning and, in fact, did so most mornings.

The ranch, I found, ran several hundred head of cattle—mostly the cross-bred shorthorns of that day before the Hereford breed had practically "taken over" the range.

But Scotty's chief love was his horses, of which he had about four hundred—or so he thought. But, as he said, horses range far and wide, and are not gathered for winter since they live out. So it was always hard to know just how many you owned, especially since prices had improved and horse stealing, he thought, had increased. Not that he had anything definite to go to the law with. The Police had an immense territory to cover, and the few Brand Inspectors at the border and at shipping points were not too hard to by-pass; if a man were bold and clever.

Scotty's riding days, he lamented, were about over. He weighed over two hundred pounds and was paunchy with it. He occasionally put his old long-seated, "A"-fork saddle on Shamrock, his ancient cow horse, but it would be only to proceed at a quiet amble around some horses in the pasture, or as he called it, "wrangle field." Shamrock, a tall gaunt Hambletonian, had, like his master, seen better days.

We finished eating, and Scotty went on to say, as he began to put the things away, "As soon as Jake gets back I'll send the two o'ye ower to Kealy Springs to pick up a bunch o' mares that Jock McGregor tells me are ranging there. He tells me they've got foals and also some following yearlings and maybe two-year-olds, and that none of the young stuff is branded. I'm not worrying about them because they'll stay wi' the mares. All the mares will be branded so that will prove ownership o' the rest, but it'll be best to get them home and put the iron on them."

He explained his brand to me—Ex open Aye (XΛ) on the left hip for horses; and Ex Aye bar (XA) on the left ribs for cattle. I surreptitiously wrote them out in my pocket book so that I could memorize them. "Besides," he went on, "I want they mares bred by my own studs. There's a sight too many scrub stallions on the range, and this year's foals will be but runts I'm thinking."

He shut the cupboard door, put fresh wood in the big range, shut it off, and took his big hat from its buck-horn peg. "Now," he said, "I'll go with you and show you how to feed and water the studs, and tell you what else to do till Jake comes."

Under his instructions I led the ranch stallions to water, cleaned out their log quarters, and fed them hay from a stack enclosed by pine rails.

Just as I was finishing I heard the clop of a horse, the squeaking of a corral gate, and a horseman rode up to the barn.

He rode a sweat-crusted sorrel with a wide blaze, and was garbed in worn leather chaps, short jacket, black neck scarf, and stiff-brimmed Stetson hat. It was obviously Jake, for he knew his way around, slipping the bridle from his horse's head and kicking the stable door wider to let the beast by in the manner of one familiar with his surroundings. He did not look at me nor speak till he'd forked some hay to his animal.

Then—"Scotty in the house?" he asked.

I said, "Yes."

<h2 style="text-align:center">4</h2>

It was dinnertime so I closed the corral gate, and followed Jake to the house, stopping to take an armful of stove wood with me. Scotty had said, "Whenever ye come to the hoose just stoop and pick up an armfu' o' wood. That way the box in the kitchen doesna get empty-like."

As I got to the door I could hear Scotty's booming voice and he seemed upset. Jake gave a low answer in a sulky way, and as I put the wood in the box their conversation stopped.

We sat in to baked beans and corn bread with syrup. Scotty's wife was keeping to her room that day. When we'd finished the meal, Scotty filled his pipe, and as he smoked and stroked his heavy moustache, Jake deftly rolled and lit a cigarette. I got out the tobacco and papers I had bought in Maple Creek and tried to do the same, but I spoilt several first attempts before I finally managed an egg-shaped affair which slowly came to pieces as I puffed.

Scotty turned to me. "The barn democrat will be here today wi' your saddle, Charlie. And from now on ye'll sleep i' the bunkhouse along of Jake. He'll show you."

My saddle was coming! With Scotty's help I had picked it out at the saddlers and paid out more than half of what money I had left. We could not bring it with us, as the saddler, at Scotty's suggestion, was going to give it a good dressing with neat's-foot oil and make some changes in the stirrups.

I brought my mind back with an effort—Scotty was still talking. "Ye can ride my old saddle this afternoon, forbye it's big for ye, but Shamrock's that easy gaited it'll make no differ'. I want ye to go wi' Jake over west there, and bring in some mares, and there's two-three ponies you'll have to ride."

Jake and I saddled up. He was so dour and uncommunicative that I did not like to ask questions, but I watched what he did. First the bridle. That was easy—I didn't quite know then *why* the bridle came first. Then the saddle blanket. Well, the one he indicated to me with his thumb was already properly folded, so that was easy, too. Then the thirty-five pound saddle, with its awkward heavy stirrups. I saw how Jake put his fingers palm up in the gullet and threw his on. I did the same, only I heaved too strenuously and almost threw it over Shamrock's back, and got hit in the eye by the oak stirrup. When I stooped for the girth—I found later it was not a "girth" but a cinch—I found two (for this was an old double-rigged Frazier saddle) and looked for straps and buckles. I saw Jake take the long "strap" which is the latigo, and put it twice through the cinch ring and rigging ring and tie it. I did the same, slowly, clumsily.

We mounted, and silent as ever, he led me over the creek and into the rolling green hills.

The horses were not badly scattered nor far away, and the sun was still high as we gathered them and drove them before us to the home corral. These mares had been brought to the studs during the early summer months and knew just where to go. The prairie grass was curled and dimpled—that's why they call it "prairie wool"; cloud shadows chased themselves over the swells and across the hollows where the longer grasses rippled in the breeze. The land lay tawny and golden in the evening sun and gray-green in the shadows. The gleaming ponds were dark with wildfowl.

Here I saw my first coyote—a gray shadow moving without effort across the hillside. I turned to look back at him, and felt my saddle slip dangerously. Shamrock stopped, and I dismounted to find the cinches hanging loose below his body. As I tightened them I felt very green and stupid. I should have known enough to check this before.

Jake kept on riding, and for the first time opened his mouth. It was to sing, half under his breath, but loud enough for me to hear—

> *A forty-dollar saddle,*
> *A twenty-dollar hoss,*
> *A ten-dollar rider, an'*
> *A hay-wire boss!*

My saddle, I thought, had cost a bit more than forty dollars and if a "hay-wire" boss meant a poor one, then I would still choose Scotty before this unfriendly fellow.

We chased the "gentle bunch" into the big corral and closed the gate. We had several teams of heavy Clyde mares, used for ranch work and breeding. A smattering of leggy foals, and half a dozen broke saddle ponies. (They were not all "pony" size, but that made no difference.) These were not the best on the ranch—the pick were out on the roundup—but useful looking animals—all geldings.

Jake pointed out a little gray, a slab-sided bay, and a trim buckskin (which I would have called a dun) that had a black mane and tail, also black legs and a "strip" down his backbone. These were to be my mounts, he stated in as few words as possible; adding, "You'll have to break out one or two more this fall—if you stay."

Just then the barn democrat drove up and we went to unhitch the team. I think I mentioned that Scotty was also the proprietor of a Livery and Sales Stable. His barn manager, Geordie Griffin, brought out supplies at intervals to the ranch.

He had brought my trunk, and here, too, was my handsome new Riley & McCormick saddle and a bridle—boots, chaps, and spurs I would have to earn as time went on. But with this heavy stock saddle I felt that at last my life as a cowboy was begun.

CHAPTER TWO

Parting the yearlings

1

Next morning, "Well, boys," said Scotty, "you better start for Kealy Springs the day. Take across country Jake, but don't put too many miles in your pocket, or Charlie here is apt to get mighty sore. You can stop at Bellinger's if you like, and make to McGregor's the next day."

Kealy Springs, it turned out, was sixty miles east, almost at the far end of the hills. We stopped the first night at Bellinger's ranch, and I wasn't sorry to bed down there. Breaking in a new saddle was not—I found—a pleasure. Only Mrs. Bellinger was at home—everyone else was out riding the south country. She gave us a good supper, showed us the bunkhouse and had breakfast ready for us the next day.

These people were English, and the lady tried to be nice to me, but I was too shy to make much response. It was my first taste of that ranch hospitality which feeds any and every visitor. Under this system the feeder in his turn becomes the fed.

Next day we splashed through the ford in Skull Creek and started to climb up into the Cypress Hills, following a rutted wagon trail. Kealy Springs was on the high bench, as the level plateau above the timbered slope is always called.

Remembering what Scotty had said, I asked my silent companion when we would get to McGregor's. He jerked his horse's mouth and swore at the animal, and, "What do you know about McGregor's?" he asked. I said I thought we were supposed to get some horses from near his place.

"Aw shucks! You green Englishmen are all the same! Why the Old Man bothered to hire you I'll not pretend to understand. Stop yapping and do as you're told and we'll mebbe get on."

I didn't feel he had much cause to say this because, much as I longed for a friend to talk to—one who would help me get to know all there was to know—I thought I had matched his reticence very well. I thought to myself—this is going to be a hard man to get on with.

We scrambled up the last gravelly pitch, with the dark pines straight and even on either side, and suddenly found ourselves on the open "bench"—that long grassy plateau which overlooks the State of Montana to the south, and the great prairies of Saskatchewan to the north.

Shortly, the trail forked—one branch to the east, the other to the south.

"I'll be leavin' you here," said my companion, "you keep a-ridin' that way"—he pointed east—"and in about a mile and a half you'll come to Geisner's store. Tell him I sent you, and I'll be there about noon tomorrow. The hosses should be south here somewheres, but if

I'm not back when I said, you just stay put." With that he touched his horse with the spur and loped away across the bench.

I felt very much alone. Here was an enormous stretch of country. If I got lost I doubted if I could find my way home. However, if there was a store only about a mile away, there must be some people about.

Had I known it, there were several ranches—including McGregor's—which we had by-passed on the ride.

Well, I thought, this is the life I wanted, and I might as well like it.

In half an hour the trail started down a coulee where, among poplar and pines, stood a low log building with a sign "STORE" crudely painted on a crooked board. Some sheds and corrals showed through the trees behind.

2

Simon Geisner, the proprietor of this backwoods store, was a strange figure. He was not really old—probably sixty—but he was the most bent and shrivelled gnome of a man I had ever seen. His nose was almost flat to his face; his eyes burned in deep sockets overshadowed by unkempt brows; his face was seamed with dirty creases. Great tufts of coarse gray hairs protruded from his wide, dirty ears. He wore shabby old bib overalls and a faded blue shirt, which may once have been clean. He met me at the door of the store—stared very hard at me, and in an unpleasant rasping voice asked what the hell I wanted. I told him Jake had sent me and I was to wait here for him.

"Well," he said, reluctantly I thought, "guess you kin stay—put your hoss in the corral thar—but I warn you, there ain't much to eat, an' by grab I ain't going to bother cookin' nothin' for a saddle tramp."

So I turned my horse in, and made him comfortable; then went to a door at the far end of the shack, which I guessed must be the living quarters—for he had locked the store door as he addressed me, and then disappeared through this other. I knocked but no one answered, so I entered.

Geisner was taking some stuff from a corner cupboard. A can of sardines. A handful of home made "biscuits." A greasy-looking plate with a dab of butter on it. These he arranged on a rickety pine table, brushing dead flies and the crumbs of an earlier meal to the floor with his sleeve. Having put down two plates, two mugs, and some cutlery, he appeared satisfied and spoke two words.

"Sit in."

The sardines were good, but I could have eaten two cans myself. The butter was rancid. The biscuits had been made a week ago and they were burned black. I longed for some tea. As if reading my thoughts, Geisner said, "Ain't got no use for tea or coffee or any ev that bellywash. There's water in the pail." I filled my mug, but noticed that while I did so he adroitly slid a small bottle from his dirty clothes, and tipped some into his mug before following me to the water pail. I was hoping he might speak; ask more about the horses or where Jake was or something. I found the silence uncanny and frightening. As I watched his dirty, clawlike fingers scratching up biscuit crumbs, I thought of Ebenezer Balfour of Shaw's in *Kidnapped* and wondered if my second name—David—was an unfortunate one.

After supper he told me I could sleep in the hayloft above the stable—"and mind you don't smoke." So I said good night and turned to go. He did not reply but busied himself putting the remains of the meal back in the cupboard, slamming and locking the door.

I went out thinking that here must be a real miser! It was not quite dark so I strolled up the hill behind the corrals, and out onto the bench. A horned owl hooted. The nighthawks were twanging their bowstrings and "peeping" as they swept overhead. The bench grass was wet with dew. Overhead the mysterious stars, which were later to be my friends and guides on many a lonely night watch, twinkled and shone.

How peaceful, how enchanting was this new country. Yet how grim and foreboding to be a stranger here, unable as yet to judge the motives and characters of a people of whom some at least seemed incapable of any gesture towards friendliness. I thought of how Du Chaillu's West African savages invariably met him with presents of chickens and fruit!

I was not to know that into this free and peaceful country had, from time to time, come some of the most unscrupulous people in North America—fugitives from scenes of former crimes, off-scourings of earlier frontiers. Nor was I to know that this man Geisner was hated and feared for many miles—if not for any known criminal act, at least

Old Geisner

for his miserliness, his bad temper, and his suspected connection with horse and cattle thieves—in fact, to use an expression of the country, his all-round "orneryness." The store was more of a blind than anything else, though I didn't know it then. He raised a few horses, a few cows. But in no sense was this place a ranch. It was, rather, a "roost."

3

Next morning the old man stumped out and called me to feed a team he had in the barn, which I did; and having fed my own horse I went to the house in hopes of breakfast. There seemed to be no signs of that important meal, but Geisner told me to come with him to the

store, for, said he, "You might as well do something for your grub."
So he set me to various small and irritating tasks, which I did with
what grace I could muster.

About ten o'clock he said, "Here's some biscuits and a bit of cheese
if you wanter eat." He set the breakfast on the narrow counter and
began to eat himself. The biscuits were dry and I started for the door
with the intention of getting a drink at the spring. I thought I would
take a lookout for Jake at the same time; he should be here shortly.

As I stepped into the brilliant sunshine, I was almost knocked over
by a horse that came around the corner at a lope. Its rider pulled up
short and shouted, "You thar—Geisner—come on out or I'm a-coming
in after you."

I had stepped back into the doorway, and I now raised my eyes
from the hooves which had almost run me down to the face of the
man who had roared. And what I saw was not at all reassuring. The
lanky frame, clad in worn range garb, was topped by a countenance
composed chiefly of scrubby whiskers, purple nose, and little red eyes
set in a mass of weatherbeaten flesh. Upkempt, grizzled hair hung from
under his battered hat.

He paid no attention to me, but repeated his challenge, at the same
time threshing his lively bay horse with a rawhide quirt till that animal
reared again and again.

I felt a movement behind me, and then Geisner's harsh nasal voice
at my elbow, "You—Coyote Bill—you again, eh? Now—git offen my
doorstep and make tracks!" This was followed by an interchange of
curses.

The bay horse was quiet now, and for a moment the two men took
a breathing space, each glaring hideously at the other. I noticed that
the man addressed as "Coyote Bill" carried a Winchester carbine on
his saddle. And then I noticed something else. He was barefoot. His
crusted, dirty toes protruded like gnarled roots from the oak stirrups.

Geisner spoke to me, "Feller, you hand me one of them forks." Just
inside the door was an empty nail keg in which several hay forks were
displayed for sale, the tines pointing upward. I reached within and
pulled one out. Geisner had not taken his eyes from Coyote Bill's.
He now reached behind and took the fork from me, presenting it at
the intruder like a well-trained bayonet fighter. "Coyote"—he spat—

"you worthless hunk er meat you—*git out,* an' stay out, or by grab I'll skewer your carcass to your saddle—git!"

With that Coyote gave way a yard or two. He began to fumble at his saddle. "I'll show you," he stated, and Geisner shrilled, "Keep away from your hardware! I kin throw this'n ten yards!" and he poised the fork like a javelin.

"Now," he said, "Coyote Bill—I've had enough of yer argifying—I ain't given' you another pair—I don't care what you say—trade is trade so quit yer yappin'. 'Sides—yer wore t'otheruns out—I kin see yer old cloven hooves plain."

"Why, y'old buzzard," retorted the rider, "I got 'em here—the blasted things giv me such a misery I didn't wear 'em but oncet!"

With that he loosened something behind the saddle, swung up his arm and woosh! whop!—a pair of boots tied together with string thudded into the dust of the dooryard. At the same time Geisner threw the pitchfork, which went yards wide of its mark. Quite casually the storekeeper stooped down and retrieved the boots. He looked them over; said "humph" a couple of times, then turning to me, "Pick up that damn fork," and re-entered the store. Coyote sat on his horse, motionless except for the movement of his jaws as he masticated his cud of tobacco.

Geisner reappeared. He carried another pair of boots. He flung them down at the horse's feet. "Try thes'ns," he said, "they'r a size larger—an' by the Almighty Jehosephat if yer come a-bothering me again, I'll cut the gizzard outa yer—no foolin'."

Coyote dropped his reins and slowly dismounted. Squatting in the trampled dooryard, he put his ugly bare feet into the knee-length cowhide riding boots. Then springing up with remarkable agility, he stamped around for a minute or two. Finally—"They'll do," he said.

"That all what brings yer here?" asked Geisner with a curious look.

"We'll want some grub and blankets I guess," replied his erstwhile enemy in a sulky tone. "They'll be here today, and we got a long ride before"—Geisner interrupted him angrily to bark at me.

"What yer hangin' around fer—git in the store and start to hang them harness up."

I re-entered the building feeling very much not wanted. But my curiosity was roused, and I made as little noise with the heel chains as possible. I heard the words "across the line," and something about a moon—or the lack of one. Presently, the two came in and some groceries were spoken of—"sow belly" and "a bit o' flour" and "plenty tabaker," and something like "we kin pick up the other stuff later." Twice I thought Geisner seemed to nudge his companion, and each time that worthy lowered his voice. And with that Coyote Bill rode away.

As I watered the horses—Geisner's and mine—at the bubbling spring, I fell to wondering if all was well here. However, with the resiliency of youth I soon threw off that feeling, and chided myself for trying to see high adventure when there was only sordid trade carried out with no saving grace of good manners. Two things did puzzle me, new to the range as I was. One was that the corrals were in such good repair considering the obviously few stock kept. They were equipped with a strong squeeze gate, which judging by the number of small piles of ashes, must have seen considerable branding done. The other was that not a blade of grass grew in these corrals at that time of year. They were churned to a mixture of dust and horse dung for the depth of six inches or so. The corrals at Scotty's ranch were not like this. It looked as if these were in constant use.

Half the afternoon was gone, and still no Jake. I tried to talk to Geisner, but he replied only with grunts. To my inquiries as to whether any of Scotty's horses were around he would only say, "Mebbe."

4

Near sundown we had another visitor. I was sitting hungry and disconsolate on the corral fence considering whether I might not saddle up, leave a message for Jake with the old miser, and take a ride around with an eye for Ex open Aye horses and perhaps better quarters. Having no money with me I could not buy anything from Geisner, so I had to depend on someone's free hospitality. It seemed that anyone would be better than Geisner. Then the horses in the corrals raised their heads and my buckskin whinnied.

"Jake at last," I thought, but it wasn't Jake. The rider who approached on a fine black horse was tall and dark—French looking—

and wore a neat Stetson and gaudy scarf. He rode easily to the bars and dismounted as gracefully as a cat, regarding me with the first pleasant look I had seen for some time.

"Hello, my frien'," he said, and I said, "Hello—have you seen anything of Jake Meldrum?" The new arrival gave me a curious look and finally shook his head, then—"I think mebbe he be back west where he work." I said no, and told him who I was and that Jake was supposed to be here today.

"Oh—I guess he come allright den," said the rider. I asked him who he was. "Alex LaFromboise," he said, as if I should know. "Me—I'm rider-broncobuster. Everyone know Alex LaFromboise! I come now for get some tabac from de ol' diable here."

I followed him, and while Geisner was getting the sacks of Bull Durham, I noticed Alex looking at my New York boots. I was feeling quite self-conscious about them anyway. Finally he spoke. "Wat kindu boots? Mebbe Boy Scout?" I felt my cheeks burn, but he went on, "By gar is good boots, too—good leather. Good made . . . wat you want for trade dose boots, eh? I can see they goin' fit me good? Eh? How about leetle trade?"

I knew nothing of that great western pastime called "trading"—i.e., exchanging. Before I could speak he said, "Come wit' me. I got good rifle on saddle. She make good trade. She's Winchestair—pretty ol' but is bon fusil—come." So I went with him and he took the old '95 Winchester from under his stirrup, "See, she got two—t'ree shells to boot—you trade, eh?"

I said I liked the rifle, but if I traded him my boots I'd have to go barefoot—I thought of Coyote Bill. "Huh! Dat's notin'," said LaFromboise—"me, I'm not cheap. Me, I'm not old Geisner—*ce sacre voleur!*" He began to take off his own boots—first carefully laying aside his silver-inlaid spurs. "See," he said, "I got plenty dis kin' boots. Dese ol' wons pretty near finish' anyways—you tak' dem—you can get better pair when you go to Maple Crik."

By this time he was in his socks, and he held out the boots with such a friendly grin on his dark, handsome face, that I had to grin, too, and take them. The boots were worn alright, but still had plenty of service in them. They were ankle-high gaiters, with elastic sides, and I was amazed that they fitted me snugly. I soon found that most riders in the West had small feet—from lack of walking I supposed. While he laced my footwear on his own legs, I stumped around on the unaccustomed high heels to tie my rifle on Buck's saddle.

"I got to go," said LaFromboise as he mounted. "Mebbe I see you again. We live about four miles north"—and with that he was gone. I was sorry to see him leave and suppressed an impulse to call him back and ask if I could go to his place for the night.

That was the first, but not the last time I met that champion bronco-buster and later Rodeo Star—Alex LaFromboise, the French half-breed. It was also my first introduction to that gay, kindly, and im-provident race which had been in turn *coureurs de bois, voyageurs,* and plainsmen. A race whose achievements as fur traders, explorers, and scouts are only now being recognized by the more aggressive peoples who have supplanted them.

There was still no sign of Jake at sundown, so once more I rolled up in the hay with my saddle blanket. But sometime during the night I heard a trampling of hooves, the whicker of foals, and heavy thuds as corral bars were let down. Then a confused murmur of voices, and presently three men climbed the ladder and threw themselves on the hay.

"That you, Jake?" I asked.

"Yep," came from the darkness.

"Did you get some horses?"

"Yep," again. Then a voice, "Who the hell is that?" and Jake's voice, "Oh, some English kid the old man hired. He don't know nuthin'—he's supposed to help me with the horses."

I thought it the best policy to go back to sleep and see what morning brought.

It was barely daylight when the men roused and started feeling around for boots and spurs. Jake shook me. "You git up, Charlie, and tell the old feller there's three more for breakfast."

"He doesn't seem to like—" I began, but Jake interrupted me.

"He'll feed *us* alright—git going." So I slid down and woke the house.

5

The old man was in a worse humor than usual and cursed for a minute or two, but finally got a fire crackling in the stove and sent me with two pails to the spring.

I noticed that the main corral was almost full of horses—there must be about fifty head, I thought. They were standing in groups in the hip-shot attitude of animals which are glad to rest.

When I got back Jake and his companions were squatting on their heels along the wall of the bare room, rolling cigarettes. Few Westerners of this type remove their hats inside, and these gentlemen were no exception; their only concession to the rooftree being to tip their head gear well back.

As I lifted the dripping pails to the low plank shelf Jake spoke— "This yere is Charlie from the Old Country—meet Mr. Myers and Mr. Preston."

Those two nodded and I said in my best Canadian, "Pleased to meetcha."

"Best eat if y'r a-going to," said Geisner, and put on the table—to my surprise and joy—a big frying pan full of sizzling bacon, and a platter of "hot cakes."

"Got any coffee?" said Mr. Myers.

"Darn near out, but guess this brew'll do," he was answered, and bang! a big, black coffeepot hit the table.

Mr. Preston speared about six hot cakes with his fork and transferred them to his tin plate, looking vaguely around as he did so. "Efn' its syrup you'r a-lookin' fur," said Geisner, "there ain't none."

"Hell! Come on, you old skinflint. You got plenty in the store. Go git it!" and Mr. Myers glared so furiously at Geisner that the old man—to my astonishment—answered never a word but departed, to return in short order with a new can of "Lily White" which he thumped down on the table as much as to say, "This is done under threats, but I'll put a good face on it."

While we ate I studied the two strangers. The one called Myers was middle-aged, thick-set, with dark iron-gray hair. He spoke thickly. He wore a biggish gold ring which I thought must indicate membership in some Lodge, but I could not see it clearly. Preston was a very different-looking individual. He had the same lithe bearing and catlike grace that I had observed in Alex LaFromboise—a bearing which I afterwards found indicated a good rider. This man was younger. Tall and lean-thighed, he appeared quite dandified beside the others. His fair hair had been combed and tidied, his hands washed. His clothing was neat, and while showing signs of wear also showed signs of careful repair work. His boots, spurs, and hat were all new looking. Like the rest, he was, of course, unshaved. I had got used to that by now, in a country where once-a-week-if-you-need-it-or-not was the rule. In fact, Alex LaFromboise was the first clean-shaved man I had seen for a long time.

While they ate they didn't talk much, but communicated their needs for sugar or hot cakes by making motions towards those requirements, which were promptly passed. Each as he finished eating produced tobacco and papers and rolled his morning smoke.

Jake spoke when he had finished his and ground the stub under his heel. "Well, fellers, we better git them strays cut out and me'n' Charlie can hit the high spots with the rest." With one accord they lunged to their feet and tramped out to the corrals. I started to follow. "We don't need you, kid," suddenly said Jake—"you git back in and help the old buzzard with the dishes." I didn't like this, but my job was to do as I was told, so with bad grace I returned. Those dishes got washed in double time, and I went out again. In the melee of dust and confusion at the horse corral, I wasn't noticed as I climbed up to the top rail to watch. The gate to the second corral was open and the man Preston stood by it, evidently ready to shut it when needed.

6

Jake and Myers were both on horseback, trying to cut out what I took to be a yearling filly from among a bunch of mares and foals. The filly would get going down the side of the corral towards the far gate, but time and again she spun around at the last minute and dashed back between the riders, whickering frantically and always heading towards the same bunch of mares and young stuff, which answered shrilly. I took particular notice of this filly, for she was a picture. She showed a good deal of breeding and was a smoky buckskin with black points like my saddle horse. She was as quick on her feet as a cat. Only one thing spoilt her appearance—both her ears were shot as if they had been cut off halfway up with shears. Each time she passed I looked for a brand, but could see none. Whenever she got back to the bunch she would hug up close to an old sway-backed buckskin mare.

With the mare was a foal and another mare also with a foal. This group all showed the buckskin coloring in some phase—in the case of the younger mare she was a buckskin pinto with a walleye; and so was one of the colts. I could see the Ex open Aye quite plainly on the two mares. Presently the riders were able to cut out the filly again, and this time they got her through the gate which Preston fairly slammed on her heels.

As the dust settled I saw that about fourteen young horses were in the second corral, all blowing and sweating and nervously circling the corral. These had evidently been cut out of the main bunch while I was doing dishes. These must be the "strays" Jake had mentioned. The two men rode through the bunch again. This time it was a bay two-year-old gelding standing between a dark brown mare and a bay foal that they started to "chouse," using the loops of their ropes as stock whips. They got him running for the gate when "look out, Chinook!" cried Jake, for the brown mare had followed, too. Myers swung his loop to the near side, thrashing the mare across her nose, and she dropped back. The yearling's momentum carried him through the gate, which was again slammed.

I left my perch and went around the outside of the main corral until I could peer between the bars of the smaller one. As far as I could tell not one of the young horses within showed any sign of a brand.

When I returned and hoisted myself up again I found myself looking into Jake's face. "Quit pesterin' around the corral," he said, "we can't work them broncs if you git frightening them."

"Say, Jake," I said, "those horses you are cutting out—who's are they?"

Jake turned in his saddle quickly. "Why—ranchers' horses, o' course—got to running with ours, and a damn nuisance, too. If we

don't cut 'em out now an' hold them back, they'll foller us home."
He lifted his bridle hand to go.

"But, Jake," I said, "those horses don't have any brand, so how—"
Jake stood in his stirrups and rocked.

"D'ye hear that—Chinook, eh? Charlie yere says them old plugs
ain't branded!" They laughed together. "These yere green English!
Couldn't read a brand on a whiskey bottle—har-har!"

Well I thought, that's funny. Those are young horses, not "old plugs,"
and I was sure they were not branded. And why had I been introduced
to "Mr. Preston" and "Mr. Myers" in a country where I had found
already that first names or nicknames were almost exclusively used.
What was more, Myers did seem to have a nickname—"Chinook."
I'd heard the word already of course. The chinook wind. Perhaps Myers
was a "windy" talkative person. But I knew there was also a cow town
south of the border called Chinook.

In rapid succession the two men proceeded to cut out another seven
or eight young horses. At least two more were geldings, and I thought
since they had been altered, why hadn't they been branded at the same
time? I noticed, too, that since my brief conversation one or the other
invariably mentioned a brand when cutting out a horse. It would
be—"Hi, Jake—git around that running W cayene." Or—"But git rid
of this yere angle-bar mare." To my eye, this "yere angle-bar mare"
was an unbranded young filly.

7

Finally the job was completed. Twenty-four fine young horses had
been cut back. In the main corral were now left thirty-two head. Twenty
brood mares with long manes and tails, of which fourteen had foals
at foot. All the mares carried the Ex open Aye plain for the world
to see on their left hips.

"Git your horse saddled," said Jake to me, "and we'll pull out with
this bunch." Glad to be active again, I soon returned with Buck. Jake
opened the corral gate. It stuck and squeaked, and he cursed and
wrenched like a man in a hurry. When he got it open he shouted,

"Charlie! You git behind them broncs and chouse them out. I'll turn them down the trail."

I did so, and as they streamed through the gate I saw Myers and Preston squatting outside the store talking.

Just then a rider leading a pony with an empty packsaddle rode up from the south. He dropped the lead rope in the dust and dismounted slowly. Myers and his pal rose from where they were squatting and the three entered the store. But before a curve in the trail hid the buildings from view I had recognized the new arrival. It was Coyote Bill.

Our trip back to the ranch was uneventful. Since this was the first time I had trailed range horses I was nervous and afraid of doing the wrong thing, but once clear of the buildings, the mares kept the trail well; and by the time we had left the bench and were clattering down the steep hillside, the sway-backed mare had swung into the lead; and thereafter she kept it. The whole band swung along at a steady trot for the most part, sometimes breaking into a lope on the up-slopes. Range horses are beautiful creatures at any time, but they never look better than when traveling at a good clip in single file, with each mare's foal running at her flank. Their glossy coats shine in the sun, their manes and tails stream behind, their heads are up, ears pricked, nostrils wide open and their liquid eyes alert to all they see.

A ruffed grouse, dusting in the trail, whirred into the pines, and the whole moving line of horses shied sideways as one.

We splashed through the first two creeks, but by the time we reached the third, the horses stopped with one accord and put their muzzles to the sweet water. The foals splashed and then took fright at the cold spray that drenched them and their dams' flanks, or blew at the water and then wrinkled their velvety noses at the coldness of it.

One by one the mares heaved themselves up the far bank and again broke into a trot while Jake and I relaxed in the saddle with the cigarettes we had been able to roll as the band drank.

We camped at Bellinger's again, and I thought Jake was somewhat relieved when the good lady said her menfolk were not back yet. Late the second day we turned the mares and foals into the home wrangle field and went in to our much-needed supper; for, as commonly happens on the range, our noon meal had been a tight belt.

CHAPTER THREE

A mite scary

1

I came in from feeding the saddle stock next morning just as Scotty's voice boomed, "Come and get it!"

Jake seemed sulky and lost in thought, but bestirred himself once or twice to speak to me far more civilly than he had done the previous day.

"Reckon you got a hand coming up, Scotty," he said, as we finished the meal. "Young Charlie yere's doing right well—knows how to do what he's told and *keep his mouth shut.*" His eyes darted across to me as he fumbled for tobacco. Scotty, who was filling the kettle from the water pail, only grunted, but I was well pleased, and my doubts and fears began to vanish. I had lain awake the night before trying to puzzle things out, but the pieces wouldn't fit.

So now, sitting in the comfortable kitchen, in the clear light of day,

I determined it was my newness and ignorance that was at fault, and felt better.

Jake was sent riding again. He turned at the door and said, "Best come along, Charlie—I'll likely need help."

But Scotty said quietly, "I got a job for Charlie the day—I want him to bring in that old brindle cow from out on the flat and try his hand at milking her. She was tied up once or twice they say, before I got her from that nester in trade. She isna' so wild, but I reckon she could be milked, and Charlie says he knows how. I'm fair tired o' canned milk."

Jake started to expostulate, "Ain't going to turn this spread into a cow hospital, surely? If you do, we'll not keep a man!"

But Scotty calmly turned his back; and Jake, after a long look at him and then at me went out and slammed the door.

I had just saddled Buck and led him out when Scotty stumped up, puffing a little. He looked old and ill. "Charlie," he said, and sat down heavily on the hewn log that formed the stable doorstep. "Charlie, laddie, I want to talk to ye." I dropped Buck's reins and sat down, too.

Scotty was silent for a while, looking out across the prairie; then, "Charlie, how many horses altogether did you fellers bring into the corrals at Geisner's?" I told him I had no hand in bringing them in. "Why not?" he asked. So I told him how I had been left at the store and how Jake and the two others had brought in the bunch. I added that I thought there were about fifty head. "How come ye didna' stop at McGregor's? He knew them horses." I replied that I simply did not know. "Weel," Scotty went on, "I don't like to speak to one man about anither. But I ken ye have an education, aye and a noticin' eye—even if ye are green! So now I'm going to ask ye something. Maybe ye'd be too young and inexperienced to gie' me the answer—but, did ye obsairve anything—*anything,* mind ye—that didna' seem just right on this trip?"

I thought for quite a while. Would I be simply making a fool of myself if I told him all that was said and done that day at Geisner's corrals? Finally, I said, "Well, Mr. Gow, I saw and heard things that didn't seem right to me, but I could have got the wrong idea, and I don't want to make trouble between you and Jake—or Jake and me,"

I added. Scotty looked serious. When he spoke again I felt that he was angry—whether at me or not I couldn't guess.

"Charlie, my man," he said, "troubles come in every man's life. Jake an' me are having trouble now. He was damn ornery with me the morn, when ye were out feeding the horses. We had a fair set-to. For d'ye see, he makes but a poor accounting of my horses, and it's like to break me." He sighed. "Aweel," he continued, "it's an awfu' thing to suspicion anybody, and I'll not question ye further the noo—hitch up Kip and Bunco to the buggy, Charlie—we're for town."

The drive to town was a silent one. Scotty was plainly upset. Twice he pulled the ponies to a halt, and seemed about to turn back for home—twice he chirruped again and the little team trotted on. Late evening found us at the livery barn. Scotty gave me two dollars. "Ye can get a bed at the Maple Leaf," he said, "and your supper and breakfast. Be at the barn tomorrow at eight sharp." I bid him good night, and turned into the B.C. Café, to be served by the smiling and pleasant young Chinese.

Eight o'clock found me at the barn, where Geordie was hitching up the team. "Scotty going home so soon?" I asked. Geordie's reply was cut short by the arrival of my boss himself. He looked better. He was freshly shaved and his heavy moustache was neatly combed. He wore a new fawn Stetson, and a handsome old gentlemen he was.

"Get in, Charlie," he took the lines and clucked.

"Are we going home?" I asked.

He looked at me from under his bushy eyebrows, "No, laddie—to the Barracks."

As the buggy swayed and bounced Scotty broke the silence. "It's my belief, laddie, there's been some funny work going on, and I'll get to the bottom of it if I can. So maybe the police boys will want to ask you a few questions, and dinna be afraid to speak up." I did not answer, for we had swung into the entrance of the Barracks square, and a corporal approached.

"Howdy, Scotty," he grinned, and, "Howdy, Corporal," returned Scotty. "What's on your mind?" the policeman went on.

"Want to see the Sergeant if he's not too busy," returned my boss. "Staff Sergeant Flint, I mean—d'ye think he can see me?"

"Surest thing you know, old-timer," and the corporal clanked ahead of us through a big building, down a corridor to a door marked "Staff Sergeant Flint—Please knock."

The corporal rapped, and "Come in," answered a pleasant voice. I felt nervous. Scotty seemed quite at ease. "Hate to bother ye, Staff," he began, but Staff smiled and said, "No bother. Sit down, won't you?" motioning to a chair. "Who's your young friend?"

"English feller I hired a week or so ago," said Scotty. "He's been riding with Jake Meldrum, and that's what I want to see ye about."

The Staff Sergeant looked mildly surprised.

"Never had *you* come in before with hired help trouble," he began.

"Och now," laughed Scotty, "it's no' the like of that. It's—I'm mortal afraid it's horse stealing!"

"Tell me," said the Staff Sergeant, in that gentle and reassuring voice I have so often heard from men of his profession.

2

Scotty told how he'd had Jake with him for five years. He was a good horseman in most ways. But—for some time now—the tally never seemed to jibe. He'd send Jake out to where he was positive so many horses should be running, and Jake would come back with few or none. Only last week the boys from the East and West had sent over word that about twenty head of his horses had been seen in Medicine Lodge Coulee. Jake came back and said there were none.

Then two years ago—or maybe eighteen months—Alex LaFromboise had told of seeing some mares and foals and a few yearlings ranging at the head of Skull Creek. Jake had gone right away—been away a week—and came back empty handed and cursing the lying half-breeds. Later Dan McGregor had met him (Scotty) in town and told him about the same bunch. By now the mares had newborn foals again. Then just within the last few days he had sent Jake and "this young feller" over to get them. Apparently Jake didn't go near McGregor's but instead chose to go some miles further, leaving "this feller" with "that awful old Geisner." From there on, he said, "Charlie here can tell ye more." He had only to add that only mature brood mares and this year's foals came back.

"Naturally," he concluded, "them yearlings and two-year-olds wouldna' be branded, but they'd stay with their mothers, and anyways McGregor gave me a rough list of the ones he's seen, and here it is." So saying, he searched through his waistcoat pockets and finally produced a creased bit of writing paper folded very small, which he handed to the "Staff."

"Thanks, Scotty," said that gentleman. "And now," turning to me, "could you tell me exactly what happened from the time you left the ranch with Jake, till you got back with the horses?" I was silent—trying to collect my wits. As if sensing my nervousness he smiled again, held out a packet of cigarettes and said, "Haven't been out from the old country long, have you?"

I told him.

"Well, my boy," he continued, "you seem to have landed into something. Now, take your time and tell me in your own way. You have nothing to fear, and if there's trouble I don't think you'll be in it." Thus encouraged I told him all I knew, omitting details. When I had finished he was silent for a while, still making notes on a scratch pad.

Then, "Do you mind if I ask you some questions?"

"No, sir," I answered.

"Right"—he suddenly smiled again. "Let's see now"—he consulted his pad—"first off, did you have anything to do with horses before you came here?"

"Yes," I replied.

"Where? On farms and so forth I suppose?"

"Yes—I rode a little. Then I used to help the plowmen feed their animals. And—the New Forest ponies. You know—they run loose and wild like the range horses here. My father took me there a couple of times sketching," I finished.

"I see. And now," he went on, "you seem to be pretty observant. Would that be to do with the sketching trips? Your father was a painter, I take it."

"Yes," I replied. "He wanted me to be one, too, and he always said the most important thing for a painter was to notice *everything*."

The policeman said, "I see. And now tell me some of the things you noticed about New Forest ponies, will you?"

To this somewhat unexpected question I replied that they always ran in family groups. "My father would say, 'See that old mare with the long tail? Now, see, she's got a sucking foal, a leggy yearling, and a two-year-old with her. That's all one family.'"

The Staff Sergeant and Scotty exchanged glances, and the latter said, "Didn't know they had horse ranches in the Old Country, but that's the way of it alright."

"Right," said Staff again. "Now, would you say that those young horses the men cut out from the mares were actually the offspring *of* those mares?"

I said, "Yes, I would think so, but of course I couldn't swear . . ."

"No man's asking you to swear, my boy," interrupted the Sergeant. "Swearing's a bad habit. Now—about brands. Have you any reason to suppose that these horses which the men called 'strays' were *not* branded except for the fact that you could not *see* the brands? Brands are mighty difficult to read sometimes, you know."

"No," I said slowly, feeling uncomfortable at being engaged with experts on a technical discussion of "The Horse." "No—only that I did look very closely—on both sides. Those geldings had been attended to lately—they were not comfortable yet—so I thought they ought to be branded, and recently enough to show up. They tell me branding and altering is often done at the same time."

"With cattle—yes," stated the Staff Sergeant, "with horses—not necessarily. They are commonly branded as foals and altered as two-year-olds. However, if they had been recently cut, it does point to them being young horses. Young studs are hell to part from the old mares, and the men might have had them in the corral to alter recently which would explain the way you tell me the corrals were mushed up. But we mustn't jump to conclusions. Now, another question. Think well. Do you know the looks of a broke horse—for saddle or harness? I am assuming these horses *might* really be strays—older than you think, and perhaps some of them broke."

"Well," I said, "I don't think a 'broke' horse would be so wild, but perhaps I'm wrong there. Anyway, most of the ones I've seen have an odd little white patch—a saddle or harness mark, I suppose; and then again the tails are usually trimmed and often the foretop cut. None of the ones we are speaking about had the *look* of a broke horse."

"Very good," he smiled. "Tell me, the buggy team tied up out there—do they have any of these marks you speak of?"

"Yes, sir—Kip has a collar mark on the off shoulder—at least that's what Jake said it is—and Bunco has a white strip each side where the belly-band buckle rubs."

Scotty stared and then laughed—"And those are my own ponies, but I couldna' have told ye *that!*" he said.

The Staff Sergeant consulted his pad again before he spoke, then—"What do you know about horses' ages—apart from teeth, of course?"

I felt on firmer ground. "With the New Forest ponies the yearlings don't have much mane or tail compared to the older ones. Besides, they are awkward and leggy—their bodies don't seem to have thickened up to match the legs—even two- or three-year-olds look different to the grown stock. Those horses they cut out looked—as I said—like yearlings and two-year-olds. Then again, the yearlings at least, seem smaller and lighter." I concluded somewhat lamely, for how to put into words that *something* that tells you what you are looking at?

My questions began again—"And you were laughed at when you spoke to this man Jake about young horses, eh?"

"Yes," I replied.

Staff looked at his notes once more—"Now this man Myers—you said someone used a nickname—what was it again?"

"Chinook," I said.

The Staff got up and took a file from a steel cabinet. Laying the folder on his desk, he rifled through the papers, finally coming up with what he wanted, which he flipped in front of me.

It contained a photograph of a man in range garb. Above were the words "WANTED FOR HORSE STEALING." Below was printed "Anthony ('Tony') Mistral—also known as 'Chinook Tony' or 'Chinook.' This man is wanted by the State of Wyoming on three charges of horse stealing. He is believed to be headed for Canada, and may look for a job horse breaking, as he is a rider by trade. If apprehended, please notify, etc., etc." Dated about two months previous.

"That's Myers," I said. "I'm positive. I see the big ring on his finger, too."

"Thank you," said the Staff Sergeant, and flipped the sheet to himself again. He took up his pencil and wrote under the picture. I saw what he wrote—not for nothing had I perfected myself at reading upside down so as to crib from my brother's Latin—it was, "Alias Myers," and he put the file away. "One more thing"—he turned to me again—"did you notice anyone—or more particular, horse or horses that you can describe? I mean, as to color, marking, or anything outstanding?"

"I think so," I replied; and told him about the crop-eared buckskin filly.

Scotty made as if to speak but the Staff Sergeant silenced him with a motion of his hand. "I want the boy to say only what he saw," he said. I finished. The policeman looked over the paper Scotty had given him. "This," he said, "is a note from Mr. McGregor to you, Scotty, is it not?"

"Oh, aye," said Scotty.

"Right," said our questioner again. "It describes a number of horses. One is a sway-backed buckskin mare branded Ex open Aye on the left hip. She had a winter-born, or very early spring foal. It was a buckskin. Being foaled in very cold, probably sub-zero weather, both its ears had been frozen so badly that the top half of them dropped off."

Scotty and I looked at each other, and my boss said softly, "Whenever ye told me something didna' look right I was wondering, had ye seen that filly."

Staff suddenly called, "Corporal!"

The corporal entered. "Send Constables Jenkins and Mathewson at once." The corporal departed. "You better stay in town another day or two, Scotty," said the Staff Sergeant, more relaxed now. "You might as well know I am sending a patrol to the ranch to pick up your man Jake, and another to Kealy Springs. It looks as if Jake has been deliberately shifting your mares off the home range, and then stealing the increase. It's a fairly old trick, but it's caught us all napping as usual. It's so hard to get evidence as a rule. I doubt that we'll get your horses back, but will do our best. As I said—you'd best stick around, eh?"

"We will that," said Scotty, and we left. It was noon as we drove out from the Barracks, and the trumpet sounded "Stables" loud and sweet, the notes floating away over the sunlit plain.

3

The police did their best, but the odds were against them. The patrol that went out to Scotty's ranch was too late. Jake had departed. Probably he wanted me to go with him that last morning so that he could pump me. Scotty must have made some pretty pointed remarks, and when he held me back Jake must have realized that trouble was on the way. Not only was Jake gone, but his saddle and spare clothes were gone, too, and the sorrel saddle horse which was Scotty's property—the horse we called Fox.

For this last theft a warrant was sworn out for Jake. The Police rode many miles on their investigations but it was as though the earth had swallowed Jake, horse and all.

The patrol to Kealy Springs was as unsuccessful. The police could get nothing out of Geisner; and Coyote Bill and the other men had had three days to decamp, and get their "hot" horses over the line. Communications were not so speedy then as now. The various detachments here were not linked up by telephone, and in any case the N.C.O. in charge was apt to be out on patrol. A wire to the sheriffs in Montana, at Chinook, Havre, Plentywood, or Malta had to be sent by way of Moose Jaw and Minot, North Dakota, and sometimes was many hours in reaching its destination.

It is a big, wide country from the Canadian border to the Great Northern Railway line in the States—badlands and buttes and semi-desert—a country where a man can travel many miles and still keep out of sight. The stolen horses were probably branded (with a brand registered under an assumed name somewhere south of the border), and very likely herded in some quiet, grassy valley till the brands "haired over" and lost their new look. A few weeks after branding the scab lifts and leaves a vivid pink scar, which takes some months to tone down and "hair over" again. Thereafter that brand will show, either because the new hair may be a different color, or grizzled, or because of the "set" of the hair.

It was quite probable that the thieves had intended to brand this bunch of young stuff at Geisner's before moving them. My presence may have made them a bit nervous so they pulled out right after Jake and I left, for according to signs the police found, a bunch of nags had been held for some hours in a brush corral in Cow Coulee, on the south side of the bench. The men wanted them away from Geisner's, evidently, but held them till nightfall before attempting to cross the open country towards the border.

I was learning a lot of things.

As for the police and the U.S. sheriffs, they took this matter very seriously and renewed a vigilance along the border that had dropped off in the last few years.

Just before we left, Staff Sergeant Flint called us both to his office. He told us what he could of the above happenings, and ended up with some words of advice to us both.

To Scotty he said, "Old-timer, I joined the Force about the time you left it. You are the old-fashioned out-of-date rancher whose word is as good as his bond, and you think everybody else is the same. It is a good way to be. But it is expensive. If people were all as straight as you think, I would be out of a job today!

"I know that at one time you had a lot of faith in Jake Meldrum. You told me so yourself. You had no sons, you said, and here was a likely fellow, and if he'd do right by you, well, he'd probably get a share in the spread someday. Jake might have been alright once. But you see, you were too easy and too trusting, and your 'likely man' couldn't wait for 'his share.' Human nature is often like that. Just because his father was in the Force in your day—well, even preachers' sons . . .

"So you get yourself a good ramrod, Scotty—a man with references, not just a saddle tramp from God knows where who will try to 'work you' like Jake. You don't need to mind asking for a reference, and the right man will be glad to give it. Then see that he does his work. Oh, I know you're getting old and can't ride—but first off have a roundup to gather all your horses in. Put on enough men to be sure you make a clean sweep.

"Then brand everything that's 'slick'—provided you know they're off your own mares. See that all the young studs are taken care of. Then get a brand new tally book and enter up the lot, that'll give you a fresh start. And after that, let us know right away when anything looks suspicious—darn it! The police can't help you fellows if you leave your stuff all over the place and unbranded. Just trusting to people's honesty!

"What's that?—you hate writing?—no hand with a pen? Well, get Charlie here—or someone—to do that, but get those nags *tallied and branded* and *keep 'em* tallied and branded, for your own sake—else you'll go broke; and for our sake, so's we don't do a lot of work for nothing. Now, so long, Scotty! And no hard feelings, eh?"

"Man, no!" laughed Scotty. "I ken well 'tis my own fault—trusting to luck and honesty like you said! But I got to tell you I believe I *can* get the right kind o' a man. Do ye ken Lee Blackwell? Him that used to break horses for the Q?"

"I sure do," replied the Sergeant. "He's a good enough rider, I know—and honest, I am sure. We had him riding the rough string at Regina when I was at Depot coupla' years back. Sergeant Fowell thought a lot of him, and I believe he tried to enlist him in the Force, but Lee said he'd done enough soldiering and saluting in ninety-nine. But what makes you think you can get him?"

A strange horse

"Eh!—but I'm pretty certain! The wagon boss of the 76 was in town last e'en and he was telling me Lee had been wi' the Matador outfit but they were closing out some of their lease at Swift Current so he was at a loose end, and he was speiring for a job with the 76. But Galbraith says they're near through wi' the roundup, so they don't need him. I sent word back wi' him to tell Lee to ride over to Graburn and see me."

"Good—good," the policeman said, "you'll be in luck if you get him. Maybe I lectured you too soon! Looks like you mean business anyway." He turned to me. "Now, my boy," he said, "you've been a help to your employer. Go on being. You're young and you're green, but I bet you know right from wrong and don't forget it. If you ever need help—come to us!—and don't forget to write home!" he added with a smile.

4

We had been back home for several days. I had gone up the creek flats to find old Brindle, and had brought her and her husky calf into the corral. The next thing was to milk her. With helpful advice from Scotty, I finally got her roped and snubbed up to a post. She fought hard for a while, but after I had snared her hind feet and tied them fast, she gave in. Warily I investigated. I found I could milk only one teat. The other quarters were spoiled, and when I told Scotty that— allowing for the calf's share—a pint of milk a day would be about all we'd get, he said, "Turn her loose then, Charlie." Turning her loose wasn't quite so easy as catching her. She had sharp horns, and gave me a couple of nasty jabs in the ribs before I got the rope off. Finally the job was done. I turned her back up the creek, and since the afternoon was spoilt anyway, I sat smoking for a while on the creek bank, watching the sun sink slowly towards Eagle Butte. It was getting on for fall, and heavy dew was already beginning to unlock the night smells from the ground and herbage. The slightly saline smell of a marshy place by the creek made me think of looking for sea-urchins at low tide back home in Sussex. The grass, cured by the dry winds and hot sun, smelt like new-mown hay.

Somewhere a mare nickered and a foal answered shrilly. A short-eared owl—the earliest of that fraternity to be abroad, never waiting till the sun is down—beat up and down on silent wings in his quest for mice. I pulled up Buck's head to mount, and his breath smelt of wild mint. When I put Buck in the stable, a horse snorted in the gloom, and I held the door wide open to see better.

In the stall where Jake had always kept the missing sorrel was a tall bay that looked as if he had traveled far. He knew it was a strange barn and a stranger entering, for he stopped eating and turned his head to me with hay still hanging from his mouth. I spoke to him, "So—boy," and he heaved a deep, tired sigh and relaxed, burying his nose again in the sweet prairie hay.

Hanging on a peg was a heavy Frazier saddle, from the horn of which dangled a "lug" bridle (that fits just over the ears, with no throat latch). Thrown over the two was a damp Navahoe saddle blanket. On a small silver plate set into the leather behind the saddle cantle were the initials "L.B." All this I took in with the curiosity natural to one who loves horses and gear.

And when I got to the house, Scotty was smoking his pipe and talking to a tall man of about thirty-five who looked up with a pleasant face as I came in.

"Eh, Charlie," said Scotty, "this'll be Lee Blackwell you'll have heard me speak o'. He'll be straw boss from now on—and, Lee, this is the young Londoner I was telling ye aboot. I want ye to coach him like, and learn him to work wi' ye."

Lee rose, and we shook hands. I liked him at once. Inwardly I decided to tell him at the first opportunity that England was not all London!

CHAPTER FOUR

Range gate

1

For a few days after Lee's arrival I didn't see much of him. He made some long rides alone. I think he was getting the lay of the land, and listing what horses were on the home range.

In the evenings he would be closeted with Scotty, going over the old tally book and getting the picture in his mind.

Then one day at breakfast he said, "Charlie, get your spare horses up this morning and bring in the black and the two bays for me. We'll be doing a lot of riding, and they can run in the small wrangle field and come up to the bars for hay. Soon as you get that done we'll ride. I'll pack some grub for the both of us."

I rode Buck through "the little wrangle field," which contained about a hundred acres, and out into "the big wrangle field," which enclosed four sections—well over twenty-five hundred acres, and out of which the smaller field was carved in the nearest corner. The big field was a government lease, for already "nesters"—homesteaders—were pulling into the country hereabouts and filing on their quarter section claims of a hundred and sixty acres. In order to keep their home pasture, ranchers were beginning to see the wisdom of leasing and fencing some of the best grazing. It was to be only another couple of years before free grazing would be a thing of the past. Many ranchers said, "Oh, we've had a few wet years and the homesteaders will take up some land, but as soon as it gets dry again they'll move out." But big outfits like Wallace and Ross over southwest in Alberta were taking the hint, and proposed building nearly thirty miles of fence this year; so rumor went.

It didn't take me long to find the gentle bunch and bring them home. I found Lee saddled up and ready to go, so I quickly switched my gear from Buck to Tony—the little gray with the dark nose—and we rode out through the south gate with its tall pine posts and crossbars. One of the reasons for the twenty-foot gate posts one sees on the line fences is to make it easier to find the gate in the wire. You may come to a tight fence stretching out of sight to right and left. It will be of three wires, the top one about five feet above the ground. You ride to the nearest high ground and follow the line of barbed wires as it goes over hills and through hollows. Naturally, in a woodless country all fences are of barbed wire, only corrals being made of poles. Usually you will be able to pick out two high posts by eye—for most leases have a gate about every mile. This saves you from fruitlessly following a fence on horseback in the wrong direction.

That was the beginning of many days' steady riding. Sometimes we made it back to the ranch at night; sometimes we stopped at a ranch; sometimes we camped on the prairie. When we did that, it would be by a creek or spring, and where the grass was good. Usually only one (the oldest) horse needed to be picketed, for the younger one would not stray far without his pal. We carried a picket rope, and never used a good lariat for that purpose except in an emergency, for the hand-twist would kink up with night dew and be ruined. If we had no picket pin, we'd look for a survey mound and use one of the stakes, although this was frowned on by government men! Otherwise, we would try

to find long-tufted grass—Lee showed me how to plait the end of a
soft picket rope into such a tuft, which, surprisingly, would hold.

We always had coffee and Lee carried a small pot in his "turkey"
together with some sugar. And if we didn't have some cold grub with
us, we might have a little flour which we could boil up into a "dough-
god" in the same pot; or sometimes snare a sage hen or even a rabbit
if there was brush.

And then we'd lay our chaps beneath us and our hairy, smelly,
saddle blankets over us, topped perhaps with a slicker, and look up
at the indigo sky and count the falling stars, then suddenly we knew
nothing more—until the sun hit the top of the gray-green sage and
the longspurs fluttered overhead.

At times we brought home as many as twenty-five or thirty horses—
mares, foals, and young stuff. But there would be days when we drew
a blank or returned with only two or three head. Everything was turned
into the big wrangle field, where Scotty meant to keep them through
the winter—the grass was thick and abundant—and until the mares
could be bred the next spring after foaling. And Lee, with a scrap
of paper and a stub of pencil, would note the coloring, sex, and age
of each animal so they could be entered in the tally book.

Before snow flew, Lee said, he wanted everything gathered, branded,
altered, and tallied. Then he would know how many studs would be
needed next spring, and how many marketable young horses would
be on hand for sale.

The horse market was good. Settlers coming in, and farmers in the
wheat belt getting out of oxen and into horses meant brisk demand,
and matched teams of broke young horses changed hands at from three
hundred to three hundred and fifty dollars. Scotty's band, if properly
managed, should give him a good profit yet.

And so we rode, as summer gave place to golden fall, and the frost
got a bit keener each night, and the green timbered slopes of the
Cypress Hills turned to bronze where the poplars grew, leaving the
spruce and pine darker looking than ever.

2

The haying crew—made up of temporary help—which had been stacking hay on the bench, had long since been paid off and had drifted to the harvest fields of the wheat belt.

Soon the roundup wagon would be pulling in to its winter quarters at the old Oxheart; and the riders would disband and go to the ranches for winter work. The boys from the States would be on their way to Havre, to Powder River, to the Bear Paws or the Little Rockies with their "cuts" of Montana cattle which had grazed the summer away in Canada.

The roundup wagon was variously called the "chuck" or "grub" wagon, but to the cowboys it was just the "Wagon" with a capital W. For out on the far prairies, anything up to 150 miles from the smallest town, the Wagon was not only home, but town, too. Here the riders met at grub time. Here they had their turkeys with their tobacco and spare socks and perhaps a girl's photo. Here they ate, they slept, and played poker, as well as tricks on each other and the cook.

The cook was boss of the grub, but the foreman of the roundup was the Wagon Boss. He ate alone and didn't talk much, for on him was much responsibility. He'd take his mug of coffee, his plate of beans and salt beef a little to one side and seem to be looking idly over the landscape, but he was busy. He was "figgering." Not that beans and salt beef was all there was to eat, for the cook made yeast bread if he had a cookstove, and good Dutch-oven soda bread if he cooked on a campfire; and the boys liked lots of finger-licking syrup and canned tomatoes. Sometimes towards the end of a run grub might run a bit short, and sometimes (on the bigger outfits) they'd maybe kill a steer. But not on ours, which was the local "pool" wagon, that is, a wagon owned and run by a group of smaller ranchers like Scotty.

And it was the Wagon that worked—not the men. At least in conversation; for a man would say "Our Wagon was working Chokecherry Ridge" when he meant that he and his bunch were rounding up cattle on the Chokecherry Ridge. Just as he'd say, "I was with the Spencer Wagon in '13' "—which meant he was somewhere down on the Milk

River then, but he'd say it as a man might say, "I was living on King Street in Regina."

The Cypress Hills "pool" wagon "worked the country" (as they say) from the hills to the border. The Circle Diamond from Montana worked east and west along both sides of the line. The Spencer wagon worked west into Alberta, and still another, the 76 from Crane Lake, west to the Great Sandhills, north of Maple Creek, and as far as the South Saskatchewan. Beyond that river was the domain of the Matador Land and Cattle Company.

Two of Scotty's riders—Pete Lamond ("Banjo Pete") and "Chuck" Dennis—were expected back any day with the Ex Aye Bar "cut."

The boss, he eats alone

3

Lee proved the best of companions and teachers. He was quiet, calm, and evidently a master of his craft. I never saw him lose patience with a beast. Where Jake had taught me nothing, letting me find out for myself, Lee showed me something every day. How to keep creases out of a saddle blanket, how to knee hobble a horse; how to picket him to a tuft of coarse bottom grass if no pin were available, and a thousand other little essential details, which go to make the difference between ease and discomfort to horse and rider.

Before the winter set in I could use a rope after a fashion, and knew how to avoid being trapped or hurt by it, as well as to keep the loop away from my spurs and my horse's tail.

Under Lee's tutilage I broke out a four-year-old gelding to add to my "string." The pony did not buck much when I first rode him in the corral; but I thought it was bad enough. He was very nervous, but Lee said something I never forgot—"You think *you* are scared! Don't worry—that hoss is a damn sight scareder!"

Next time Lee snubbed up the colt to his saddle horn, and I crawled on somehow. The colt couldn't do much, and after about a mile Lee passed me the halter shank, and said, in that easy way of his which horses liked, "Take it easy. He don't know he's free yet. Sit tight but relax. He'll follow 'Cap' (Lee's own mount) anywhere now, so don't bother to try to rein him till he gets used to packing you."

Next day we left the colt (which I called "Red") saddled and bridled, with one rein tied to a stirrup. He was in a big corral and had freedom to move about, but always the rein brought him around in a big circle. We went about other work—we had some foals to brand—and at noon, after he'd had his hay, Red was turned loose again, this time with the opposite line tied back. It wasn't long before his mouth began to toughen up enough to bear reining on, and he knew what a slight tug meant.

Next time I rode him he went pretty well. Lee said—we were getting near a small band of horses—"See if you can work Red around to the left and bring in that there gray mare and foal." Red didn't want to leave Cap. He seemed to think his life depended on following exactly in his tracks. With some difficulty, for he kept trying to rear and throw his head, I worked the colt partly around in the right direction; then he got stubborn and started to back up. Lee said quietly—"Don't let him put it over you. Tighten your grip and then use your quirt—leave his head free or he'll start to buck around." I obeyed. With the first crack of the quirt he bucked, but I had my seat. Lee saw I was uncertain and called, "Hit 'im again—and hit 'im every time he bucks—don't stop till he goes the way you want."

If you are green and a horse starts to argue with you, you quite naturally think of his size and strength and you think you can't win. But when you get to know, you realize a horse can't think of two things at once. If you can change his thought, you are master in no time.

So I quirted that pony a couple more times, and he didn't like it and I thought, "here's where I get piled"—but just then he lunged in the right direction, straightened up, and loped towards the old mare. She ran to join the bunch and Red, right behind her, realized he had done it and was quite pleased.

In an almost incredibly short time—about a week—that colt, which was not even halter-broke when we first caught him up, was driving stock, if not quite like a veteran, at least very well. It was interesting to see how he gradually gained confidence and got to know his job. Lee said, "All this fancy breaking and lunging on a rope may be okay, but for my money take a green horse and put him to work with stock right away—that way he don't have time to think about monkey pranks." Red was always hard to catch. He had to be corralled and roped each time. But he remembered lunging and fighting against the hard-twist lariat when I had halter broke him, and after that, no matter how fast he was dashing along the corral bars, he'd stop dead the minute the noose settled over his head.

Of course, while a young stock horse was put to work right away, the actual hand work involved was not to be compared with eight or ten hours on a plow, such as would be the lot (very often) of a draught colt. You were constantly on and off for one reason or another, and the companionship with your horse was close and intimate. You would go a few miles at a jog. Then a gate to open. Then perhaps a short rest by a creek for a drink and a graze while you sat on a knoll with a cigarette, searching the landscape for the sight of some stock, so as to save miles of riding. Then away again to look through a bunch of horses. Nothing wanted there—so an easy trot over low hills to explore up draws or around water holes.

Always doing something, always looking for something, but never hurrying, for—contrary to some Western films—cowboys don't go dashing along madly all day! At noon, saddle and bridle off, and either hobbled or picketed to graze; although with one old wise horse along, the green ones could often be turned loose with just the halter shank dragging. Young horses are like young people. They like to appear very brave and dashing, but they won't often break ties altogether with their elders, and few young horses would make a dash for home on their own hook.

A young horse, perhaps the third time out, hardly knows what to do when unsaddled and hobbled. He seems afraid to move, let alone get down for a roll or start grazing. He thinks he is still under discipline.

Another thing that helped in breaking a horse—he was always in and out of strange places and seeing strange sights. A lumbering wagon or a high-top buggy might scare him the first time, but not again. Barking dogs, chickens, or geese in a strange corral would make him snort; but as soon as he got his hay, good appetite soon overcame fright. Mostly our saddle horses lived by grazing, and none of them knew what oats was; but the odd overnight or noon feed of hay at a ranch was something they really enjoyed.

We never put a horse to a gallop except when we were chasing something and were forced to. By riding at a slow trot—"*troto sereno*" Lee called it (he had been in Mexico)—our horses were always cool. Then if we spied a bunch of real "spooky" horses, led by some old ridge-running mare, we had plenty of reserve in our mounts and could usually head them the way we wanted. But those old leaders—the matriarch mares—were up to all the tricks of the trade. We thought we could "read" the country pretty well but what those old sisters knew about it made us feel pretty green sometimes.

We would start a band down a coulee which led to level ground. They'd trot along and turn a corner perhaps; and the next thing we'd know they would be clattering away up above us, headed for the broken country again. The old leader knew there was a side coulee up which she could dodge. Once in a while we would lose a bunch like that because dusk was coming early. And, of course, next time the old girl could be depended on to pull the same trick again. Only this time one of us would not go down the coulee at all but slip back and around to the head of the "bolt hole" and outwit the old devil. They usually knew when they were outmaneuvered though, and after that they'd string out for the home corral. I remembered the same sort of thing happening when I was riding with Jake, and he didn't seem to mind them getting away. It was clear to me now that this was what he wanted. It made them wild and foxy, which suited his purpose.

4

Not only did I learn a lot of horse nature, but I was able to see any amount of wildlife on these rides. Flocks of pipits and longspurs would rise out of the dry grass and sweep away like wind-blown leaves. They were migrating southward from their Arctic breeding grounds. Geese and ducks were gathering on the lakes preparatory for departure, and we would hear the sharp whit-whit of mallards' wings above as we rode home in the dark. The grating cries of south-bound cranes filled the air for days.

Once in a while one of us would pack a scatter gun and get a brace or two of prairie chicken (sharp-tailed grouse) which Lee showed me how to skin and spit above a fire of "*bois de vache*"—the plainsman's fuel which was always handy.

These buffalo chips—to use an old term—were really just that in the days of the Red River carts and hunting Indians. This had been a great bison pasture once, and the beast's old wallows were everywhere—shallow depressions perhaps a foot deep in the center and six to eight feet in circumference—now grassed over. Great buffalo stones were also here and there, where bison were once wont to rub and scratch, till they had worn a deep trench all around and polished the rock to such a patina that they shine to this day. And quite often we rode by bleached old skulls of bison that had met death here perhaps forty years ago. Indians, in pursuit of the herds, had camped frequently in this area; we often saw the stone rings marking the sites of their tepees.

One such camp, judging by the rings, must have contained about one hundred and fifty lodges. Some of the oldest camps would have been those of the Gros Ventres, but most of them were Cree or Blackfoot; for here was a meeting place of the two nations—though "meeting place" ill describes that no man's land in which these old enemies both hunted, and in which the tide of mastery swayed back and forth till recently.

Sometimes we saw pronghorn antelope, but this heavily grassed foothills' country was not their most favored habitat. Rather, they preferred the sagebrush and soapweed flats further south, where the grass was short and the wind never ceased to blow, for antelope are creatures of the wind and the empty places.

It is in the fall, too, that the eagles come here from the mountains for their winter hunting. Mostly golden eagles, but sometimes one of the "bald" kind. We could usually tell when we were approaching the carcass of a dead animal; for these birds, gorged and sluggish, would rise and sail slowly away on their great pinions.

I have watched one for an hour—lying on my back as my pony grazed alongside—without seeing a movement of its wings as it circled slowly in search of carrion. This would usually be in the mornings, and I imagine the bird was taking advantage of the upcurrents of air as the sun warms the earth. The prairies are in this way kin to any desert, for no matter how hot the day, it was always chilly at night. Late in October it might freeze at night hard enough ice to bear a man's weight; yet by noon your coat might be off and your horse sweating. And the mirages would always be there to remind us that this is part of what was once called "The great American desert."

5

Gradually the days drew in, and gradually we gathered up horses from far and near, till Lee said, "Good enough for this year, we've got in about two hundred and fifty—better than the old man hoped for." He added that by spring all but the mares could go out on the range again, as they would now be "range broke" (as they always should have been) and would not stray far as long as they were periodically gathered. The mares would stay in till after next spring's breeding season, so their foals would be dropped within the fence; and as Lee explained, "A hoss most generally will always come back to where he was foaled."

"Take Cap now," he said. "If I was to turn him loose he'd stick around for just so long. If I didn't hunt him up, in a couple of weeks he wouldn't be in Canada, but back along the Powder River where he come from—wouldn't you, old boy?" and he slapped Capitano (to give his full name) on his now not-so-glossy rump; for the horses were getting their heavy winter coats.

"Banjo Pete" and Chuck were back home now from the roundup with about three hundred head of cattle which would range on the long grass till feeding time. They had lots to tell of the roundup. Of course they had heard all about Jake's doings—news travels quickly where few people live. They all figured he'd got away to the States.

One late November morning, after weeks of clear, mild weather, during which the chinook hung on, the wind changed at night and we awoke to a snowy world. It lay for only a couple of days, then the chinook blew again, but not strongly enough to wipe the range completely clean, for the snow stayed in the shady nooks and on the north sides of the rolling hills. And, of course, on the high bench, which was always colder. It wasn't deep even there, but the white carpet served to set off the trim, purplish clumps of shrubby cinquefoil which we called buckbrush or greasewood.

Lee, riding with me in the low hills, pointed out the patches of snow on the north slopes. "Ever notice," he said, "how the grass is always heavy and coarse on the north sides? That's 'cause the snow lies there--even late in the spring. Prairie fires usually skip them—too wet to burn—so the sod builds up, and after a while, small brush. That's why any 'ole cow hates to graze a north slope. The grass ain't sweet enough and the rose bushes prick her nose."

I did notice. And I noticed, too, that the south slopes showed a sparser—if sweeter—growth; and also very often some erosion from wind, so that pebbles and small rocks were exposed, and in place of rose burrs or snowberry shrubs would be small "pin cushion" cactus and fronds of creeping juniper. I found that no matter how the fog came down you could not mistake north from south. Even on the darkest night you knew by the clink of stones, or the muffled, cushioned hoofbeats of your horse, which side of a hill you were on. Along water courses and creeks this was even more pronounced, the sides away from the sun sometimes carrying quite a heavy growth of willows and scrub.

I learned, too, to look at the lay of the grass to get my bearings. The prevailing wind is southwest, and any long, matted growth invariably lay to the northeast.

If either of the above failed, there was always polaris who never lied—and the Big Dipper to find him with. Once you got to know the movement of that group—which elsewhere is variously called Charles's Wain, the Plow, or the Great Bear—you have a clock that never fails so long as the sky is clear.

That snowfall was a warning. Winter was not far off. Soon Keewadin, as the Indians say, would show himself in his white rabbit robe.

6

And sure enough, winter set in soon after that with a cold spell followed by a deep snowfall. I was amazed that it didn't seem colder, when about Christmas time the thermometer dropped to minus twenty-five, then to minus thirty and forty, after which it slowly began to moderate. With those low temperatures the usual winds dropped, and so dry was the air under the cloudless sky, that the cold, while ready to bite unmittened hands, never got into the bones as it does in damper climes.

About five miles southeast of the home ranch the winter camp was situated. It was at the foot of the hills—handy to the haystacks on the bench above. Several springs flowed well all winter for the cattle to drink at, and there were clumps of heavy spruce to form a sheltered bed-ground for the animals. Why those springs—like many in the West—did not freeze, I don't know. Probably extra water pressure in winter caused a constant overflow.

It was customary to leave the cattle to rustle their living pretty well all winter, but enough hay was put up to take care of rough spells and deep snow. The cattle knew where to go when rustling got difficult.

A few cattle had showed themselves at the camp just after the snowstorm, so on one of the more moderate days the four of us saddled up and brought them home. Here the calves were separated from their mothers and put in the weaning corral. The calves bawled their heads off, of course, and so did the cows. The steers and young stuff had drifted back to the winter camp by the next day, and there we fed them. We also fed the calves in the weaning pen, but did not put any hay out for their mothers, who gradually got tired of standing in the snow, bawling. Next day they too, began to drift off in small bunches to join the others at the hay camp. Within a few days the rest of the cattle showed up and we had all the calves weaned. However, for pretty well two weeks, we'd suddenly hear a cow bawl; and the anxious chorus from the calf corral would start all over again. Some old cow had suddenly bethought herself of her offspring. A five-mile walk at night was nothing to one of those range cows.

Sometimes on a frosty night our sleep would be disturbed by several cows tramping around the corral, bawling and making a loud squeaking noise as they walked on the frozen, packed snow. There was a cabin and a small stable at the winter camp, and we took turns where one of us would stay there and feed any cattle that came. The hay, stacked on the bench, was about two miles from the camp. Of the three of us who remained at the home ranch, one had to go daily with a team and sleigh to haul hay for the saddle stock and calves. Whoever did this would take grub to the camp, or mail, as needed, and would eat his dinner there, for it was seven hard miles both ways.

Sometimes, if it were cold and the snow badly drifted, two of us went—usually Banjo Pete and myself. Then we would take a team and rack each and haul hay—enough to do us two or three days. That way we could build up a little reserve in case of really serious weather. The advantage of two was that if a rack upset—as quite often happened in bad drifts—there was the other man and team to help put things to rights. Some of those trips were pretty cold. The worst days were when there was a good stiff breeze at minus ten degrees. That was a lot worse than thirty-five or forty below, but calm. One or the other of us froze our faces every cold spell. I soon realized that the oldish men one sees so often on the prairies with parchment-like patches of dark skin on their chins and cheekbones had been victims of continual frostbite—and that the swollen veins in richly colored bulbous noses did not come from drinking!

The hay racks we used were made by local halfbreeds. They were called "basket racks" and the same technique was used as in making the Red River carts of long ago. The ax, auger, and drawknife were the only tools used. They were built right on the bob sleighs. The main frame was of poplar hewn by hand and bored at two-foot intervals to let in the peeled willow sticks that formed the sides and ends. No nails were used. They were commonly ten feet wide and sixteen to eighteen feet long, and one could load up to two ton of well-packed "prairie wool" as this bench hay was called. Any of Scotty's big Clyde teams could handle that easily.

7

In between cold spells we would get thaws—mostly from the chinook wind. We would go to bed at night with the thermometer reading minus thirty. We'd put a couple of big sticks on the bunkhouse stove and shut her off for the night.

The bunkhouse itself was a snug one-roomed cabin of pine logs, well chinked. With several men in the bunks and the old stove gradually burning those logs through the night, you'd think we'd be pretty fuggy, but no; the stove still drew draft enough from around the door to keep the air sweet.

But as I was saying, it might be $-30°$, and we'd roll in, with extra blankets or buffalo robes tucked around us. (Any real buffalo robes were by now pretty well worn out, but soft tanned horse or cow hides were invariably referred to by the old name.) At midnight we might wake feeling too warm, and wondering if the old barrel stove had burned too furiously. One of us would get up to investigate—no—the big logs were only smoldering. We'd try to sleep again, but sleep wouldn't come. We'd puff cigarettes in the dark and talk. Then someone would say—"Must be going to chinook."

And when morning came, sure enough that great arch would be

hanging over Eagle Butte again and the air would feel mild, always with a faint smell that made me think of low tide at Winchelsea. Then just at sunup the wind would come with a rush and a roar. You would see the pines on the hilltop bend and sway, and bits of hay and trash would be flung up and away, while every loose board on the barn roof would flap and squeak.

By ten o'clock the water would be dripping from the eaves as the snow from the last storm melted, and we'd look at the thermometer—forty above! Another thing we'd notice—smells. The smell of the barns, of hay, of damp earth, struck one with peculiar emphasis; for during the hard frosts there is an utter lack of any scent.

Sometimes it would blow for just a few hours, but often it blew for days, and left the range bare again. The cattle would low and sniff the breeze; then, leaving the feed ground, they would slowly string out in single file over the prairie. Next day would find the low dun hills all speckled with them, and they would stay out till the next storm.

Sometimes a storm came when they had strayed far off, so that occasionally we would have to ride to find them. But as they grazed north of the Hills, and most bad storms came from that direction, drifting before the wind would bring them either to the winter camp or anyway along the edge of the bush, and in its shelter they could make their way to the feed ground. We must have looked like Mongolian herders on our ponies with their wild manes and tails and shaggy winter coats, ourselves muffled in sheepskin-lined jackets, fur hats and mitts, and woolly angora chaps. In those days, when there was much winter riding to do, those chaps were a necessary part of your clothing.

8

January that year was rough; but all February was mild, and the good weather hung on well into March. We had not seen the cattle for some time when Lee announced, "I got a feeling we'd better locate them dogies—if they git too far east and a storm comes from the northwest, they're apt to drift still further that way, and if they hit the Havre trail they'll keep going through Six Mile Gap and we'll have a hell of a time to gather them."

Scotty didn't think too much of the idea. "Why, hell," he said, "in the old days we let the cattle take their chances—they never came to much harm!"

"Not even in nineteen and six?" said Lee with a grin. "Have it your own way, then."

Scotty hurriedly said, thinking of the big kill-off of *that* year, "If you've a mind to go, just take one man. Charlie better stay here and Banjo can get on down to the camp to be ready if she storms."

So Lee and Chuck went the next morning. It was still mild, but there was a hint of what Lee called "duck-egg green" in the northwestern sky which he said didn't look good to him. Also for several nights now we had not heard the merry chorus of coyotes yapping; nor had the horned owls "hoo-hoo'd" around the corrals. The wild things knew something was in the wind.

And wind it was; that afternoon. I was coming from the winter camp, heading straight into the northwest with a big load of hay. When the wind came, she came all at once—wham!—and before five minutes were up I had my ear flaps down, my mitts on, and my head tucked into the collar of my sheepskin with only one eye peering out. The team snorted and pulled for home on a half-trot. It began to snow—just fine icy pellets at first, that stung the eyeballs and made the horses arch their necks and turn their heads sideways. But by the time I got to the ranch it was snowing hard and the wind was throwing it down only to snatch it up and whirl it in my face again. I didn't stop to throw off my load. I unhooked traces as fast as I could and got the panting team into the barn. Scotty was in the bunkhouse fixing the fires. "Could be only a squall," he said, "or could be a bronc blizzard— anyways, I hope Lee and Chuck can get under cover."

They got in late that night. It is a miracle they made it. Lee said they had sighted a long string of cattle just before noon, all drifting south, and he felt in his bones that Chuck and he had better drift with them "pretty pronto." Long before they got to the timber they couldn't see a landmark at all, he said, and it was the cattle that saved them. "We just strung along behind them 'old dogies.'" said Lee, as he sat rubbing salve into his frostbitten feet, "and shore enough them critters didn't miss the winter camp by a hundred yards. I reckon if it hadn't been for the timber and old Banjo a forkin' out hay and hollerin' the feed-call they'd have gone right by 'cause their eyes were bunged up some with ice. We knew we'd make it here okay from the camp—you can't lose ole' Cap at suppertime."

"And how many—d'ye think—of them cattle made it into the camp?" asked Scotty.

"Not more'n half I reckon," answered Lee, "mebbe less. A lot more must have been way east—so could be we got to really get out and ride when this lets up."

9

The storm blew with ever-increasing ferocity for two more days; during which it was nip and tuck getting from the bunkhouse to the barn and back. We fixed up a rope by tying several lariats together, but even then the wind couldn't be faced, and going out to feed the horses we went backwards. On the third day—the worst—we couldn't get feed to the calves; but they had a shed for a windbreak, and a couple of days' starvation wouldn't hurt them, we knew. After that the wind dropped and it warmed up a bit, but continued to snow; only this time it was large, wet flakes, and sometimes cold rain. We managed to get my load of hay unloaded at the calf corral that day.

Lee decided that next day we would ride out and see what we could find, but that night the wind came out of the northwest with greater fury than ever.

Next morning it took us till noon to dig out the bunkhouse and stables; for the snow had drifted right to the top of the doors on the lee side, and it was packed so hard we shoveled it in chunks. About noon the wind dropped and the sun came out, and by evening the prairies lay peacefully smothered by a great snow blanket; all rippled and carved and sculptured by the wind. The sun set red behind Eagle Butte, and as the full moon rose, the northern lights—always a good sign—flickered and wavered across the sky.

The next day we thought, "now we can ride." But we hadn't gone far before our horses were played out and bleeding above the fetlocks from the sharp edges of the crusted snow.

"This doesn't look too good," said Lee, as we turned our weary mounts about—"its got to soften up some before we can do much."

After the storm

And so another anxious day passed before the sun finally made travel possible. And that morning a rider from the East and West Ranch made it through to us by following the edge of the timber where the snow was not so packed. Even so, both he and his horse were weary; and he was glad to throw himself on a bunk.

He told us that about eight hundred of their cattle had drifted through the hills by way of Graburn Gap—three miles west of us—and would be scattered over the open country south. Pete and George wanted our riders to lend them a hand to locate them. They were short of help, but young Mitchell (our visitor and informer) would stay over and go with us, while the brothers would join us somewhere below the gap. Mitchell added that they thought Scotty's cattle would all have made the winter camp. Lee explained the situation to Scotty.

The boss thought a while, then true to his salt, he said, "Aweel, laddie, 'twill be easier going like through the Gap, and if the boys want help, we'd better give it. Forbye, any of our cattle that have lived through the storm must have gone through the Six Mile, and if they follow the Havre trail there'll be no guessing where they'll be. However, the Oxheart riders and Badger's men will be out, I'm thinking. So we'll let the folks east take care o' ours, and we'll gie help closest to home where it'll do the most good. Take Charlie and Chuck wi' ye. Banjo can stay at the camp; and I guess I can tend the calves for a couple days."

That afternoon we set out with Mitchell through the Graburn Gap. We saw some cattle sign, but the wind had obliterated most of it. There were no horse tracks, so we knew we were ahead of the "boys," as the proprietors of the East and West were commonly called. At one place we found a cow standing upright in a snowdrift—frozen solid— she stared at us with great eyes that were as hard and glassy as marbles.

It was the warm day between the storms that had done the damage. The tiny ice particles of the first snow had penetrated through the hair to the hide, until the animals' coats were plugged full. It had started to melt on their backs that mild day.

Then when it suddenly turned cold again, it froze solid and became a heavy mass of ice, built up by the second snow.

Now the heat of the sun was thawing the ice loose—that's why we could see the cow's eyes—and as we looked at the poor dead critter, a mass of ice which must have weighed fifty pounds suddenly sloughed off her hips, taking hair and hide with it.

"Good gosh," said Lee, "if there's many more like that it'll be a real die-off. Anything still alive won't hardly be worth saving if the snow goes quick. If it *don't;* well, holler-gut (i.e., starvation) will finish 'em. Let's go."

And as we came out onto the plain beyond and topped the first rise, what a ghastly scene presented itself. It was a Dante's "Inferno"— the rolling plains, the Milk River ridge a blue knife edge on the southwest horizon, the sky blue and clear, the sun hot. The glare of the snowfield stinging one's eyes. And looking, we suddenly saw—

here—there—along that coulee edge—in the lee of that patch of brush—at the edge of that wash—dark, deformed bits and pieces of shape. All that was left of eight hundred cattle! Not lying all together, of course. We could see perhaps twenty-five from this low ridge; but we knew the scene would be repeated and repeated. Sometimes a humped-up back, and a bit of a head. Sometimes only a leg protruding from a drift, or part of a horn. These were dead cattle. But worse than the dead were the living. Poor beasts! Stuck fast in the drifts, or trying to rise from shallower snow as we rode up; feebly making a gesture of defiance, trying to give a toss of the heads at the approaching horsemen; that ultimate standing at bay which is instinctive to creatures about to die.

Many of them were practically—if not totally—blind, their eyeballs frozen. Great chunks of ice welded together ears, horns and forehead. Hair, hide, and meat was stripped in chunks from their backs and ribs. Their tails were frozen like broom handles.

Some of them had been hock-frozen, and when they tried to move, their joints creaked like rusty hinges. We looked for a minute or two. The East and West rider said softly, "Them could be any of us."

Lee slowly pulled his Winchester from under his stirrup and levered in a shell. "I'm mighty sorry, old gel," he said to a brockle-faced cow that stared at him with her sightless eyes. "I'm mighty sorry," and you felt he meant it. Bang!

We finished off several more, then went over the next ridge. We heard a couple of shots from our west and partly behind us. "That'll be the boys," said Lee.

It was dark when we turned into Bill MacRae's horse ranch near Egg Lake. But we had another long day ahead of the same kind, before we finished, "helping the neighbors."

But miracles happen, too. There's a big spring surrounded by a thicket of buffalo thorns at the head of a coulee leading west from Battle Creek. Lee and I went to investigate and found four or five big steers safe and sound, only a bit "ganted" as Lee put it. They must have been among the first to drift here, and they had found good cover. Naturally steers could live where a cow would die; at this season cows are heavy in calf. Over in another coulee we thought we saw a drift move. We picked our way between some dead critters and Lee kicked into the drift with his foot. His horse reared back as through the opening in the heavy crust a two-year-old heifer pushed an angry head.

We dug around a bit and helped her out. When she was free she promptly charged the East and West man, who just made it to his horse in time. Then, looking thoroughly pleased with herself, she turned back to the snow cave and uttered a low note. What should stagger out, bright-eyed and all licked dry, but a newborn calf. "I allers say," Chuck spoke gravely above the cigarette he was rolling, "I allers say it takes a storm to start the calves a-coming."

Just then, too, a little company of horned larks—first sign of spring in the cow country—dashed twittering from the same cave. We drove the cow and calf to safer ground, and I dismounted and saw how she had sheltered against a cut bank, half roofed in by overhanging juniper. This had held the snow till it finally drifted over the entire company— for I could see that it was among the roots of the creeping-juniper shrubs that the birds had huddled for several days. That incident somehow cheered us all up. It was nearly Easter. Out of eight hundred cattle we finally gathered about five hundred.

10

When we finally got back to the ranch, Scotty told us he had word from the Oxheart that about a hundred and fifty of our cattle had holed up in the breaks of the Whitemud, having drifted through the Six Mile Gap. A few were dead, but "the big end would make it, as the storm had not been so bad further east."

It was nearly April now, and the snow was rapidly disappearing. In a few weeks we would have green grass, so Scotty decided to let those cattle stay at the Whitemud till after calving. Then the roundup wagon could pick them up in the fall.

In the meantime, many Indians had arrived with their light wagons and tenting gear. They got leave to skin the dead cattle and take what meat they wanted. So they soon had racks of willow sticks set up and strips of meat hanging to dry. They worked fast against the warm weather and the competition of the coyotes and eagles—not to mention the big lobos.

CHAPTER FIVE

Range mother

1

Within a few days a chinook had mopped up the snow and again the prairies lay drab and dun under the spring sky. All the little hollows brimmed with water. Great skeins of geese passed noisily overhead by day and night. We heard the clamor of their voices faintly at first, then clear and loud. Gazing upward we saw the straggling arrowhead formation. Always one side of the angle was longer than the other, and the formation appeared to rise and fall like the beat of a waltz tune, as with steady wing beats' and thrust-out heads the great birds disappeared into the north, while their honking continued to beat faintly on our ears.

One morning there was a querulous quacking of ducks, and looking up, we saw mallards and pintails in their nuptial flights, their wings whit-whitting as they cut the air, till with a noise like tearing paper they suddenly swooped downward to a pool, parting the mirrored surface with their breasts and sending oily ripples to agitate the withered herbage at the shore.

The little folk, too, arrived in flocks great and small—juncos with their black suits and white waistcoats, tree sparrows with russet caps, neat white-crowned sparrows wheezing their brief song. All these scratched and twittered in the brush or fluttered in the willows, bending down the sprays of pussy willows, which already the early bees were exploring.

On the bench tiny phlox made a carpet of mossy greenery all spangled with white blossoms that faded with time to mauve.

Early calves slept curled up for hours, never stirring till their dams came with the evening hours to nourish them. Unless you ride many miles and know where to look, you will not see many cattle on a ranch—except in winter when they are on the feed ground, or at roundup time; but they are there, in the folds of the prairie. Cows do not normally feed in a herd. Rather, with spring they find their way in small groups to favorite nooks of other years; places they know of, where the first green grass shoots forth. And as the ponds—sloughs we call them here—dry up, the cows gather in small groups and claim a grazing ground not too far from a spring or waterhole.

When a cow is about to calve she leaves the society of her friends and finds a quiet spot where she will be undisturbed. Should wolves be about she is safer, for the gray lobos are attracted by the stronger smell and presence of a number of animals. I have trailed cows and young stuff, and I have seen where one of the cows has had to turn aside up a dry wash because her time was upon her. The rest kept going, and the wolf swerved neither to left nor right, for I could see his big pad marks in the soft ground over the last of the cattle tracks. And I found the cow licking her new born calf as calmly as if murder on four feet did not exist.

In the chosen spot, within a day or two, the calf is delivered, and only minutes after, the queer, wobbly, wet creature, with its drooping ears, staggers to its feet under the comforting application of its mother's drying tongue and her low murmur of encouragement. It may fall at first, but it always rises again and persists in seeking its food. It may suck on the hair of the cow's brisket for a start, and finding no comfort in that, wander aimlessly back and forth, butting feebly at a bush or its mother's leg. But in time, when you think it is exhausted and cannot possibly remain on its legs another minute, it will discover the right place, and having taken the full teat between its leathery little lips, it sucks with joy till contented, wagging its still wet tail and straddling its knobby legs. Thereafter, it knows where to go. Having fed, it crouches in the grass, or is pushed by its matter-of-fact dam into some low brush to lie hidden. After a parting lick or two the cow, too, lies; for she needs rest now, that her body may assume normal proportions. Having rid herself of the placenta, she will rise and dispose of it by eating it, so that the trampled area of her labor is sweet and clean, with no odor to attract any inquisitive predator. Later, she will graze slowly, never wandering too far till, in a few days' time, the calf will follow her by stages, as she returns to the bunch to which she belongs.

When several cows have so returned with their young hopefuls, they form a matron's club, bedding down together at night after the calves have had their evening romp, and in the morning, having suckled them, off they go, ranging far and wide to seek the sweet young grass. The calves bed down in a little herd of their own. Once down they disappear. Always one cow remains nearby as nurserymaid, ready to come on the prod if danger threatens. But even if she should graze out of sight behind a knoll, nature takes care of these babes of the grassland, who lie so absolutely immobile—heads stretched flat in the herbage— that a padding coyote or lean lobo may trot by within a few yards, unconscious of the proximity of the warm meat. Many a time my horse has stumbled on a newborn calf determined to "play possum." Sometimes even when I have earmarked them, they never heeded the knife and lay limp and apparently lifeless.

Most ranchers earmarked. At branding time this helped you to decide quickly who the owner was if the calves were separated from their mothers in the confusion of the milling herd. The ultimate test of ownership was, of course, the mother's brand, and earmarking had to be done as nearly after birth as possible, otherwise the cattle would have to be gathered. So cowboys always carried a sharp knife at calving time and attended to all calves they came across in their daily round. Some of the marks used were the swallowtail, the under crop, the over crop, the grub, and these could be used on different ears. You'd hear a roper call "left ear grub" as he dragged up a calf, and the equivalent branding iron would be put to use.

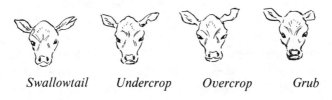

Swallowtail   Undercrop   Overcrop   Grub

Some earmarks—all left ear, but could be either or both.

Once the calves join the communal nursery they no longer lie supine if one rides among them. Aroused from sleep, they break cover in all directions, with high-pitched bawls which bring nursey a-running and bellowing till a troop of cows come charging over the skyline like arabs among the dunes. Their horns are curved like scimitars against the bright sky, and you don't dismount.

It might sound a sort of peculiar relationship in which men practically risk their lives for their cows, while the animals look upon them as enemies. It isn't really, of course, it's quite natural. Often the most quiet and dependable bitch becomes a regular devil when she has pups! As Kipling says, "The female of the species is more deadly than the male," and I would rather face a bull than a real "proddy" cow. Yet I don't know of any case where a man was badly hurt as long as his horse was active. I was once thrown under such circumstances, but I laid still and the cow just looked at me and then spoke softly to her calf and led it away.

2

Chuck and Banjo were at the bunkhouse oiling saddles and repairing gear. They were getting ready for spring riding in earnest. It was also time to gather more saddle stock and fit them, too. About twenty head had already been brought into the small wrangle field, and early one morning I saddled up and opened the big corral gate to bring them up for hoof-trimming and mane-pulling. It was one of those pearly, windless mornings when, as they say, you could hear a gnat scratching itself.

Just as I swung to the saddle I heard the click of a hoof south down the creek. "Who is riding this early," I thought, and reined in my pony. He, too, had heard the sound and turned his muzzle to the south with a forward flick of his ears. And simultaneously we saw the phantom that approached. Stumbling, heaving, checking; then wearily dragging itself forward, was the very skeleton of what had been a horse. Hip bones stuck out like a steer's horns. Matted unshed coat, brittle and dry: whitewashed by the magpies that had feasted on the running sores that rode his gaunt withers and defaced the stretched hide of his ribs.

The animal stumbled to a halt by the lower bars and stood swaying. My pony whistled softly, and the derelict answered with a sound like a dry sob. I looked at the sunken eyes, the drooping lip all scaled with dry alkali dust. My gaze wandered down the thin neck to the shoulders and saw the weary muscles that fluttered like poplar leaves in a wind. Down the forearms to the scabbed knees and finally to the broken hobbles which dangled above the hooves, hobbles which but recently had parted company with each other, for a trailing end of tramped-on rawhide still remained, and the early flies clustered and crawled, black and loathsome about the festered forelegs.

"What devil did this?" I said aloud. And then I thought. Do I know this horse? Was this dry-coated, earth-colored cadaver once a bright sorrel; an eager, full-eyed cow-horse? I moved to see the brand, if any. It was Fox, the XA plain on its lean haunch. Fox, the good horse Jake had taken to make his getaway nearly a year ago.

I let down the bars. Fox stepped forward, swayed, recovered himself and was in the corral. I went for an armful of hay and the horse rewarded me with another dry whisper from deep in his scraggy throat. I was looking him over again when Chuck came up, followed by Banjo. "Hello! What the hell—" said Chuck, and then stood silent, taking it all in. Banjo just stood and stared.

"The Grim Reaper for sure," breathed Chuck finally. "Yep. The Grim Reaper. The Walking Boneyard. The Skeleton in the Closet. Geez!"

Banjo spoke next. "It's 'ole Fox, ain't it? I'd like to git me hands on the fox that rode 'im, and then turned 'im loose with a saddle and hobbles—yep an' a bridle, too—see that tongue a-hangin' to one side plumb cut in two?" And sure enough, Fox, having taken a mouthful of sweet hay, was unable to eat it, and as it drooled from the side of his mouth the damaged tongue was there for all to see.

"Well," chipped in Chuck, "we got some oats we c'd cook up till it heals a bit and with new grass a-comin', if we can keep him alive for a week, he'll make it. I allers say a merciful man is merciful to his horse. Let's go!"

Old Fox

While the two went about their task of kindness I called Scotty out. "Yes, laddie, it's Fox sure enough, and if I can read signs he's come a long ways. See them hooves, the way they're worn down? He's been in the mountains I doot—probably the Bear Paws. See those seeds in his tail? The big flat black anes? That'll be Spanish bayonet and they dinna' grow hereaboots, but I seen them on the Missouri breaks. Ay, he'd ha' come from way south and it's a wonder he got through the winter. What happened to Jake, then? I'd be guessin' he maybe got dry-gulched at a noon camp. It suspicions me he'd maybe had a fall-out with his scalawag friends. That way he'd hobble his horse and leave the bridle on for a quick move.

"How long the poor beast carried the saddle 'tis hard to say. What with rolling and all it likely got under his belly, and he kicked till he got loosed of it. He'd maybe be longer with the bridle, and ever time he'd jump his hobbled feet he'd likely tear his mouth. Poor beastie, poor beastie. Well, now, laddie, I maun notify the police, though I doot they'll make much o't." And shaking his head the old gentleman returned to the house.

Fox responded to careful and tender treatment and was finally able to limp out to crop the rich juicy grass with the brood mares.

3

Lee had been away for a week, attending to the cattle which had drifted before the blizzard. They would be calving, too; and the thin and weak would probably need help and attention. The cows at the home place were in good flesh, and we had had little trouble. So one morning Scotty said, "Say, Charlie, I want you to pack a horse and ride down to Whitemud. Lee sent word by one of the 'breeds that he needs help. Better take blankets and some grub. Likely Lee will be running short, and I can't send a wagon out from Maple Creek till the creeks go down a bit." This just suited me. To "ride line" from the Whitemud cabin would take me away from the home ranch and right out into the blue.

So I caught up my best pony—Buck—to carry me, and a little roan mare called Maggie to carry the pack saddle and load of necessities. In addition, I took two spare mounts which I "tailed" to Maggie. Into the pack-panniers I wedged a chunk of "sow belly" (as we called salted side-pork), some flour and baking powder, salt, coffee, sugar, and a bag of black Mexican beans. Over these my bed was thrown—three good blankets and a tarp—the whole roped on with a squaw-hitch. Into a spare shirt I crammed a cheap notebook and a pencil stub. And so I rode away proudly on my first solo assignment, as a plump robin shouted like a Sussex missel-thrush from his perch on the corral gate.

It was better than a day's hard riding to Whitemud cabin; and as I did not get away from the ranch till nearly noon, and could not travel fast with a loaded pack animal, I decided to camp at Clear Springs that night. I knew the way, having been there while riding for horses. Clear Springs was about twenty miles from the ranch, well south of the Cypress Hills, and from what Scotty told me I should find a faint trail heading east by south that would take me to my destination. It was easy to keep direction without a compass because the sun was shining and, also, I knew the ridge of the Cypress Hills lay to my north.

The rolling country had burst into life. The south slopes of the knolls were washed with emerald-green. On the flats, the feathery, aromatic sagebrush showed a livelier color as it budded. Always a tireless bird's nester, I kept alert as I rode. A pair of horned larks, sitting side by side on a flat rock, seemed to scold me, and I slid off Buck, who set the example for his followers by immediately thrusting his muzzle into the grass. I searched the curly prairie wool all around the rock, the birds watching me in a detached way. Either it was too early in the season, or the nest was too well hidden, for I found nothing. Chiding myself for my delay, I remounted.

The trail followed a wide, shallow draw that led up into higher land. Presently sagebrush and soapweed gave way to clumps of cactus, green-gray and viciously thorned. Now they looked like dried-up toad skins, warty and dry, with little promise of the profuse mass of golden, silkly blossoms they would put forth later. Now the hard-baked gumbo soil—which can be like stiff glue after a rain—was replaced by gravelly patches interspersed with small, crumbly hillocks, all dotted with round stones, flattened on two sides like the cookies baked by the ranch women. As we climbed higher and the draw narrowed to a coulee, the neat clumps of shrubby cinquefoil began to appear; just nicely budding to a rich green. To my left was a towering butte, craggy-faced and eroded into fantastic shapes. High up on its face I saw a huge huddle of small brush and dead sage twigs, which I knew was the nest of a buzzard. Not the turkey vulture which is called buzzard hereabouts, but a member of the Buteo family, great hawks that wheel and scream always above the prairies. The commonest of the tribe is the Swainson's hawk, but this nest belonged to its peer, the ferruginous rough-legged hawk, exceeded in size only by the golden eagle. Like that bird, its tarsus is feathered to his toes. He is truly an *Archibuteo,* as his latin name tells us—*lagopus;* well, that has to do with his pants; and *sancti-johannis* must be a reference to his lonely perch on a high butte, whence he surveys the endless prairies, just as Saint John once gazed across the Grecian seas from his aerie on Patmos.

I heard that long-drawn whistling scream, and looking up saw the two great birds, wheeling in solemn arcs. I longed to have time to climb to the nest, but the sun was declining, and I said to myself as I have so often been forced to—"Some other time."

The coulee brought me out upon a small bench over which I jogged, following the faint wagon tracks till they turned down the head of a similar ravine running the opposite way. This coulee was narrow at the top, with steep walls down which overhanging branches of juniper crept. The dried skeletons of older limbs disposed themselves, gnarled and crooked, writhing like snakes among the green and living.

Where the coulee opened out on the rolling plain, among a score or so of wind-bent willows, lay Clear Springs; twin pools of bright, cold water. The numerous ashes of dead fires, the trampled grass, and old picket pins against which one stumbled, bore witness to the many times folks had camped here.

4

I made a comfortable camp after picketing my horses and laying my cherished saddle properly on its side. While water boiled for coffee I began to make biscuits, as we call the baking powder scones so universally used as a bread substitute in the cow country.

Using one frying pan to make a lid for the other, in which were my round biscuits cut out of the dough with the baking powder lid, I carefully scraped a hollow in the hot ashes in which I placed the contraption as Lee had shown me, then drew the ashes over it—a primitive type of Dutch oven. I had never made biscuits before; and alas, when I finally removed the lot they were as hard as Hudson's Bay Hard Tack—which is *hard!*

As I was ruefully surveying my handiwork, Buck and Maggie suddenly raised their heads and pricked their ears to the southwest. Following their gaze I could just see a rider's head approaching from behind the clump of willows. That head wore the smart, stiff-brimmed

Stetson of the Royal North West Mounted Police. I jumped to my feet and called a greeting. The horseman, now completely in view, raised a hand. To this day I think the grandest uniform of all is the Stetson-hatted, red-tunicked get-up of the Mounted Police, with the boots, the jingling spurs and the blue breeches striped with cavalry yellow. And the men who wore them were worthy of the outward glory.

This particular long-legged, handsome constable dismounted stiffly by the campfire. "Hello," he said, "you beat me to it—was going to camp here myself. My name's Merrik—from Pend d'Orreille detachment. Who're you?"

His pleasant English voice sounded so much of home that I could almost see the tea table. I said, "I'm with Scotty Gow—from the ranch on Box Elder. I'm heading for the Whitemud."

"Oh, I see," he replied, "you're the young chap that rode with Jake Meldrum, eh? The corporal at the Ten Mile told me the horse he stole came back—but, by the way, when did *you* leave the shores of Perfidious Albion?" I told him.

"I was just going to eat," I added. "Coffee's ready and the bacon is all right I think; but I'm afraid I'm not too good at biscuits."

"Um-m-well, they *are* a bit rocky, aren't they?" he replied, after trying one. "Just wait a jiffy while I look after 'Bobs' here, and I'll give you a tip or two."

He turned to his horse—a fine blood bay, which I noticed carried Scotty's Ex open Aye as well as the MP which was the Forces' brand. As he unsaddled and hobbled the tired beast he remarked, "Yes, he's one of Scotty's raising, but I assure you he was legally obtained! The Force buys quite a few from him—good stuff, too." That made me realize how these quiet gentlemanly young men of the Old Police could observe without seeming to pry, almost as if they could read your mind. Returning with his saddle pouches, he flung them over the willows, adding his pistol belt and scarlet "serge"; and squatting by the little fire of dung and willow twigs, he proceeded to mix a batch of biscuits with all the effortless ease of the experienced bachelor, all the time explaining with the utmost gravity that the main point to observe was not to mix the dough too well, but to let it remain slightly crumbly.

His biscuits were delicious, especially when topped with the marmalade which he, surprisingly, produced from his pouches. He admitted

A member of the RNWMP

that he had a sweet tooth. If in my day I have been spoken of as a light hand with dough, I give the credit to Constable David Merrik, one-time Sandhurst Cadet, later a "rider of the plains" and, as the cowboys said, a humdinger on the piano, whenever he could get his hands on one.

We talked of many things that night. I, of Sussex; he, of the tidy vicarage in East Anglia where his father still gave spiritual comfort to the sturdy farm folk; both, of music and books. Beethoven, Conrad and Kipling, King David of Israel, Homer, Shakespeare—how the names of the Great Ones fell away from us to be wafted away among the whispering sage of this distant land. "Some day," Merrik was puffing his last pipe, stretched out at ease against his heavy Police saddle, "some day, laddie, an immortal will translate all this"; and he waved the brier root vaguely towards the naked, darkening plain. Talked out, we finally rolled in our blankets while the western stars winked and twinkled overhead, and the horses stumbled about with a clink of tether chains, or stopped their regular cropping to stare and snort into the darkness as coyotes flung their dirges from knoll to knoll. I lay awake a long time.

5

It was noon of the second day when I arrived at Whitemud Creek and the cow camp.

This watercourse is also called "Frenchman's Creek" from the number of French "half-breeds"—as we (and they) always used to say, with no thought of disrespect—who had once settled there. The "white mud" (a gumbo clay) hereabouts was famous for plastering log buildings; setting like cement when properly applied—i.e., first puddled up with chopped hay and then applied with the hands.

The metis people, as we now call them, even perhaps if they are Scotch half-breeds, worked for the ranchers in fits and starts, doing a little trapping and hunting between times. They did not fancy regular work and regular pay. They preferred "contracts" for fencing, cutting logs, or building; activities in which whole families took part, from the aged grandparents to the youngest dark-eyed boy who could harness a horse. Many of them were first-rate horse breakers—like Alex LaFromboise—and good cowhands; deft and graceful with a lariat or a branding iron. The cabin itself was an old breed building, the sod roof overcrowded with silvery sage. Half the mud chinking had fallen out.

Behind, closer to the creek bank, stood a dilapidated barn and a crooked corral. The whole establishment occupied a small blue-joint flat, where the creek made an oxbow curve.

The tinkle of a horse bell told me where the saddle stock grazed. Dismounting, I unpacked the mare, carrying the supplies into the dim interior of the cabin. Just inside the threshold and to the right lay something furry. I set down my burden to examine it. It was a fat prairie badger, marked like any Sussex brock, but much wider, heavier, and more powerful looking; with a blunt, bearlike snout. Well, I thought—Lee must have been hunting, but I never knew badger was good to eat. Out in the bright sunshine I mounted Buck and led my little string in the direction of the bell. The spare horses were grazing on another small flat separated from the buildings by a low hill. Lee's own pack mare—Jill—lifted her head and shook her bell at my approach. The "spares" looked, too. These geldings would never leave the mare, and were left to run loose, while the mare was hobbled by day and picketed by night.

Thereafter, we always knew if anything was around between sundown and sunup, for we would hear snorts and stamps, and then the bell would stop ringing, which meant that the mare was looking and listening.

This camp did not belong to anyone in particular. Its original owner had departed long ago. Various ranchers used it as a camping ground from time to time as we did now. There would be cattle from many outfits all around us, and we would give them the same attention as our own. One of the unwritten laws of the range was that a cowboy helped any animal in distress—friend's or enemy's—regardless of the brand it carried, knowing that men from other outfits did the same.

Lee returned about five P.M. He seemed glad to see me. As we went in to get supper, I asked him if he was going to cook the badger. "Hell—no," he grinned, "they're too fat to eat. But they's so many badgers about it's hardly safe to ride. Otherwise I hadn't too much reason to kill the poor devil. Ole' Cap fell in a badger hole this morning and sprained himself.

"Coming home noontime I met this one out in the grass, and feeling sore on badgers I took down my rope. He tried to make it up onto a knoll, and I said to myself, 'Ah ha, my fine and feathered friend, that's where your hole will be.' So I hazed him back into the long grass and put my loop on him. Not the first time, mind you. He'd go through it before I could pick up slack—but finally I got him. Well, I drug him a ways, and he sort of curled up; so I hopped off, and doggone if'n he didn't come to life and make for my legs. So I got on Cap and drug him up here. Had to drop a stone on his head afore I could get me rope off. Yea—he's a big fellah, isn't he? You can skin him if you like."

I did like, and while Lee was cooking sow belly I began to sharpen up my pocket knife. "Come and get it," called Lee, and I dragged a stool over. Just then there was a sort of scrabbling noise.

"What's that," I said.

"Oh, pack rats I guess," Lee replied. "This old roof is a regular runway for the varmints. They kept me awake all last night; and this morning my boots had the top all chewed, and they were half-full of rice." But it was not pack rats; for after supper I strolled over with my knife intent on turning Brock into a rug—but that gentleman was not there.

We ran outside, and following Cap's intent stare, saw our erstwhile prisoner ambling like an animated doormat over the prairie, his long silky coat parted neatly down the middle of his back and sweeping the grass on either side. He stopped near a rocky place on the knoll, turned his mild spectacled face towards us for a second, and then quietly disappeared into the bowels of the earth. "Well, I'm damned," said Lee. "Chuck always said you couldn't kill a badger, and now I believe him."

I put my knife away—half disappointed at the loss of a "specimen," half glad that what had been a mere brute corpse was again a living creature.

One day we rode many miles east of the Whitemud to see if any of our cattle had got that far. We found none—only a few head with an East end brand on them. But that trip will always live in my memory.

We came to a great butte, almost pure white on its steep south side, all stratified in delicate pastel shades. Lee said, "That's purty, isn't it? I drove a wagon one year for a geologist fellah, and he told me that butte was 'pale cretaceous'—what they show on maps as Irvine Pale beds—though it don't look like a bed to me—more like a fort. We should find some rock roses here."

We dismounted and searched around the buttresses that had been carved at the base of the pinnacle by wind and water. He showed me the "roses" (low evening primrose). They grew sparsely on the white gumbo, flat to the slope, their long rubbery stems ending in pear-shaped buds or waxy blossoms—white as paper when fresh-blown, but soon turning to pinkish violet.

All around us rose the bubbling songs of the rock wrens, as the little birds crept around the gumbo knees, or disappeared into crevices, reappearing unexpectedly many yards away. Bank swallows had bored so many holes in the upper face of the butte that, to quote Lee, "it looked like a colander."

Still higher we could see hundreds of the gourdlike nests of cliff swallows.

Further down the creek, on a bare alkaline flat was a colony of prairie dogs, the fat, plains marmots that rear their mounds so that the mouth is well above any flood water. These little animals would stand on their mounds staring at us till we got too close, then with that barking note that has earned for them the name of "dog," they would flick their tails and disappear, only to pop up again after we had passed.

I would have liked to spend many days here, but the evening breeze was freshening and we started back. On an abandoned mound a burrowing mole slowly descended backwards down the mine shaft. I thought of *Lorna Doone* and of Quennie Fairfax's father—the Cornish miner who John Ridd likened to a kobold of the earth.

A clump of silvery wolf willow stood behind the cabin. Soon it would blossom with masses of tiny yellow flowers giving off a sweet but pungent odor. From a later experience, I have found it to be like the smell of phosgene gas, so that now when I smell it I think of the Somme.

But now the bushes acted as a clothesline and held our spare socks and shirts.

7

Our chief job at this camp was to make daily rides to keep cattle out of the worst "sink holes" and dangerous places along the swollen creek; or if a critter did get bogged down, to tie onto her with the rope and pull her to dry ground.

Cows sometimes needed assistance at calving. Sometimes a calf died or was born dead, and if the mother's bag was badly swollen she had to be tied down and milked a time or two so her udder would not become cracked or spoilt.

Also we were supposed to keep the cattle more or less in the White-mud Valley and try to prevent them drifting east, or south over the border. We fed passing friends or strangers alike; but the latter were given a pretty good (if not noticeable) scrutiny, because the cow thieves weren't all dead yet, according to Lee.

Lee himself always went armed, and insisted I do the same, so I found a use for the old thirty-thirty Winchester I had traded my boots for, and it lived under my saddle flap (of course, revolvers were banned by the RNWMP). Not that I ever expected to have to fight cattle thieves! But there were still a few buffalo wolves about. We called them lobos.

One day we heard cattle bawling at dawn. Lee hurried out with me. We rode rapidly north in the teeth of a spring gale. The bawling sounded urgent—and closer.

Soon we topped a rise to see before us what I was often to see in later years.

A bunch of about twenty head of cows and calves were standing tightly packed and bawling "fit to bust." About one hundred yards to the west two gray wolves were running a yearling heifer which they had cut out of the bunch. One wolf kept snapping at the heifer's flank, the other was trying for her throat. The heifer—tongue out and flanks heaving—dodged, twisted, and kicked, bawling lustily. But it could not last long.

Lee quickly dismounted, levering a shell into his breech as he knelt. He pulled the trigger just as I threw myself at his side. The wolf at which he had aimed was not touched, but at the swish of the bullet it stopped dead, and faced us for a moment. That was the beast's undoing. A second bullet caught her (a bitch she was) in the throat. Meanwhile, I had shot at the dog, which was streaking away over the prairie. My bullets only sent up puffs of gray dust, but at least they hastened him on his way.

The heifer was a loss. Although she was still alive when we reached her, the long gashes in her side had let some of her innards out; so we shot her. We didn't let her go to waste, though, for we immediately skinned her out. When the meat was cool we took it to camp. Fresh beef was a rare treat, but as the weather was turning warm we only had a couple of feeds of it.

The rest we cut in strips for "jerky." Hanging on a rope stretched between two high corral poles with a smudge fire underneath to smoke flies away, and subjected to the dry wind and hot sun, the meat soon dried as hard as a board, keeping, however, a juicy red interior.

During supper Lee talked about South Africa. He had served in the Boer War with Lord Strathcona's Horse. "I liked it all right," he said, "it's just like this country. Lots of good grass, and you can always get a view from a kopje—that's what we call a butte here. Only thing was—it wasn't *home* or I might have stayed." (Many people tend to become "insular" if far from seaports or coasts.)

"Look south, out the door," Lee said. I looked—far and away over swell after blue swell to the hazy tips of the Bear Paws. Meadowlarks fluting. Plovers lamenting. Gray sage burgeoning to purple and gold; greening prairies merging into violet distance. "That's what South Africa looks like," Lee went on, "that's the Transvaal, the Karoo brush and the grass and the plovers and 'way back, the Drakensbergs."

By now grub was running short—except for meat—and the creeks had gone down. And then, on a gusty day of the first spring rain we heard the sound of wagon wheels and the thud of hooves down at the ford. As the wagon drew up before the cabin of bleached cottonwoods, we saw that the driver was none other than "Old-Joe-From-the-Crow"—one of the last of the half-breed scouts of the Old Police days—Old Joe, son of a French father and a Crow mother.

He greeted us with old world courtesy—"Bo Jo', fellahs, I bring plenty grub. Dat sacre' trail she bomp me and bomp me so I got good h'appetite. Better we cook some dese stuff."

8

It rained all that night, but next day was sunny and hot again. The grass seemed to have grown an inch, and all the prairie was bursting into flower.

The bare gravel banks of yesterday became blue carpets of a flower I was to know later as hairy beard's tongue. Another slope shone yellow as butter with the dwarf buffalo beans, while still another knoll would be wine-hued with the shy-faced Johnny-jump-ups.

Everything on these short grass plains was dwarfed and flattened, hugging the earth in escape from the ever-present wind. The delicate mauve prairie anemones, which the cowboys called windflowers, were scarcely three inches high. Rose briars, which elsewhere might be up to three or four feet high, hardly attained a stature of six inches; while the tall asters of the long-grass prairies were here the merest pygmies, with stalks too short for picking—one only got the blossom.

That prairie wind—you got tired of it, yet when it dropped and calm fell you missed it; for the air lost its sharpness and the mosquitoes hummed in vicious clouds. A strong wind would sweep them away, and many other things along with them—a water bucket left outside the cabin, my socks from the shrubby clothesline.

After a big wind I often went down on a gravelly flat where stone rings marked an old Indian camping ground. Here, on the new swept earth, I would search for Indian arrowheads and artifacts. I managed to gather some really nice ones. Arrowheads of chalcedony, others of flint; a broken lance head and a stone for grinding pemmican.

These Stone Age people had certainly combined beauty with utility—some of the arrowheads were exquisite. Nearby grew a thicket of saskatoons (service berries) from which, no doubt, the hunters had made their arrow shafts, for this was the wood they favored.

A calf nursery

9

Towards the end of April calving was pretty well over. On the whole we had not experienced as much trouble as Lee and the boss expected; no doubt due to the good weather and early grass.

Lee said, "If we'd had a week's cold wind and some wet snow, the grass would have been held back and the cattle chilled. We were lucky, is all." Weak thin cows can have trouble in many ways when their time comes.

A calf may be presented the wrong way. A strong cow can usually deliver it, but not a weak one. We'd find, perhaps, a thin heifer with her first calf, down on her side in a hollow, vainly trying to give birth while the inevitable coyote licked his chops on a nearby knoll.

On our approach she would struggle to rise, but fall again. This was a pull job. Lee would throw me the loop of his rope, I would get in on the calve's leg or legs, and he would ease his horse back to take a pull on the calf each time the cow heaved. To pull at any other time would be to injure the cow. Meanwhile, I would bear *down* as hard as I could on the tight rope so that the pull was more downward than backward. Finally the calf came with a plop! and lay, a wet glistening thing choking for its first breath. We could usually get the cow up then. If not, we rubbed the calf with dry grass, wiped the mucus from its nostrils, and left them to be revisited on a later round. Usually we found mother and baby up and about. Sometimes we had to "tail" the mother up and hold her there long enough for the calf to suck. "Tailing" up a cow consisted of lifting her hind end by the tail—for a cow, unlike a horse, gets up hind end first. Once she's up you can steady a weak cow by an upward pull of the tail. I have heard it said "raising cattle in the old northwest manner—by the tail." The cow, of course, would try to hook us, but her weak attacks were easily evaded.

I marveled at Lee's quiet patience and sympathetic regard for these patients. It was always, "Well, Mamma, how are we today?" Or, "Been over on your side, old girl, eh? Well, well, we'll just bank you up on that side so's you don't roll again—Charlie, pull me some dead grass to soften up these yere rocks, will you?" Or, "Easy—e-asy now,

Indian Camp

Mamma—don't you fret. We'll have you right as a trivet," and so on.

We only lost two calves and one cow and that, Lee said, was pretty good going.

Also, one cow we found dead without a mark or a sign of a struggle. "Poison weed, I reckon," said Lee, "prob'ly death camus—that one I showed you the other day." I remembered the narrow green blades we had looked at; and could understand how a cow, hungry for something green when the grass had barely started, might be tempted to eat them.

It was around the first of May. Soon the roundup wagons would be rolling, the crews assembled, to commence the long months of gathering and branding. Old Joe told us that Scotty sent word we were to meet our wagon between Graburn and Cypress Lake within the week.

With a few days to go, Lee said, "Reckon we might as well take a ride around the Old-Man-on-His-Back fust. It's pretty rough country and cattle don't usually drift in there till late summer, but there's a couple small outfits on the west side. Or we could make a camp at Antelope Springs. That way, if any of our stuff—steers and such—is there, we'll know. The wagon won't work that stretch till late; and there's always a chance, too, we might find some horses."

So we said good-by to Old-Joe-From-the-Crow, who headed his team for Maple Creek; and with our stuff on the pack mares, which we led, we set out south by west, the spares running loose. The ground rose gradually and the going got rougher. We seemed to be continually crossing coulees, invisible till we came to them, so deceptive are these apparently rolling-to-level plains. The south facing slopes of these ravines would be almost bare of growth, exposed as they were to the hot sun. The slopes facing north, however, were matted with growth— saskatoon and chokecherry bush and thorny clumps of rose canes and buffalo bush. The floors of these narrow, tortuous, and high-banked drainage courses were littered with water-worn stones that the horses hated. Lee said this was good antelope country, but all we saw that day were some tracks in a shallow draw where a local shower had dampened the ground.

10

We made Antelope Springs early that evening. We had hardly got settled, and the sweated horses had only just finished rolling, when we were surprised by the sound of horses neighing, the thud of hooves, and the creaking of an ancient wagon. Looking up, we saw approaching us a wild-looking cavalcade, consisting of two mounted Indians, followed by a light "mountain" wagon drawn by two creamy pinto ponies, each with a tiny foal following. The wagon was overarched with leafy boughs under the shade of which could be seen some squaws and children, and was followed by a motley collection of dogs and loose horses.

The wagon stopped. A small boy with pigtails stared at us. The women drew their blankets more closely around them. The two braves rode up, dismounted, and led by the elder, approached us. At close quarters they did not look so wild. The traditional leggings and robe of the plains Indians had been, I knew, pretty well discarded; and these two were garbed in overalls and shirts, but they retained much of the old spirit in their erect and dignified bearing, as well as in the smaller matters of dress. The older man's battered felt hat was set with a nodding eagle plume, while the other's was encircled by a band of rattlesnake skin with the rattles attached. Both wore their long black hair in plaits. Both had beaded moccasins, wide leather belts studded with brass, and carried braided quirts.

The leader dropped his trail rope and held out his hand to Lee, his white teeth gleaming in his leathery face. *"Tansee—Tansee Nishtas,"* he said, and *"Tansee Mooso,"* answered my companion. The younger man's greeting was more subdued—a smile and a nod. We all sat down. Lee produced tobacco. *"Wha, wha! Stamow,"* grunted the two, and proceeded to fill pipes.

All the time the wagon stayed where it was; the weaker members of the party sitting patiently; the harness horses grazing as far as they could stretch their necks; the two foals lying flat in their mothers' shadows.

The Indians smoked in silence for a while. Then the older man began to speak. He'd say a few words and stop. Lee said, "Uh-huh," and after a bit the red man would speak again. Each time he paused after a sentence I thought he had finished, but each time Lee gave that affirmative grunt and the old man would continue.

Lee turned to me. "This is an old friend of mine," he said, "his name is Mistaha Moostoosisowyan which means Many Calf Robes. The other is his son, Wolf Dreamer. They are Crees, and have been visiting relatives across the Medicine Line. They're on their way back to Woody Mountain.

"Meantime," he added, "if we've got enough flour we'll make a couple big bannocks, and you open that new can of syrup. Indians always fed me, and I reckon I can do the same by them." He turned to the two men and said something like, *"Kapawawow oma,"* and then rose and beckoned to the women who drove the wagon closer and, choosing a spot to the far side of the spring, began to put up a small tent. The youngsters scattered to gather what small twigs and *bois de vache* they might find.

Lee called out in friendly tones to the eldest and stoutest squaw, *"Tansee, Tansee Nokomis,"* whereat she laughed, showing a fine row of teeth.

Of the two younger women, one turned out to be Wolf Dreamer's squaw, who took as little notice of us as had her husband.

Apparently only the quite young and very old are supposed to show any curiosity or feeling. The other young woman flashed the ghost of a smile at Lee from under the bright yellow head scarf which accentuated her dark eyes and gave her features an almost classic beauty. Lee greeted her, too, with *"Tansee Neechimoos,"* but she pretended she didn't hear and bent low over a cooking pot.

"Known her ever since she was a papoose," grinned Lee, "but I guess I better quit calling her sweetheart!" *Mooso,* he told me, meant grandfather, *Nishtas,* brother-in-law, and *Nokomis,* little grandmother. We had a good square meal. The four of us menfolk at our camp; the women and children at theirs, but the women waited on us first. They had some dried berries which they mixed with flour and tallow and boiled. It tasted like a sort of plum duff and was, I suppose, pemmican without the meat. We drank a scandalous lot of hot sweet tea. Indians don't care for coffee.

Pipes were filled and cigarettes rolled. Lee put a question in Cree to the older man. Again a long oration with the usual pauses, which I found that I, too, was filling in with the inevitable double grunt which means "yes."

We said good-by and left. Those were the first real Indians I had met.

Lee now said, "That old fellow thinks there might be a few cattle south of Buzzard Coulee. I'll make a circle back that way and pick up your spares and mine at the line camp. I'll meet the roundup somewhere, but I think you'd better just high-tail it for Graburn so as to make a report to Scotty." We said "so long," and I turned my horse to the north.

CHAPTER SIX

Heading them

1

When I got back to the ranch, Scotty told me to ride over to where the roundup was starting. He told me the wagon was south of the gap, and I'd better get some sleep so as to make an early start. My string should already be there with Lee. Banjo Pete had left the day before with his string.

So next morning I made up my turkey—two blankets, tarp, spare socks and shirt, tobacco, and papers—plus a cheap copy book. Pencil stubs were always in my pocket. All this, with my slicker, made a heap of bulk behind my saddle cantle. Buck didn't like it and snorted and let on he was going to get rid of it, but I finally got mounted and headed for Graburn Gap.

Graburn Butte was soon above me. The trail followed the windings of the creek through the parky country of willow and poplar with open grown spruce at intervals. High up on the slopes the pines sighed in the wind.

Near here, in the early days of Fort Walsh, so Scotty had told me, a Constable Graburn had been killed by an Indian, and his name is commemorated in the butte and local post office.

Scotty said the Indian killed the wrong man. Some of the Police boys had been herding remounts up the valley. Among the Police was a young fellow who'd been trying to flirt with an Indian woman at the camp outside the fort.

When the boys brought the horses back a halter was missing. Next morning Graburn was detailed to return to the grazing ground and find the missing equipment. The squaw's husband ambushed and shot him there, thinking he was his wife's lover.

The valley lay so peaceful in the early summer sunshine that I found it hard to imagine that any scenes of violence had taken place here. Yet only four miles to the south was the old "massacre ground." Here, in 1873, a party of Montana "toughs" who called themselves wolfers had wiped out a peaceful Indian camp. They accused these Crees of having stolen horses from their camp near Earing Coulee. Denials were useless, and the Indian camp was attacked at dawn. All the braves and most of the women and children perished, and their horses were run off across the Border.

It was deeds such as this, plus the scenes of debauchery and chicanery at the American trading posts in the Blackfoot country to the west—Forts Stand-off and Whoop-up—that brought home to the government at Ottawa the need for a Mounted Police Force in the newly acquired territories of the Northwest.

In 1874 the famous march across the plains of the North West Mounted Police took place. Among the first superintendents was Major Walsh. He built the fort that carries his name as close as possible to the massacre ground. This greatly impressed the Indians who now realized that they had protection against the border thugs.

Most of the perpetrators of the massacre were tracked down by the Police, but few came to trial. Extradition from Montana was not easy in those days, since the powers-that-be in that territory didn't see eye to eye with the Police. "Why make such a fuss about a few Indians?" At least one arrest was actually made, but the state of Montana could not stand for that, and he had to be released as he was taken on U.S. territory. For lack of co-operation the prosecutions petered out. But a start had been made, and thereafter the Queen's law would ride the Border for fifty cents a day.

No wonder the wise Crowfoot—at the Treaty of '77—said, "As a bird's feathers protect her, so do the police protect us."

Fort Walsh was headquarters for the North West Mounted Police till the '80s, when the commissioner and his staff moved to Regina on the new railway. Thereafter this area was served from Divisional Barracks at Maple Creek. Up till a few years ago—perhaps even today—you could still pick up grim souvenirs of that murderous action—empty cartridge cases, buttons, and bones.

2

I got to the wagon at noon. Only the cook was there. Further west on the flat I saw the cavvy under guard. The cavvy is the term we use for the herd of spare saddle horses—from the Spanish *caballo*. The nighthawk's snores came from the bed-wagon. I untied my turkey and threw it up among the miscellaneous assortment of sleeping gear. The snores stopped for a while. Riding out to the horse herd, I greeted Sonny Myers who was day wrangler. I told him I wanted a horse. "Can't you wait till I bring in the bunch tonight?" he replied. "Some of the boys will be picking up their right hosses then."

"Well, if you can't drive them in now—suits me. I can't ride Buck any more," I said. "I'll take it easy for a while."

Back at the wagon I unsaddled Buck. I waved my arms and chased him for a bit. He started out for the cavvy. The old boy was pretty tired and needed a two- or three-day rest.

But when I sneaked around to the bed wagon with the idea of forty winks, the cook spotted me and it was—"Hey! Young fellah—go git me some firen'. I got oven bread a-bakin', and the boys didn't git me enough—as usual."

So I chored for most of the afternoon.

It would be "Kid! Take a couple of pails and rustle some water fr'm the crick. Might as well wash me some underwear while the bread's a-bakin'." Or, "Fellah, would you mind to give them wagon wheels a bit o' grease? You'll find the grease tin in back," and, "Just hang them harness straight will ye? An' well off the ground. Them pesky foxes'll be eatin' at 'em if not." (He meant the little kit foxes—not red foxes who would be too wary to enter a camp ground. They tell me the kit foxes are gone now—I wonder.)

The cook—like most plainsmen—was a fussy housekeeper. He never had to straighten things up. They were kept that way. Every tin mug or plate, every bowl and skillet had its place. His array of butcher knives were held by a leather strap on the wagon's side, with a square of tarp nailed so as to hang over them.

This passion for neatness was noticeable in all the cowboys and range men. Any one of them, making coffee on the prairie, did it in an easy methodical way. No movement was wasted, no "muss" made. A can was dipped in a spring with no splashing, no overflowing. The little fire of cowchips—not much bigger than a plate—was kept neat, and all trash swept away to avoid a grass fire. Afterwards everything was left tidy, with the coffee dregs dumped on the smouldering ashes.

I remember calling at a rancher's house years later, and being quietly amused by his concern for traditional tidiness.

He was well-to-do, and had a German woman to keep house for him. His home was commodious, and after a good supper, he and I went into the sitting room to smoke and chat.

I noticed that Bill didn't seem to be concentrating on the conversation. His eyes kept turning kitchenwards and he seemed to be listening. We could hear Lena washing up. After a bit she popped her head around the door and said, "Vell, I go to bed now. Good night." We bid her the same.

As her footsteps retreated upstairs, Bill rose, and took two or three lithe strides into the kitchen. The door was open.

I saw him look around as if sizing things up. He evidently noticed that something was missing. He turned to the big corner cupboard, got out the dishpan, and hung it on a nail behind the cookstove. Then he hunted around till he found the dishrag hanging on a line. He took it down and draped it in its proper place, over the pan. A touch here—a touch there. I knew Bill had "batched it" for years, and he wanted his kitchen kept just right.

Soon he rejoined me, quite contented now and full of anecdotes and humor. I expect that game had been going on for weeks.

The cowboy's idea of housekeeping could be summed up as follows:

(1) Don't have too much junk around.
(2) *Keep* everything in its place.
(3) Do it now.

Charlie Wilson, an Oxheart rider, used to say, "A woman plumb loves to make a hell of a mess, and then have a grand time tidyin' up."

3

The camp was well south of the hills, but still on high ground, so you could see a lot of country. About five o'clock a little puff of dust

The chuck wagon

showed to the east, and I knew the first lot of cattle were coming. Soon little bunches began to appear from the south and west. You'd see the blur of moving beasts and be able to pick out the riders as they weaved back and forth from drag to flank.

As each bunch came in they were herded into the low ground, and soon the shallow valley was full of bawling cattle. Cows ran hither and thither looking for their calves, while the same calves hunted around on the opposite side of the herd calling for mamma. If a cow recognized the voice, she'd walk slap through the bunch, making a way with her horns, and as soon as the reunion was accomplished you could hear the smacking and drooling.

The first boys in were first to be put on night guard, so they didn't waste much time eating. By the time they had washed down the last of the beans and hot bread and syrup, the cavvy was run into the rope corral between the chuck wagon and the bed wagon and held up at the sides by a few metal posts easily diven in or removed, and the boys changed saddles to fresh horses. They'd roll their after-supper smokes as they rode out and relieve the boys holding the herd. Then they would gallop in, fling their reins to the ground, and start to fill up.

That particular night the wagon boss, who himself came in early, said, "You got here, eh? Catch a horse as soon as the cavvy comes. You'll take first guard with Pete La Vallee. He'll tell you what to do."

The wagon boss is an important man. You don't talk to him, but when he talks *to you,* you keep your ears clean, and you do exactly what he says without question, and right now—or you find yourself riding home. There has to be discipline with a big crew like that—even though it's hardly noticeable. I was to find later—both in the army and out—that if only two men are on a job, it's best if one leads and makes the decisions; and the other follows.

I saddled the gray gelding. Pete showed me how to pull to a walk on approaching the cattle. How to ride around not too fast, not too slow. He would ride one way, I the other. We would meet, make a smoke, and talk about the herd. I could hear him when he was on the other side as the dusk deepened. "Move in a bit you dogies and settle down," I'd hear him say in his quiet voice. Or else singing—more humming—singing any old thing.

It seemed to settle the cattle, and one by one they lay down with great gusty grunts, and if you stopped your horse you'd hear the chewing of hundreds of cuds; the soft blowing; the occasional click of horns. After a while, when it got really dark, you'd pick up other night sounds. Pete's horse clinking his bit away to the left. The buzzing drone of a great beetle. The wailing song of a coyote, or the sobbing cry of a rail from some swampy place up the creek. Sometimes your nose caught the spicy smell of smoke from a prairie fire; and perhaps you'd see the skyline flicking red.

Nights can be awful dark, but you get used to it and wonder why you used to think you had to have a flashlight or lantern. Once you know how, you can saddle or hobble a horse just as well in darkness as by daylight. It's the fingers do it—not the eyes.

This night the moon rose early, and flooded the whole valley with silver. I could see the cook's fly-tent gleaming in the brush a quarter of a mile away, and the gray's long shadow walked before us.

I tried singing—I think it was "Flow Gently Sweet Afton," and the gray horse—I called him Monte—pricked his ears and blew, and the cattle turned mild countenances towards me. But I had been warned before by Lee—"Don't make no sudden movement nor noise. Don't flap nothing. Sing low and easy and talk so the dogies'll know you're there. It only takes one ole' mossy-horn to take fright at his own shadder to start the whole lot off."

"Flow Gently Sweet Afton" came to an end. Quite near me I heard the last verse of "Chisholm Trail," and Pete's horse whinnied gently. "Our guard's up," said Pete, looking up at the Dipper. (Few cowboys use a watch.) "Let's go," and we walked our horses quietly to camp, woke the next guard, and rolled in.

Thereafter one day was much like another. It was ride a circle in twos, gather all the cattle you saw and head back to the wagon. You'd see those little strings of cattle coming from every direction. Then a day of branding, the herd held by mounted men while the "heelers" rode their best ponies into the herd, picking out a calf, roping it by the hind legs and dragging it to the branding fire to be branded, earmarked, and (if it was a bull) castrated.

We had four branding crews, each one consisting of a "heeler" (mounted) and four men who worked on foot. Two of these seized the calf as it was dragged up. They threw it, slipped off the heel rope and flung the noose back to the heeler. He would catch it and lope back to the herd for another. Another man "ran the brands" according to the brand called by the heeler, who quoted the brand worn by the calf's mother. The fourth man did the castrating, and earmarking. An extra man—sometimes with the help of cook—tended the many irons heating in the fire. His was the most exacting task of all—for an iron too hot or an iron too cold is anathema to the man who has to use them.

I was used as a spare at first. I'd help tend irons, or run with them to the brander and so on, but pretty soon I was given a knife—first to earmark all calves that had been missed by the spring riders. I cropped and undercut and swallow-tailed and dewlapped and was soon covered with blood and satisfaction.

Next I was initiated in the operation of unsexing the young bulls. Since that day I suppose I have done many thousands. Wounds heal quickly and blood poisoning is rare in this dry, sunny climate. No disinfectant was used and no losses occurred.

All the riders were from local ranches, the owners of which were the proprietors of the wagons and equipment. Expenses were shared on the basis of the number of cattle branded for each shareholder. The big outfits like the Circle Diamond, the 76, and Spencer's put out one or more wagons for their own exclusive use, but the ranchers here were not large-scale operators.

There must have been about one hundred and fifty horses in the cavvy. When one lot of calves were all branded, that herd would be turned loose, and the wagon would move on to work another stretch of country.

4

Our outfit was short-handed. A couple of weeks before, the news of the declaration of war with Germany had burst among us like a bombshell and already seven of our men had left in answer to the call from their units—the 22nd Light Horse and the Alberta Dragoons. I was eager, too. Letters from home brought the news that one of my brothers had already seen action near Le Cateau, and another had volunteered. But Lee had said, "Wait a bit, Charlie. You're pretty young yet, and they might not pass you—you're hardly tall enough. It'll probably be over soon, and if not you'll be needed more next year and they may not be so particular about anyone being five-foot-seven or -eight by then." I was not yet eighteen and his counsel prevailed.

That morning we left the wagon in the gray dawn of what promised to be a blistering October day, and headed towards Egg Lake to see what we could find. The wagon would be at Battle Creek that night, somewhere this side of Badger's Ranch. The branding had been done and now we were gathering beef.

By ten o'clock we were well into the broken country. We headed up a long coulee with steep gravelly sides and a dry creek down the center. Lee said there were springs about two miles up, and any cattle in what he called "this neck of the woods" would probably be there.

Lee was a man of many parts and we enjoyed each other's company. He had been born near Medicine Hat, Alberta. His father had been a railway man. After a sketchy schooling he had started his cowboy life; while quite young he had gone to an uncle in Texas. He could describe that country well; and told me many tales of the Vaqueros, of the turbulent country west of the Pecos. I think he spoke Spanish well, and often broke into "Mex," as he called it, under stress or excitement.

He looked about thirty-five, but he told me he was over forty— "Though if and when I go to join up, I won't tell them that," he added.

What he lacked in formal education was made up for by a natural sensitivity to his surroundings and an acuteness of perception. Coupled with his love of extensive reading, this gave him a general knowledge and a charm of personality, added to a quiet restraint which impressed me then. I know now that I owe much to him.

He rarely spoke of his mother, but I sensed that he had the greatest love for her. He was always a bit shy with all other women, I think as a result. And it must have been his mother's influence that prompted a habit of which he never spoke, or encouraged others to speak.

He said his prayers.

Of the many nights I have camped with Lee on the lone prairie—in summer's heat or winter's frost—I cannot recall once that he did not

Antelope on the hill

kneel for a moment by his saddle and tarp before pulling off his boots and settling down.

Now Lee said suddenly, "Fellah—I think we are in for a snow storm. Ever' time it gets this sultry in the fall it's breeding weather."

I looked up. A perfect October day. Indian summer, not a cloud in the sky. That's when I got my first close-up look at antelopes. Looking up the coulee side to the left, something got between me and the sun. Lee reined up his horse—"Pronghorns," he said. Then they came in single file, clitter-clatter among the small pebbles and scraggly sage bushes.

What beauties they were!

A big old buck on the lead with shiny black horns, sharply hooked. Does, fawns, a sprinkling of young bucks. All intent on following-my-leader to the bottom of the coulee.

And then, suddenly, they saw us. Our horses pricked up their ears and stared. The big buck stared back, wrinkling his nose. The sun was bright on his cinnamon back and flanks. The white of his throat brought in strong relief the chocolate brown, slightly roman nose, his liquid eyes, and polished horns. For a second he stood thus. Then in a flurry, with great bounds, the herd turned and flung themselves over the top, their white rump patches extended like great flowers. We raced up the stony slope and topped the crest onto the level prairie lying all dappled and tawny. There were our antelope—about seventy-five of them—running all out in that wonderful rapid gallop—like tiny ponies but faster—thin bodies appearing to float easily above the blur of their rapidly moving legs. Their coloring blended so well with the sere grass, that when at last they stopped, nothing could be seen of them but the flashing of their white rumps as they sent their helioscope signals to another band. We sat our horses and looked for some minutes.

"Not as many as there used to be," said Lee. "I mind the time there would have been seven hundred instead of seventy-five. The spring blizzard of nineteen and six cleaned up a heap of them; and what with the range getting fenced and nesters coming in, I wouldn't care to be a pronghorn. If they *do* go—well, this life will be gone. They are part of it." This was undue sentiment for him. He turned his horse impatiently, and I followed.

5

We soon ran onto our first bunch of cattle; an old cow with about fifteen followers near the first spring. Two or three big steers, four to five years old, were with this bunch. "We'll leave them old mossy-horns and pick them up after we work the head of the coulee," said Lee.

The long, winding ravine headed up in a bunch of wild cherry and thorn bushes under a steep cut bank at the foot of which clear water seeped into a small pool. It was much tramped by cattle. We found about thirty head here. Quite a number were really big steers—the kind that, till the war came, had been shipped on the hoof to England. Some of these animals resented being pushed out of their haven.

One old steer in particular would not leave the shelter of a tangled clump of gray thorn bushes. These were loaded with the red buffalo berries. They make the best jelly in the west; and if you are brave enough to face the two- or three-inch thorns, they make good eating raw. The Indians get them by cutting off the laden boughs, which they take to camp on their wagons. Then they beat off the berries with a switch, above an outspread blanket.

I had been thinking of this and let my mind wander when Lee shouted, "Look out!" Old mossy-horn was glaring at me as if daring me to get off my horse and go in after him. If I didn't—well, he seemed to say, *he'd* come out after me.

I backed up my pony—I was riding Red—and reaching up the cut bank behind me I broke off a chunk of dry gumbo. Taking good aim I conked him just under one eye. With a snort he charged out the other side where Lee caught him a good thwack with the honda of his rope.

All told we gathered five small bunches and headed down towards the first we'd seen. Then as we came out of the shelter of the wash I suddenly shivered and looked up. "Reckon I was right," said Lee. "Knew those antelope weren't moving for nothing. We'd better ride pronto, Charlie, if we're going to make camp tonight."

And ride we did, as the wind increased and the gray clouds lowered. You could feel the temperature dropping. The cattle seemed anxious to move, too.

Luckily the wind was behind them—and us. It began to get dusk with still several miles to go to Badger's Crossing.

Then the snow came. Fitfully at first, then with increasing steadiness. We urged on the cattle and donned our jackets, turned up their collars, and pulled our Stetsons down as far as they'd go. My ears were getting cold, so I tied my neckerchief over my head, under my hat. Lee did the same. Our leather gloves weren't much use, but by alternately shoving first one hand and then the other down inside our chaps we kept them fairly comfortable.

A big roan steer took the lead. We reckoned he'd hit for the shelter of the Battle Creek breaks, and somewhere along there would be the wagon.

On ordinary occasions cattle seem to move with exasperating lethargy, but when the critters really want to get some place they'll pretty near outwalk a horse—even breaking into a smart trot on their own hook. Then, if they are going the right way, you don't drive—you follow.

By now the storm had become a blizzard and the wind cut like a knife. The cattle became barely discernible in the gloom ahead. Suddenly even they vanished and we were alone. But not for long. In a few more steps our ponies began to plunge downhill. We were over the breaks of the creek. We could hear the cattle tramping and breaking twigs among the willows. Here in the shelter the force of the wind was broken; nevertheless Lee had to ride knee to my knee and shout to make me hear.

"Reckon the wagon's somewheres to our right. This must be the thick bush north of Badger's where they winter-feed."

So we turned right-handed. We knew the cattle would not move till the wind let up anyway. Presently we realized that cattle were standing in the brush all around us. "Must be the herd," said Lee, and it was. We caught a beam of light in the willows ahead. We rode up to the camp. The wagon boss stood up with a coffee mug in his hand.

"You boys okay?" We said we were. "Better eat," said the wagon boss, "but keep your ponies saddled. Chuck and Sonny Myers aren't in yet with the cavvy. And the boys from the south circle aren't back either. Likely they'll be in at Badger's. The cavvy probably won't make it against the storm. When it lets up we'll have to locate 'em, but right now it 'ud be wasted effort. No guard tonight boys. The cattle won't likely move out of shelter, and if they did we couldn't stop 'em. I'm turning in. Good night."

Lee filled his plate and took his mug of coffee to one side. I joined him. We squatted on our haunches and ate. After the cold and gloom of the dark prairie, that little fire in the brush with the faithful wagon standing in the glow was our own bright happy home.

I reached for tobacco from my inside shirt pocket. No papers. "Give

me a makins' paper, Lee," I said. No answer. I nudged him—or where
he should have been. He wasn't there. "What the—" I started up.
"I'm a-coming, Amigo," I heard the voice from below and there
was Lee's face about a yard away and level with my toes. "Bank
broke," said Lee, as he hauled himself up. I looked again. We hadn't
seen the five-foot cut bank behind us. Lucky it wasn't fifty feet.

6

Smoking contentedly, Lee told me about a similar "weather breeding" October day about 20 years previous. A policeman from Fort
McLeod with dispatches for some place on the border got caught in
just such a blizzard. He and his horse strayed for two days with the
storm. He was dressed for warm weather. Boots, Stetson, and leather
gloves. It got really cold as it cleared, and the sun rose the third day
on a glittering white world without a landmark or a bush showing.
On the fourth day they were picked up by the mail stage on the Fort
Benton—Sweetgrass run—'way over in Montana. The policeman had
no recollection of crossing Milk River. By that time the man was
completely snow blind.

He was taken to the Seventh Cavalry Barracks at Fort Benton and
was well cared for by the Yankees. "Barring losing both ears and a
few fingers and toes from frostbite," Lee concluded, "young Parker
was fit in no time. I knew him—was at Spion Kop with him.

"He told me he'd got off his hoss for something the third or fourth
day, and he was that cold and weak he couldn't get on again. So he
put his arm through a stirrup and the hoss would stop every once in
awhile to paw for grass. Parker wanted to go to sleep but ever' time
he slumped down the hoss'd nudge him. He kind of went off his head,
he said, and next thing he knew the hoss whickered.

"Then he heard a mule bray. He thought 'this must be hell.' Next
thing he was lifted in the stage. When he came to in the hospital he
asked for his hoss. Didn't get much of an answer. After another sleep
the colonel came to see him. After a bit of chat the officer said, 'I
believe there's a visitor to see you.' With that two troopers led in his
hoss—Custer was his name—all curried up and the saddle all polished,

and Parker said old Custer walked just like he was on parade between the rows of cots and then stopped and nuzzled him for sugar. Well, if them Yankee boys didn't run up with half the sugar bowls on the place."

We unbridled our mounts and turned them, saddled, among the cattle. As I rolled in I was glad I wasn't out in that blizzard.

7

Next morning our tarp was heavy with snow. We crawled out, stiff and sore, and hauled on our frozen riding boots with numbed fingers.

It had stopped snowing, and the wind lessened at ground level, although the gray heavy clouds still traveled southward at a stiff pace.

"Come and get it," called the cook, and we made no delay. As we gulped hot coffee and fresh biscuits soaked in syrup, the wagon boss, coming from a stroll around, summed up the situation and began to give orders for the day.

"Fust off," he said, "we gotta locate the hoss wranglers with the cavvy. Reckon they drifted a long ways and the boys'd have to follow. With any luck they got into bush some'res. We'll camp right here till the weather lets up. The cattle won't move for a bit, but if it warms up they'll be apt to drift. Jack"—this to a lean rider from the El Anchor Bar—"you and Gooseneck each take a couple men and git around them critters now. I'll send out some more boys 'bout ten o'clock. Lee—you take Charlie with you and follow the crick east and try to locate the cavvy. Me, I'll take Ellison and ride south side of the crick in case the cavvy crossed. The rest of you boys help the cook. He'll want plenty of wood, or whatever you can find."

Lee and I hunted among the willows for our tired saddle horses. They were pretty well among the cattle, and the snow had crusted hard on their manes and rumps and over the saddles. These same saddles had proved a boon to the poor beasts by keeping the snow from freezing over their backs and kidneys. The ponies had spent a long night pawing in the little openings among the willows for the good blue-joint grass laid flat under the snow. The cattle, not understanding how to paw for feed, looked pretty gaunt and stood mostly humped up in groups, but the rim of snow around their muzzles and eyes showed that they had been rooting around, too.

As we caught our mounts, the cattle began to move about uneasily. We were unfamiliar to them on foot. On the high ground we could see Jack and his riders loping easily through the snow to head off the cattle from the west and turn them back down the creek bottom.

Once mounted we, too, loped our horses for a mile or two, to warm both them and ourselves. It is wonderful how a fast canter takes the stiffness from your limbs and the fug from your head.

The clouds were beginning to break a bit now. We crossed the dry wash, which ran into the creek about a mile below camp. The cook had told us that the cavvy had been grazing here—in the angle formed by the wash and the creek—when the storm broke. Then everything was blotted out. We looked for sign, but the storm had wiped that out. Nothing lay before us but the plain, as white as this paper, with only the purplish willows to our right—all bent over and bowed down with snow—to indicate where the creek lay. The Hills were still obscured by the cloud rack.

"We better keep close to the crick," Lee said. "That way if the hosses crossed, there might still be some broken bushes to show us. I hope—" His voice trailed off and we rode in silence. I suppose we were both thinking of Chuck Nelson and Sonny Myers, the two nighthawks. True to tradition they must have stayed right with the cavvy when the horses drifted before the storm during the night.

"The wind's plumb dropped," was the next thing he said. So it had. "If she starts again from the east," he went on, "we'll get a chinook after a bit. Always has to go from north to east, *then* to southwest to make a chinook. Cain't make it the other way."

8

Another two miles in silence. Then we both saw something moving in the brush. A rider! Hurrah; one of the boys! The rider was Chuck. He was riding a mean black from Sonny's string.

Hadn't the cook said that Sonny was riding "that knothead"?

"Something plumb wrong here, fellah," said Lee, and gave his horse the spur. Together we raced up and surrounded Chuck.

"Hullo, boy," cried Lee, "Sonny hurt?" Chuck reined to a halt. His usually rubicund features were gray with fatigue—his eyes red from the sting of snow.

"Well," he replied slowly, as if he were trying to recollect something, "Sonny, now? Well—" he paused, and went on, "not hurt much I reckon. Looks like a broken arm an' a couple ribs."

"What happened?" Lee asked.

"Well," said Chuck, "I told him not to ride this dam' bastard of a knothead. 'You càn only die once, Chuck,' Sonny allus said. Guess he was right at that."

Then Chuck told us how the storm had suddenly struck like a serpent while he was in charge of the cavvy. Sonny had been out with the cavvy the night before and was supposed to be sleeping, but awakened by the storm he had rightly thought that Chuck would need help.

Sonny had joined him, but all their riding was of no avail. They couldn't turn the horses toward camp and shelter. The beasts had simply turned tail-to-storm and plunged away.

Chuck told us how they two had followed—sometimes seeing a horse's rump; more often not. *They* could never have kept in touch, but their mounts had followed and followed, while the storm grew worse and the cold more bitter. How they finally caught up to the bunch, now standing irresolute at the top of a cut bank which Chuck reckoned must be by Battle Creek. With the thought of shelter in the brush below, Chuck had yelled to Sonny to get around the left flank, while he himself hazed the bunch along the top of the cliff; and to try to turn them down at the first opportunity.

"We was going on the high lope," went on Chuck, "I couldn't see Sonny. But he must have been close because all at once I heard him yell, 'I got 'em turned, Chuck,' and sure enough them ponies went down over the bank like them whatsin-names swine what they tell of in the Bible—me with 'em. Well, they calmed down some when they hit the brush, and I reckoned they were okay for the night. I figgered we might make a camp till the storm cleared. I yelled for Sonny. No answer. I thought, that's a funny thing, he must have come down with the broncs. I rode a circle—no Sonny.

"Then Pet looked up the bank and I said, 'Go on girl'; so she scrambled up, and at the top there's old knothaid, and he's worried about something. I try to catch him, but he makes off in the dark spookylike—and I got to stalk him agin. Finally I grabs a line, and he snorts and jerks back. And then I see—well, poor Sonny, his foots' in the stirrup and he's been plumb dragged and tramped on. Like as not old knothaid got in a badger hole and rolled on him first. Or could be he spooked at something. Sonny's a good enough rider, but you all seen this black bastard pitch—and when a fellow's all bundled up and cold and not a-lookin' for it . . .

"Well, I always say, there ain't a hoss that can't be rode, and there ain't a man what can't be throwed."

"What then, Chuck," from Lee.

"Well, I was scared he was dead, so I packed him on Pet—she's gentle—and put my saddle on the knothead and we got down into the willows. Wouldn't have known where the creek was at; on'y Pet knew alright, so I let her go ahead. I'd only a few dry matches and the bush was wet, so we camped under the willows with saddle blankets over us. Sonny came to alright, but I guess I hadn't helped him, packing him down like that—but I couldn't leave him up top or he'd have froze.

"Yep, he came to okay, but he can't make it to camp the way he is. So I made him as comfortable as I could and started for help. If I keep a-going for a rig, can you fellows stay with him—it's not but a couple of miles back down the crik, and the cavvy's all there. I shore need to eat."

And Chuck rode for camp.

We found Sonny in pretty bad shape, but kept the fire going and stayed with him till the Police buckboard from the Ten Mile came to take him to Maple Creek.

Then we started back with the cavvy, and Chuck's mare, Pet.

9

That night there wasn't the usual hum of conversation around the wagon. It was still cloudy and raw, but the wind was now southeast, and it wasn't so frosty.

Somebody said, "How about a hand of poker?" but no one answered for a bit. Finally, an oldish man—Abe Trewitt, an old-timer who'd had a spread in the Chin Coulee country of Alberta till he was sheeped out—spoke up.

"Yep, boys. That's a good idee. A hand o' poker now will do us all good. While we're about it, let's start a good pot and don't be shy on your bids. I know Missus Myers, the boy's mother. She's in Medicine Hat since the old man cashed in, and she ain't what you'd call well-heeled. That's where Sonny sent his wages. It'd do no harm if we helped like—on expenses. All life is a gamble anyways—but I reckon the Lord plumb knows what He's a-doin'—see what I mean. Winner can do as he likes, only I say—send it to the woman."

That was quite a poker game. Saddles, chaps, spurs, even horses, were all thrown into it, plus the few creased dollar bills and small coins and I.O.U.'s the boys rustled up. And we played—a gray saddle blanket spread on the trampled ground for a table, and the feeble light of a stable lantern to see the pips by. As we played, Banjo Pete—who never owned a Banjo and couldn't play one if he did—took his battered mouth organ from his chaps' pocket. After much blowing and cussing he brushed it across his lips. Just any old bits of tune at first. Then presently we began to recognize "The Cowboy's Lament." And as the notes wheezed around the game, we began, one by one, to hum the tune so well known in the cow camps from the Rio Grande to the Saskatchewan. Shamefaced at first, and then with more confidence, one or two began to say the words, too, as the battered cards slithered across the smelly blanket and the carelessly tossed pile of bills and coins began to grow.

"Won't somebody write to my dear old mother,
My dear old mother and sister so dear?
But there is another much dearer than mother
Who surely would weep if she knew I was here.
So beat the drum slowly and play the fife o'er me
And play the dead march as
You carry me on.
Take me to the prairie and throw the sod o'er me, for
I'm a poor cowboy an' I know I done wrong."

Following the cavvy

10

Next morning the chinook blew. Away in the southwest was her great arch, all edged with hanging liver-colored clouds from beneath which the warm wind blew, sopping up the snow. The Sweetgrass buttes looked so close you could touch them, and the Bear Paws were clear-cut and blue.

It was two days later that the boys from the south got in. They, too, had been caught. They drifted and by luck struck the Circle Diamond wagon near the Old-Man-on-His-Back.

They brought a few head with them, but had lost some big steers. The Circle outfit promised to pick them up if possible and their wagon boss would see they got shipped from Chinook.

It was quite customary for any stray beef steers to be shipped by another outfit. They would notify the Brand Inspector and have the brand put on the waybill with the owner's name and address. The commission firm buying the animals would send the check direct to the owner.

Scotty one time got a check for nearly a thousand dollars from Clay Robinson & Co. of Chicago. It was in payment for so many steers received. Scotty never found out who shipped them till a year later when he met Fred Craig of the 76 at Maple Creek. It seems the 76 wagon had picked them up near Eastend. As long as everyone was honest this system saved a lot of trouble.

We had six weeks of perfect weather after that, before freeze-up finally brought the wagon—and the beef—home.

CHAPTER SEVEN

1

Back at the ranch again the beef cut was corralled to get acquainted for a few days while preparations were in hand for the drive to Maple Creek. If a bunch of steers have been scattered over a wide range all their lives, it helps a lot to hold them together for a while before trailing them. Cattle are just about like humans—they have their own friends, and they look with a jaundiced eye upon strange and foreign beasts.

The trail herd consisted of about fifty big steers and a few dry cows. Not a big drive. These old girls are quite a help at holding a bunch together. Also, they are pretty good to lead out. Having been driven before, they have a wholesome respect for a man and horse, and the steers, of course, having followed cows since they were calves, would usually go whenever the cows did. In those days no steer under three years old was considered fit for market. Most of them would weigh anything over one thousand pounds—to twelve or thirteen hundred pounds—but on most beef drives there was apt to be a sprinkling of older steers up to seven years old and weighing up to fifteen hundred pounds or more. These would be animals that had got away on previous roundups, and they were the fellows to watch. A few winters "toughed out" on the prairie made them full of independence and initiative. We had a rangy, one-horned critter who'd escaped the herd for two seasons by breaking on the high lope. Usually, when a steer did that a couple of boys would take after him with ropes swinging. They'd catch him and bust him down and leave him hog-tied till he thought better of it.

This particular steer had made his first getaway so quickly that he was let go. The next year he tried it again. When he was finally roped he came down so hard he bust one horn off. At the same time the rope broke, and before they could get another on him he'd headed up a wash, so again they let him go.

Loading steers on the C.P.R.

This year the boys watched him pretty close. You couldn't mistake him with that one long horn all lopsided. He'd mosey along nice and easy for a bit. Then you'd see his head turn, looking up every coulee and scanning the country for a getaway place.

One of the swing riders would yell at him and maybe pop his rope. The steer had learned respect for that. He'd sort of hide himself in the crowd till he was able to work his way to the other flank.

The boys called him "Slinky," and every once in a while you'd hear someone call out, "Look out for ole' Slinky—he's on your side."

By good luck we had brought the steer up to the ranch this year and the boss was pleased. It wasn't so much the dollars, but it's a reflection on a cowman for him to have an "outlaw" on the range. Old steers, if you left them, got mean, and were a darn nuisance when the boys were working cattle. These old mossy-horns could start a stampede as quick as look at you.

2

Up to that time a good many fat steers had been going to England on the hoof. But the market had been fast swinging to the States, and of course the war stopped the overseas selling completely. As more and more went to the Chicago market the various ranch outfits would make up big trail herds and move them across the Medicine Line to Havre or Chinook. Then they went direct to market by the Great Northern Railway.

Our lot of steers was also destined for Chicago, but they would be part of a train of cattle which the C.P.R. would pick up along their line between Maple Creek and North Portal by way of Moose Jaw.

Lee and the boss were going with the train to feed and water the cattle en route. They'd travel in the caboose and cook their own meals. We envied them the chance of a few days in the Bright Lights, and we thought of them touring the city in a big car. Cars were then unknown in the cattle country although common enough in the cities. The only one I'd seen in Maple Creek was a new Model-T Ford just purchased by the Dixon boys who kept a store there—the place where I got my first blue jeans—actually the first store in that town, started before the steel went through, about 1881, I think. It's still there. I don't think they trusted the stink-wagon on the prairie trails, but I remember it around town, usually followed by a group of young boys trying to bum a ride—which they usually got.

We were three days on the forty-mile drive. A light wagon accompanied us and kept us supplied with grub. For the two nights we spent on the trail we were able to corral the steers at ranches, and we had permission to unroll our beds in hay lofts or barns.

We had a little trouble at first, but soon old Slinky stopped trying to break, and the herd had forgotten home and were trail-broken when we got to Maple Creek. We held the herd on the flats along the creek about two miles from town, in sight of the red-roofed Police Barracks. Lee and the boss went in to see about box cars. It was pretty cold, but the steers settled down well, picking a good bellyful of buffalo grass from among the clumps of sage and cactus.

About three hours before sundown Lee galloped back to tell us to gather the steers and head for the stockyards. We were to swing west of town, between the outlying houses and the creek. Lee said he'd have some men to open the pen gates and help get the steers in.

We had no trouble till we got to Railway Street and had to turn east. The pens were away down right alongside the track, of course. We could see the cars spotted along the loading platform. Cars carrying brands from all over. Chuck pointed out "Great Northern," "Grand Trunk Pacific," "Erie and South Shore," "Chicago, Milwaukee and St. Paul," and even a lone "Santa Fé." When the great romance of railroading is written, it will be interesting to know how the outfits kept track of their brands. Chuck figured they'd need a roundup. The

The mossy-horned steer

locomotive was filling its tender from the coal shute about three hundred yards away.

Those steers didn't like the looks of those whitewashed pens, but we crowded them along with many a yip and yell. Old Slinky had worked his way to the lead. Two or three men from the livery barn were blocking the street to turn the bunch. Slinky stopped. Then he looked at the open pen gate. Maybe it was a trap. Just then some cows in another pen moved, and one of them bellowed. Slinky thought it was safe then and he took a step or two forward. His head and shoulders were in and he was snuffing the cow smell. Two more steps and he'd *be* in, and then the rest would follow.

"Of all the good luck," breathed Lee. "If he'll only keep moving."

Just then the locomotive let off steam with a gusty sigh. Old Slinky moved alright. But he moved the wrong way. He just wheeled and drove himself through the herd like he was loco, swinging his one horn ready to hook anything that side.

That did it.

It took us till dark to get the steers gathered up again. One or two crossed the bridge and started loping for home, but our horses were good and soon got around them. The townspeople helped a lot, too. This was a cow town and knew what to do and rather enjoyed it. I remember seeing one woman attacking—with a broom—a couple of steers that had broken into her house yard, and from the way she cussed I think she rather enjoyed the whole thing.

We finally got them all on the train—all except old Slinky. He'd landed at the foot of a cut bank where the creek bends south of town, and he defied one and all to come and get him. Some of the boys were for roping him, then dragging him through the water and up the bank, but Scotty said, "We can't waste time fooling around wi' a beast like yon—I'll see Bently."

Bently, the butcher, was there on his own horse, enjoying the fun. "You don't have to look far, Scotty!" said he. "I'll give you thirty dollars for that steer where he's at."

"Tis a bargain," replied the boss.

Bently turned to a youth. "Run tell Mac to get down here right off with a block and tackle—tell him to bring a couple knives and the rifle."

3

Just what started the old feud that raged between cowpunchers and freight hands, I don't know. But a feud there was—and is still, probably. I suppose the train men who had their own houses at the divisional points got a feeling of superiority from their settled, "civilized" town life—complete with daily papers.

Anyway, they looked on the cowboys as rather smelly and shiftless vagrants, who didn't know any better than to spend all summer sleeping on the bald-headed prairie. And they were ready to fight at any remarks regarding their ability to "spot" a car so the side door was exactly opposite the gate of the loading chute. They certainly seemed to take a delight in being as slow as possible and as noisy as possible; and if they could leave a car a foot or so out, it seemed to tickle them.

Especially when a foot-sore bunch of hot, tired men—used to working from the saddle—had to goad the unwilling beasts up and around the loading chutes through too narrow a passage. The cowboys wanted to get it over with and head up-town for a drink. The railway boys knew this; and if they could make the work drag on they were one up on us, for the longer it took to load, the more the boys realized that this wasn't their way of life and under the discomfort tempers got pretty brittle.

Perhaps a railroader wouldn't see it from their angle—there's two sides to everything. There weren't many actual fights. The boss on the one hand and the freight conductor on the other saw to that. But many a piece of coal was chucked slyly into the face of a steer just when he started to behave. And many a cow pat left its mark on a brakeman's pants.

Finally the last car door was secured—the last compliments exchanged between the feuders. We jumped on our ponies and raced to the livery barn to unsaddle and feed them before we hit the hot· spots. The train wouldn't move out till midnight—after the Transcontinental left the line clear for Moose Jaw. So the boss and Lee said they'd meet us later at the hotel to give us our pay.

In those days there were barrooms in every prairie town, and Maple

Creek was no exception—unless by virtue (so its citizens bragged) of the fact that its bars were bigger and better. Maple Creek was the supply point for an immense area then; from the South Saskatchewan to the border. The next town south was Havre, Montana, way below the border.

The old Haver trail has seen plenty of cow men and cowboys. Lots of families from the States had trailed their wagons and their herds up it to Canada.

The Cheesmans, the Gaffs (they came from the Nebraska sand hills), the Lawrences, the Coney Campbells at Skull Creek, and a host of others—all cow people like the Hesters and other Texas folk (or as they said, "Texians") who came into the wild horse country. There were plenty of English and Scottish families, too, as well as "Down East" Canadians. But they all got along.

4

The Maple Leaf Hotel had one of the longest and most showy barrooms—plenty of "gingerbread," plenty of shiny mirrors and gleaming mahogany. A row of polished brass spittoons were spotted at intervals for the convenience of the "chawing" public. Along the front of the bar ran the usual brass footrail.

It was customary to belly up, nominate your "pizen," drink fast, and make room for the next comer. The "bar keep" didn't put the "likker" into the glasses. If you asked for Scotch or what-have-you, he'd grab the bottle in his right hand, a glass in his left, cross hands, and plunk the two down before you. You took a small or a big drink as you wished—for ten cents the tariff didn't vary.

Over this particular bar were many reproductions in color (I think they called them oleographs) of such subjects as underclad females and well-rigged race horses. One large picture used to interest me. It was about three feet by two feet and was entitled "Custer's Last Stand." It, too, was in color and showed General "Long Hair" Custer of the U.S. Cavalry. He was still swinging his saber while most of his troopers lay in their gore being scalped by Sioux. Those braves not engaged in this grisly pastime were intent on cutting down the hatless General. The date—1876, and the place, of course, the Little Bighorn.

It was not long after that victory for the Indians that the sagacious chief Sitting Bull brought his people across the Medicine Line into Canadian territory; seeking asylum in the land of the Great White Queen whose ancestor, George IV, had decorated the chief's grandfather for his adherence to the British, in the War of 1812. In that war the great Tecumseh struck a blow for the "Old Northwest" (Ohio, Indiana, Michigan) which had been promised as Indian territory by George III.

Colonel Walsh, Commissioner for the North West Mounted Police (they hadn't the "Royal" then) left Wood Mountain post and met the famous chief surrounded by his braves near Buffalo Gap. Straggling for a mile behind came pony *traveaux* laden with cooking pots, gear and children; some women walking but many riding. Sitting Bull showed his grandfather's British medal and was allowed to stay in Canada, at least for a few years. Walsh, backed by only a handful of Police troopers, made it very clear to Sitting Bull that his stay in Canada was conditional on his good behavior.

So this picture took me into an earlier day—a day still remembered by men like Old Joe from the Crow and the older ranchers. It belonged to the days when Fort Walsh on Battle Creek was Police Headquarters—before the railway came to Pile of Bones (Regina) and the move to that point took place.

I believe these old barroom pictures, put out by the brewing companies, are valuable now. This one advertized Budweiser beer and lager. Don't think the cowboys' only relaxation was drinking, however—most of them were moderate drinkers.

There were plenty of gambling games—poker the favorite, of course. But King Pedro and Monte also had their devotees.

Some of the boys spoke of going to the house beyond the tracks—the one with the lace curtains—but they were having a good time and few of them got around to it.

The gals beyond the tracks actually filled a gap, because women were few and far between in those days and mostly married, anyway. So more than one little gal from behind the lace curtains ended up as a rancher's wife.

These gals and the Madame did their shopping on Saturday afternoons, and no doubt some of the lady pillars of Maple Creek society were not above taking a peek at them from behind *their* curtains.

Five riders from the 76 were in town that night. They'd been whooping it up at the Jasper Hotel down the street, and decided to raid the Maple Leaf. They allowed that the feller who played the piano at that joint was a tinhorn gambler in his spare time. Their horses were still at the hitching rack, as they figured to head back for Crane Lake that night.

They started up the street. Suddenly one of them—Buchanan, I think—said, "I gotta have a horse"; so he got his and clattered up the wooden sidewalk, sending the splinters flying. First thing we knew he rode into the Maple Leaf with his rope down. He made a swing at the pianist, but that worthy ducked behind the bar, so Don Quixote roped the piano instead.

His pony hunched down and dragged it to the door, but there it stuck. About this time the bartender had got hold of the pickhandle he kept for such emergencies, and the 76 boys were cheerfully trying to hold him back.

Just then a voice from the sidewalk said crisply, "What's all this?" It was Constable Greyson on night duty from the Barracks.

"Well," said the culprit—pushing back his Stetson and scratching his head—"it's what it looks like, I guess."

"Very good—how would you like to look like a fellow in the clink? You come along, boy, and the rest of you put that piano back."

"Say—have a heart—we was only joshing," said the united 76.

"Hell—say," said the bartender, "no harm done. That hombre was reckoning on leaving town tonight, wasn't you, boy?"

"Uh-huh," said the repentant roper. "Sure was—'less I stayed to join up."

"Well, in that case," said the policeman, "seeing the house isn't laying charges, be on your way. Come around to the Barracks at noon and pay for the sidewalk—and let's see you in uniform. Good night," and he jingled away.

Of course, there was a good sprinkling of khaki that year. Lean, tanned, young cowboys and homesteaders strolled about in the smart breeches and bandoliers of the Twenty-Second Light Horse and other

Cavalry regiments. There was a Recruiting Office in the town with a young officer in nominal charge, and an "Old Sweat" British Cavalry Sergeant-Major, who really was. He was back in his beloved uniform after a few years as butcher in Moose Jaw.

Well, we had a merry night and no harm done. If it all sounds pretty tame after seeing the "Horse Operas" of the American West, the lack of gunplay and so on in Canada is very easily explained.

In the United States the "Mountain Men,"—beaver trappers, mostly—penetrated the western wilderness at an early date, before and during the middle years of the last century. In Canada most of the actual trappers and hunters were the native Indians, harvesting their own possessions. The role of the white man was to be a trader, a member of a responsible body, such as the Hudson's Bay Company, who set up permanent trading posts, exchanged value for value, and used no liquor in trade—except in very early days, for they soon realized what rum could do to their Indian hunters. For the sake of trade, this Company maintained a tolerant law and kept good order, so much so that in all of what was then British North America there was no such thing as an Indian "war."

In the States, individual white men or groups of them penetrated the hunting grounds of the Cheyennes, the Sioux, the Crows, Shoshones, and Flatheads, and lived by stealing the animals that really belonged to these people. The natural resentment of the Indians to this was the cause of frequent friction and not infrequent war.

Soon, too, came the gold seekers, to be followed by the cattle and sheep men, who followed similar tactics. For example, the early cattlemen helped to destroy the Indians' meat—the buffalo—to have more grass for their herds.

Thus, in the American West a quite numerous population of reckless, daring frontiersmen already competed with the Indians and against one another *before any sort of law became established*—a law that has only within living memory brought true respect for human life and property among a people accustomed to protecting their own property and dealing out their own harsh justice.

The sad and shameful story of the red man's degradation south of the border was the natural result of a lawless frontier.

By contrast, the Canadian West was opened up more slowly. Here the law, in the shape of the North West Mounted Police, came to the plains ahead of the march of progress. From 1874 the Mounted Police kept order in the Canadian West. From then on law and order did not have to be imposed—it was already there when the settlers moved in.

This meant that life was different on either side of the border. For instance, the "Reps" from the American outfits used to ride up from Montana in the full glory of gun belts and pistols. They were supposed to report at Maple Creek Police Barracks to make arrangements to clear their cattle from Canadian territory at a payment of so much per head. "Dad" Whitney, ex-foreman of an outfit across the line told me, "Fust time I came into the office at 'the Crick' a pink-faced boy in a red jacket asked me to hand over my gun. Well, say—I'd never been asked such a thing in my life."

I said, "What for?"

He said, "Oh, over here we don't need them—nobody uses them. *We* do the shootin' around here."

"He spoke real soft and nice, but there was something about the way he said it—so I took off my belt and holster. I hardly knowed I'd done it, and I felt plumb naked. The feller hung them on a nail with a tag on them and wrote me a receipt like he was selling me a pair o' boots—and then said: 'You can turn that in and pick up your hardware when you're ready to go home. Good day.' We soon found out there was no bluff 'bout them boys in red. I liked them good. I was a-gettin' along in years, and a bit tired of brainless hombres always wanting to go a-gunning somewheres."

He added, "I ramrodded the Circle Diamond for quite a few years after that—back and forth 'tween Montany and Canady. Finally, I liked it so well up here I stayed for keeps; and I reckon I'll lay me old carcass here when the time comes." He did.

The newspapers were full of news of the war. It wouldn't last long, the papers thought, now the French were making a stand.

I paid a visit to the Recruiting Office. The height standard was five foot seven inches. I was afraid I was going to miss it all and envied my two brothers, and the third who was training for the Royal Flying Corps; piloting those nickel crates called Sopwith Camels.

It was back to the ranch for me.

5

With the beef drive over and the mild weather continuing there would have been time on our hands before snow came, had not the British and French armies needed remounts.

Two veterinary officers of the French cavalry were in Maple Creek for the purpose of purchasing horses, for this part of the West was famous for its good horseflesh.

The days on which they would inspect horses at the stockyard were advertised. They paid a flat price per head and specified geldings only, from five to eight years old; sound, and of solid color. For cavalry they wanted mounts from nine hundred pounds to eleven hundred; and for artillery and transport, heavier by about three hundred pounds or more. The British demanded slightly bigger horses for all arms of the service. All horses had to be halter-broke and ridden enough to be at least bridle-wise and not too apt to buck.

So Scotty had us all breaking horses for the next six weeks.

Most of the other ranchers did the same; and in addition to the ordinary help, a fair number of good riders—regular broncobusters—traveled from place to place, "topping off" the tough ones at so much per head.

All cowboys are not bronc peelers. All have to be good riders, but many of the older men wouldn't have a horse in their string that had the bucking habit. This applied especially to men with wives and families; and it was not timidity that kept these men back, but a decent sense of responsibility. Many a budding top bronco man quit the business at his wife's insistence, or had to make a promise to quit when he got engaged.

In those days the Welfare State had not even been thought of. There were no pensions, no free hospitalizations, no widow's allowance, and no unemployment insurance. Few sedentary jobs awaited the cripple in a country where agriculture was supreme, and the small urban centers only existed to sell sugar and matches and plows and saddles. There was no Workmen's Compensation Act.

A man has to think of his family. It may be fun to ride a bronc, but being thrown is part of the game, and a bad throw could leave

you a cripple or your wife a widow. Better play safe—there are risks
enough on the range, anyway.

Like Sonny, who had his widowed mother to think of. He got healed
up all right, but he got him a safer job than riding. The last time I
saw him he was driving a dray team in Medicine Hat.

A pinto mare

6

The range horses of the Canadian prairies were mostly descended
on the distaff side from the native stock that were roaming the plains
of North America when the ranching industry started in the late '70s
and '80s.

The Indians owned large bands of these "ponies" (for ponies they
were in size).

The history of these hardy beasts has been written: descended from
stock turned loose by Coronado on the plains of New Mexico, in 1540,
they had, within two centuries, increased and multiplied till they ran
in the thousands on the short-grass plains from the Rio Grande
northward and westward.

The Comanches were among the first Indians to make use of
Coronado's gift. Later, by trade and theft, other tribes began to use
the fleet-footed mounts. The Crows were great dealers in horses, and
through them they spread north to the Sioux and Blackfoot.

The Crees of the Saskatchewan country were among the last to acquire horses. From 1740 on they began to adopt them, but it was another hundred years before they were generally mounted.

It was the adoption of the horse as a means of travel and transport that made possible the Golden Age of the plains Indian—alas, so brief! Mounted, and with their necessities loaded on travois ponies, they could now leave the shelter of the wooded valleys and the edge of the forests, and penetrate as far into the plains as they cared to. The Sioux, the Assiniboines, and the Crees threw down their crude digging sticks, abandoned their half-hearted attempts at agriculture, and with enthusiasm rode into the west on their buffalo runners, as they called their best hunting horses. Where before they had made short forays into the sea of grass, they now made their homes with the great herds that provided them with food, clothing, implements, and fuel. The birch-bark wigwam gave place to the airy, romantic buffalo-skin tepee. And when the American Army waged its fiercest war against the red man, it was the red man's horses that they destroyed with the greatest fervor.

These ponies were variously called "cayuses," Nitchie ponies (Nitchi—Indian, from Cree *"Nihio"*), or mustangs. They were *not* called broncos. Bronco is Mexican for a wild (i.e., unbroken) horse.

They were smallish. Many years of summer droughts and winter blizzards had done that. But the large liquid eyes, the scanty mane and tail, the well-shaped limbs and hooves, the flaring nostrils, and small scimitar-curved ears betrayed their Arab ancestry. And it was no uncommon thing to find one dimpled on the neck by the thumb mark of Allah. The gray horse in my string carried such a mark. Pound for pound there were no stronger mounts to be found. They could carry a man all day over country that would finish an English thoroughbred. And at the day's end, their reward was whatever dry bunch-grass they could reach at the end of a picket rope.

This, then, was the foundation stock from which most western horses stemmed.

In the beginning, most ranchers, like the mountain men before them, were content to use these horses as they found them. But the many Southerners who infiltrated into the trans-Missouri country after the Civil War took good stallions with them (thanks to the generous terms whereby Grant allowed Lee's men to keep their horses). By the time that the cattle tide began to spread into Canada, the lean riders who spurred them on were riding some splendid horses whose male parents had been foaled on the Blue Grass.

And as the long-grass prairies of first Manitoba and later Saskatchewan began to be farmed, there arose an ever-growing demand for a good commercial type of horse—heavy draught for farm work and use in the woods. The demand was soon keen, too, for a medium but not too light a horse for police remounts; as well as a steady call for a more limited number of first-class light saddle and buggy horses.

To anyone brought up in the age of the internal combustion engine, the number of light buggy teams and single drivers then flourishing in any of the prairie towns would be an eye opener. It must be remembered that the motor car was well established in Europe and Eastern America long before it came into general use in the sparsely inhabited and roadless West.

Every town had one or more livery and sales stables. The proprietors were of a type rarely met with now. They knew every man and nearly every horse in the district. Those were the days when all classes of people had direct contact with each other. Now, you pull up to something called "Ford Dealer. Gas, Oil, and Repairs. Used Cars." Flags flutter, but Mr. Ford is not there.

You don't know who owns the place and the chances are he doesn't know you.

But when you drove into the yard of Noland's barn, Mr. Noland was there, tipped back in an old chair in the sunshine or the shade depending on the thermometer. Bill Noland looked at your horses, and having done so knew them thereafter. If you were broke he gave you leave to sleep in the barn "office"—all smelling of horses, hay, and harness leather. Perhaps he loaned you a crumpled dollar and said, "That enough, bub?" Bill had hunted buffalo in the States and had known "Buffalo Bill" Cody. At least so he said. And if he hadn't killed the number of buffalo he claimed, he certainly had been with Cody's Wild West Show. He was a great long, lean man with a white "Texas" mustache, and I know about the dollar because I was the recipient. His fine old lady wife died only a couple of years ago.

Every doctor, lawyer, parson, and storekeeper had a shiny buggy and a team of fast-trotting drivers. Every civil servant, be he Land

Inspector, Sheriff, or what have you, used this method of transportation. And farmers did all their work with horses, including the
hauling of the many loads of heavy grain over the winding prairie
trails to the new-built elevators by the railroad.

Some eastern horse dealers shipped cars of heavy draught horses
from the East, but they didn't do well in the prairie climate. They
couldn't live out and rustle their living in the slack months like the
native-bred, and besides, too many of them had worked in the lumber
woods, and were "burned out" with heavy grain feeding.

The ranchers of that day brought in many stallions from the East,
from the States, and from Britain. This was done in the hope of adding
size, bone, and weight to the native stock, while retaining the sure-
footedness and ability to "tough it" that was their birthright.

Broncobuster from Dakota

On the whole, they succeeded remarkably well. The result was not always easy to look at, and they were rough and with their mother's wildness at first, but they pulled the wagons, the mowers, and the binders on the prairie farms for years. Yes, and they pulled not only Canadian, but British and French guns, too, when the need arose.

To provide lighter saddle and harness horses, blooded stallions were used—the largest that could be obtained. English thoroughbreds, Irish hunters, American saddle horses—all got good colts by native mares; while Standard bred, Morgan, and Cleveland bays sired the best of the driving horses. Some of the most outstanding saddle horses I have known were bred three ways. A native mare would be mated to a short-coupled Clyde (or Percheron). The resulting cross (if a filly) would be mated in her time to a thoroughbred. The result would be a horse with size, bone, and conformation coupled with stamina and hardiness. While very spirited, such an animal usually had a good disposition. Many of the Mounted Police horses were of this stamp.

And it was horses of about this breeding that we started breaking out that fall. The lighter ones would be offered to the French, the heavier to the British; and Scotty hoped that from the sale of these horses he would be able to retrieve some of his earlier losses from the mishandling of his horse herd by the man Jake, including the many obviously stolen.

7

Breaking these range broncs was no cinch. We would run a bunch of horses into the big corral and slam the gate. Round and round they'd go, half hidden in a cloud of dust, while we dismounted and loosened cinches. Our ponies were puffing from the hard run. Although the end of November, it was as warm as summer. "Purty, ain't they?" It was Chuck who spoke. And pretty they certainly were. The old lead mares—typical wiry cayuses with tossing manes and trailing tails—had never known bridle or spur, and were as beautiful as any wild creatures. Many of the younger brood mares showed a little feather and the bay coloring deepening to black at the hocks and above the white socks. That, and a tendency to be Roman-nosed and to carry wide blazes betrayed their fatherhood—one of Scotty's Clydesdale stallions.

Among the lot was a four-year-old gelding about the size of a Welsh pony. How he was bred or why so small we didn't know. But he was a wiry, bright-eyed little fellow, dappled gray with wide, soft nostrils. "What'll we do with this insect?" Lee asked.

Scotty pushed his hat back and scratched his head. Finally, "Break 'im oot real good an' gentle. Superintendent West at the Barracks has a laddie aboot ready to go to school. This will make a real boy's horse for him." (The boy who rode that pony from the Barracks to school is now a top executive of the nation's business.)

And with the bunch was also an old friend—Fox. Fox, now fat and filled out, bucking, jumping for sheer joy of living; Fox, sleek and shiny. His appearance spoke well for the good hardy stock he had sprung from; not less than for the prairie grass, which had rebuilt him.

From this bunch—about eighty head—we cut out seventeen head of five-, six- and seven-year-old geldings of the type we wanted. They mostly showed the three-way descent and would not have been shamed in an English hunting field. The big end of these horses were sorrels and bays with a few dark browns and blacks and a buckskin. Also there was a pinto. This last wouldn't pass the solid color test, but we corralled him with the rest, because he was old enough to be broke out and the ranch could use him if the French could not.

We spent the first week halter breaking this bunch. We'd drive a horse into the circular breaking corral with the stout snubbing post in the center. Then we'd rope him and snub him up, the breaker putting a couple of "dallies" (or turns) around the post and holding the free end in his hand. The horse could leap and lunge, or plunge this way and that, but the cowboy kept close to the post and avoided the taut rope by turning as the horse did. Usually after a few leaps and lunges the horse would simply lean back against the loop, half choking till he was given some slack—when he might repeat the performance; but he soon gave up. Either that or he'd throw himself and somebody would have to jump on his head to slack the loop before he really choked. In either case, as soon as it was possible, a halter was worked over his head. After finding he couldn't get away (the rope being still on him, of course) he pretty soon found that a sideways pull would take him off his balance till he moved to face it. It wouldn't be long then before he'd start to lead straight ahead.

Some would fight much harder than that, and very bad ones were best roped by the front feet and brought down a time or two at the gallop. They soon learned that trying to "stampede" and throwing themselves and roaring and striking and generally raising hell didn't fizz on the quiet-spoken and even-tempered horse breaker.

It was rough. It was also kind. When breaking a horse a cowboy talks quietly to him all the time. That keeps the horse's attention. This is when most horses got their names. The cowboy would probably call him what just came to his mind. He might say, "Sho' now, Chief—take it easy," and that horse would ever after be "Chief."

But the language of the range is salty and here are a few names by which I have heard horses christened in the whirl and dust of the breaking corral. "Knothead," "Pretty Bay," "Snakeeyes," "Rock Buster," "Scarface," "Walleye," "King Pedro," "Ace High," "Star Shooter," "Sage Gnat," "Gold Dust," "Rain-in-the-Face," "Mojave," "Piegan." For fillies the cowboy waxed quite poetic: "Redwing," "Jeannie Girl," "Prairie Rose," "Pet," "Birdie," "Nellie," "Swallow," etc.

After the horses were halter broke, they were saddled and ridden. Surprisingly, some of them didn't indulge in anything more than token bucking.

Each horse was handled at least once a day. At the end of a week, what with the handling, the confinement with plenty of feed and water, and the constant presence of humans, they had gentled down out of all resemblance to the wide-nostrilled, red-eyed, roaring, kicking, pitching broncos they had been when we ran them in off the range.

Rodeo, as we know it today, was not known. The Calgary "Stampede," the Cheyenne "Frontier Days," and the Pendleton (Oregon) "Round Up" were in existence to be sure. They were the offspring of the great traveling exhibitions—"Buffalo Bill's Wild West Show" and the "101 Ranch." But the nearest thing to modern rodeo were the local "bucking matches" held among neighboring ranchers or at country picnics.

Sometimes a broncobuster would hit a town, and over drinks would do a bit of bragging. Then he'd probably be asked to show what he could do, and the bad horses of the neighborhood would be brought in. I saw one exhibition of this sort in front of the Huron Hotel in

Moosomin. The rider was a tough fellow from North Dakota. (It turned out afterwards that he was lying low after a spot of horse stealing.) He advertised in a loud voice, surcharged with alcohol, that he'd "ride anything with ha'r on it," for five dollars. They brought in some bad ones—spoiled old outlaws—and half the population of the prairie town came out to watch.

They'd bring a mean-looking horse up to the sidewalk outside the bar. The bronc rider would come out wiping his mouth on the back of his hand. Then he'd put a "chaw" in his cheek, hitch up the belt of his leather chaps, walk up to the horse, "cheek" him with his left hand, bringing the animal's head around, put his foot in the stirrup, grab the horn; and he'd be astride the hurricane deck as easy and light as a feather. That bronc would squeal and buck and sunfish and swap ends and do his darndest. He'd be ridden to a standstill, and then the rider would step off and say, "Five dollars, folks!"

He made twenty dollars that day and wasn't thrown once.

CHAPTER EIGHT

1

As the days of my second winter became shorter, the ranch hands began to settle in for colder weather. Extra help was paid off, and all but a few "winter horses" were turned out on the range to rustle till spring. But our winter horses were well stabled and well fed. It took a "grained" horse to travel through the deep drifts.

The calves had been weaned, and it was my daily job to hitch up a big team of half-Clydes and haul hay down from the high bench to feed the little fellows. I would start off before daylight with a big basket rack made by a local 'breed; and it was a long hard pull up the hay trail, through the fragrant pines to the level bench above. I would put on a big load—probably between a ton and a half and two tons, and I was glad of the hard work with the pitchfork, for on this open plateau the wind cut like a knife. Sometimes it would be calm and clear, and I'd rest on my fork and look down over Montana to the Bear Paw Mountains and see their peaks slip free from their bases and slide sideways in the winter mirage.

At other times it would be foggy and all the great world that lay north to the Saskatchewan would be blotted out and I felt I was all alone on a great cloud. But the worst were the days when a ground blizzard whipped the gritty snow into my wrist bands and neck; when the wind tore the hay from my fork; when the sun lay close to the noon horizon, pale and wan; when the snow writhed across the bench and filled the sleigh tracks as fast as they were made.

Prairie hay had a smell of its own, a sort of muskiness that I liked, and was so matted together and heavy that the wind didn't bother you too much when you were forking it from the stack. Soon the load was put on, and then came the long haul back to the winter camp, the horses holding back on the neck yoke in the steep places, the stout sleigh groaning in protest against the logging chain rough-locked

Hay from the bench

around a hind runner. Many horses hate holding back into the breeching, and will bite the neck yoke in their frustration.

Small bands of mule deer would look at me askance, twitching their big ears and stamping their feet at my intrusion; for with nightfall they would visit the stacks, and sometimes even sleep on the hay.

After forking out the load to the calves—keeping enough on the rack to fill the mangers of the work team and saddle stock—I had to take an ax and open up the water hole in the tiny creek that ran through a corner of the corral. The ice on this was about eighteen inches thick, but since the water hole was opened daily, a few strokes of the ax each morning would be enough. The water, however, remained a foot below the surface of the ice, so that horses went through strange contortions to drink, sometimes going on their knees, sometimes straddling out like giraffes feeding from the ground.

This done, I turned the team loose to drink while I carried hay to their stall. Then in they would clump, water dribbling from their hairy lips and forming little icicles, harness swinging musically, heel chains clinking. Up to their manger they would shoulder themselves and start to crunch the curly hay with slow and rhythmic movements of their jaws, their ears moving in time. At intervals, as I tussled with the heavy harness snaps, one or the other would heave his head and shoulders against the log wall, rubbing ecstatically up and down to remove the crusted snow from jaw and mane and poll. A final heave and the harness would be off and on its peg. A look at the bedding, a last pat on smoking rumps, and I was free for the evening.

2

The bunkhouse was about fifteen feet by twenty-five feet. It was built of logs, of course, with a good pine floor, a roof of poles and sod, and two small windows in one wall. The other wall was occupied by a row of bunks, three lowers and three uppers, which allowed for extra hands or visitors.

At one end was the door, and just to its left was a rough shelf for water pails and washing facilities such as tin washbasin, tobacco tin lid for soap, and a couple of towels on a string. We washed these towels once in a while, as well as our socks and shirts; so across the other end of the room was a line which usually contained some kind of rags. In summer we tranferred our "washstand" to the outside, washing under the overhanging eaves.

As to plumbing, that of course was the same all over the rural west. A little house standing coyly in a patch of chokecherries with past years' Eaton's catalogues hung on a nail. Here, at 90° above or 50° below we had to repair when called, but we thought nothing of it by night or by day.

After the cold outside, the warmth of the bunkhouse was pleasant.

Contortions of a horse

A big coal-oil lamp hung from the ceiling. A pot-bellied stove burning split logs gave plenty of heat. A few bunks on one side, a table on the other was about all the furniture; except for some shelves holding an assortment of tobacco tins, sacks of Bull Durham, razors, writing paper, and a few books and magazines.

We ate in the house—Scotty constituting himself cook, since his wife was not able to work—or so it was said—nor would she consent to a "hired" cook.

Scotty's beans, baked in the oven in an enormous flat roasting pan—all sweet with syrup and topped with thick rashers of salt side pork—were famous for miles. His bread would have won a prize anywhere. Scotty had joined the old North West Mounted Police as a constable-cook, so he had had lots of experience.

He used to amuse us with stories of old Fort Walsh, which lay only a few miles away on Battle Creek, though abandoned over thirty years ago.

Once, he said, in '81 he thought it was, the orderly-sergeant had accosted him as he was starting to cook breakfast. "Scotty," he said, "the Injuns have us surrounded. Go on quietly with your work, but keep your carbine handy in case we need you." Scotty said that certainly scared him. The North West Rebellion was brewing, and he felt pretty uneasy about his scalp. It was a common saying that the red man could raise hair without irrigation. Finally he took a peep out of the window. There they were! It was awful foggy, but he could see them all right. They were creeping up, hugging the ground. He pretty near dropped his frying pan as he hurried through to the N.C.O.'s mess hall where some of the boys had already gathered.

"Quick, you fellows," he said, "them Nitchies are crawling up all around. Ain't we going to *do* something?"

"What the hell?" said a corporal.

"Look oota the windy," pleaded Scotty. "Do ye no' see them?"

"See hell, Cookie—who's been stringing you?"

"There—and there's another," stammered Scotty.

"What—them things?" said the corporal, "sage bushes. Let's go eat."

And sage bushes they were. The same ones Scotty saw every day; only in the mist they came and went, grew larger and smaller and seemed to move—to crawl.

I could tell a tale of a night patrol in Flanders, and some willow bushes in a fog—perhaps I shall some day.

3

In describing the sparse furniture of the bunkhouse I may have given the impression of a bare and empty sort of cabin. Such was far from the case. There were always saddles hanging on pegs or lying on the floor in process of repair. Cans of neat's-foot oil lay in a corner with cleaning rags. On the numerous spikes driven into the log walls hung a varied assortment of gear all smelling strongly of horse.

Bridles, bits, spurs, hackamores, odd bits of rope, hanks of whang-leather for repairs. Chaps, heavy checked shirts, Stetson hats of every hue and age, from Chuck's new pale fawn to Lee's battered black "four gallon." Fur hats, mitts, and sheepskin jackets for winter use hung near the stove to dry out and warm up. Oilskin slickers were hung out of the way till next summer, and in their pockets mice made nests.

The long winter evenings were spent playing cards, reading, repairing gear, or perhaps making a hackamore or braiding bridle lines. All cowboys excelled at some such hobby. On a typical evening Banjo might be cleaning his beloved thirty-thirty Winchester, lovingly wiping away excess oil and polishing the stock. Chuck would be braiding a bosal (a nose band for a hackamore). Lee, replacing the stirrups of his saddle. My hobby being natural history, I was skinning out an antelope head with a good set of horns which had recently fallen a victim to the aforesaid thirty-thirty. There was much disgust when I boiled the skull. They called me "gut eater" and threw boots at me. But when I finally sewed up the skin, fitted the eyes I had sent to Chicago for, and mounted the finished product on the wall, their praise made me blush. I had also tanned the skin of a bobcat with the head fully mounted in a vicious snarl. His latin name was *Lynx Rufus,* but when an Indian said they called it *pah-pah-kao-pisoo* or spotted cat, I thought that much the better name.

Mending his saddle

Once I packed a big buffalo skull back on my saddle. Lee said, "What in tarnation do you want that thing for?" I didn't quite know myself. But it was a beauty.

In between times I used to make sketches—birds and animals mostly, but quite often of some little incident on the range. The boys were kind about them and said I was as good as Charlie Russell, but I knew I never could be.

And as our fingers worked with oil or leather or brush, the talk invariably turned to horses and cattle, grass, and gear. The merits of Hambley and Company's Ellensbury saddle tree would be totted up against the Visalia or the Cripple Creek. The great saddle makers, Frazier of Pueblo, Riley and McCormick of Calgary, Adams and Great West were names that could start an argument.

Cowboys love a fine saddle. Good craftsmanship and durability comes first, of course. Many a man has owed his life to the faithful hidden work of a good saddle maker. In those days only the best seasoned oak must go into the tree, to be covered with heavy green hide sewed on wet. Then the saddle leather proper—best California oak-tanned. Having got your basic saddle, high in the cantle and with an adequate horn in front to hold the dally of your rope, you could then have your choice of a A-fork or any of the more up-to-date swells. You could have a plain or a roll cantle. One fellow always said, "Give me a Cheyenne roll—one hand on that and one on the horn an' they really *got* ter buck."

Horns could be squat and broad—Mexican style—or high and slim. They could be rawhide wrapped, leather covered, or just plain shiny nickel or bronze. The latter were cold in winter. Skirts could be square or round.

Rigging—what holds the saddle to the horse—could be double, three-quarter, or center-fire. Cinches could be mohair, fish cord, or cotton. Latigos did not vary much and were of two-inch oil tanned. They were not buckled but tied to the cinch rings. Neither were the stirrup leathers buckled. They were laced to the rider's fit; much safer, with no danger of a buckle tongue tearing out.

Stirrups could be Oxbow (round bottoms) or Cheyenne (flat). Mostly they were of oak, either brass-bound or covered with rawhide, but some of the boys favored a simple metal ring about six inches in diameter.

Finally, the saddle could be perfectly plain, or "basket stamped" or (final glory) decoratively hand-tooled into a design which might embody prairie roses, bucking horses, or lovely girls, or all three.

Saddle blankets came into the discussions, too. One fellow would say he favored a genuine Navaho, thick and with an Indian design, from New Mexico. But they were expensive. We looked at them in the "States" catalogues and wondered could we spare twenty to thirty dollars when our old wool blanket seemed to suit the horse all right. These catalogues were thumbed and rethumbed during those discussions.

"See what I mean?" Chuck would say, "Frazier's a-puttin' out a new tree with a low cantle—that may be jake for a flat country, but if you wanted to get to the top ole' Eagle Butte you'd be a-slippin' off your hoss's rump."

Boots then were mostly soft-topped and to the knee, with rather higher heels than now. Chaps—or to give them their full Spanish name—*chaparajos,* were mostly of the "shotgun" type—plain leather leggings like pants with no seat and a fringe down the side. The various fringes on western gear of those days were not for ornament. Your chaps' fringe hastened the departure of rain water down the sides. The fringes on buckskin coats by their constant agitation when you were moving kept the snow from settling on your shoulders. Heavy winter chaps of long curly, glossy angora pelts with leather inside the legs were standard for winter riding. Nowadays they are rarely seen. The need for them has passed. (My old ones hang today in my study, and visitors ask "what are those *sheepskin* things?")

One thing that amuses me today is to see in magazines and on the screen how little resemblance there is to what cowboys actually wore. The so-called "Western" style in shirts was unheard of then. As to the women, they wouldn't have been seen dead in the "pant suits" sold by "Western" outfitters. We had no silk shirts or pearl buttons and were glad enough of a good gray flannel shirt and perhaps an old sweater or waistcoat.

A great help in the bush are the teather toe protectors or tapaderas. Most people think that they, like chaps and other things, are an affectation. Let them ride all day and half the night in wet willow bush or pouring rain and they would find their feet as wet as if they had waded in a stream, and bruised and buffeted to boot; while their expensive riding boots would be worn out at the toe.

Bits and spurs came mostly from the States, and the best were made by Crockett. A little silver inlay was nice, but the main thing was to be sure they were hand-forged.

Quirts and hackamores (Spanish *jaquima*) and such braided stuff were often homemade, but it was a tricky matter to draw too much attention to a man's technique in this regard. It smelt of Deer Lodge, for prisoners in the Montana State Penitentiary were taught this work and earned their pocket money by supplying the big saddlery firms with their handiwork.

A horseman's gear seems to be one thing where handwork is essential, and as long as cattle run on the range, the saddler will be at his bench. The men who make the saddles are craftsmen of the highest order. They know horses and cow work, they know stress and strain, and they build for strength. They build for weather conditions and for comfort, too. And having put the best of the craftsmanship into the utility end, they start on the artistic part; scrolling and carving the good leather (poor leather cannot be worked) and adding the gay conchos, perhaps inlaying with silver, or etching designs into bits and spurs.

For they know that the cowboy has no home, no furniture, no fine chinaware. His saddle is his investment, his sole possession, his necessity, and man's nature cries out for that extra touch put there simply to beautify.

Most cowboys wore a neck scarf of silk—usually black, probably another legacy from the Dons who gave us the cow industry and all that goes with it. As Charlie Russell said, "If they *wasn't* silk, we *thought* they was!"

A waistcoat—he called it a vest—from an old suit was his most universal and useful garment. It had so many and such get-at-able pockets for his makin's—tobacco and papers—for matches, and for other oddments. It was not too hot but gave him protection where he needed it most—over the lower back. In summer a slicker was thrown behind his saddle cantle and fastened with the tie strings.

For winter, he had a "sheepskin" coat of heavy canvas lined with fleece. It was roomy and warm with big pockets low enough to reach

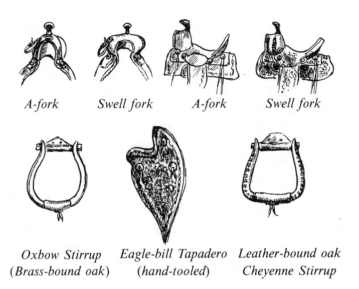

| A-fork | Swell fork | A-fork | Swell fork |

Oxbow Stirrup   Eagle-bill Tapadero   Leather-bound oak
(*Brass-bound oak*)   (*hand-tooled*)   Cheyenne Stirrup

Some old-time saddle types—not much resemblance to today's "low roper."

with ease. One sheepskin-lined coat with a heavy shirt and sweater under it, plus fur chaps, was good for $-40°$. A cowboy of those days wouldn't look twice at any of the so-called "Western" styles of windbreakers or what-not that are sold now. A leather jacket is stiff and confining. The various so-called "parka" type coats with their high or backward pockets and those useless zippers would not have found favor. They snag in the bush, the padded lining can't "breathe" like a sheep fleece, the pockets can't be got at by a man in the saddle, the zippers won't work for a bit of twig or snow; and, worst of all, they are hard to get into and worse to get out of. (More than one man has frost-bitten his fingers trying to zip a zipper that wouldn't.)

4

Banjo was telling us about the English officer who was buying cavalry remounts in town. "We were all down at the stockyards and this here officer says, 'Let's go, boys. I'm in a hurry.' So we all got ready. There was a nester's kid from up near the sand hills with only one hoss—a pretty good looking one, too. The nester was a Dutchman and couldn't speak English, so he sent the kid—who'd had a little schooling—to sell the horse for him. So we let him go in first. He rode that cayuse in on a halter and just stood there. The officer walked around him. The old hoss just stood hipshot an' easy; a-whiskin' his tail—though there weren't no flies—and with his eyes half shut. 'Do you want I should trot him?' asked the kid—'but I ain't got no saddle.' 'No,' roared the officer. 'Take him out! You're just wasting me time—I want to see some *horses!*' So the kid takes his hoss back kinda disappointed. After a bit he gets talking with Frenchy—that Oxheart fellow—said he needed the money bad and wished he could sell the hoss. The Oxheart man looks the hoss over. It carried a Q and that's a top brand. 'Tell you what,' says Frenchy, 'for five bucks I'll sell that hoss for you.' 'Done,' says the kid, 'if you can, that is.' Frenchy waits his chance. Then, with his saddle and his best bridle on the horse, he sees an opening. He jumps on the Q, neck reins him into the ring, walks, trots, and canters, then pulls up short.

"The officer took it all in. Horses was supposed to be *led* into the ring first off, ridden later; and the officer barks away at Frenchy, but that boy's got a nice grin, an' sitting there so easy like, with the hoss's head up and ears well pricked, he just talks sort of apologetic and soft and says, 'I know, Kernal, but Kitchner yere he like to tramp on my feet—not mean you know, but he's got lots o' gimp, so I . . .' 'Never mind,' says the officer and walks around the horse. 'Now boy,' he says, 'take him around again. I want these gentlemen to see what I see. *That's* the kind of hoss we're looking for. Don't waste my time with anything else.' They to the cowboy, 'Take him over to the vet's corner and soon as he's passed you'll get your check.' Maybe the name 'Kitchener' helped—cowboys usually think in a hurry where five dollars is concerned."

Chuck piped up, "That reminds me of the time Jack McCrimmon was ramrodding that same Q outfit. We was breaking a snaky black which they figgered to sell to the railway outfit. We had a mate for him—well broke, too, we'd worked him on the mower all summer. Jack figgered they'd make a matched team. So we caught up this yere 'snake eyes' and went to work on him. Mostly, we got the harness half on him when he'd fling it across the corral 'fore we could buckle the hame strap and pull the breeching down. Finally, we tied up a front foot and that helped. Sure he fought like hell still, but barring throwing himself a coupla times he couldn't do much harm. He was running sweat and breathing like a bellows, and we figgered he'd about give up.

"So we tied him to the big stud's hame, got a trip rope on him, and got 'em hitched to the wagon. Would he move? Not an inch! He'd had his fun and now he'd gone plumb cold. We tried everything but ole' 'snake eyes' just stood.

" 'Unhitch 'im,' says Jack.

" 'Okay. You lay on that trip rope while I do.' Jack hung on.

"I got the tugs undone and the neck yoke down. Still no move. All at once down he went, ker-plum. 'Prod 'im up, Chuck,' says the boss. No good. 'Leave 'im here for now,' says Jack. 'Take the stud and tie 'im up some'eres.' I tied the ole' stud to the corral. 'Now get the big team,' says Jack and hurries off. By the time I gets the team out Jack comes a-running with a log chain. We takes the eveners off the wagon and puts the chain around ol' hoss just back o' the front legs. 'Where to, Jack?' says I, thinking the black was either dead or going to be. 'The boneyard?' 'Boneyard hell,' says Jack, 'the cutbank by the crick.' He leads the way and I foller, the team a-diggin' in their toes. The black was a big devil and a dead weight and the harness scrattled and jangled as he was dragged. Jack says, 'Right here, boy! Crowd that team as close the edge as you can.' I did.

"He starts to take off the chain. The black hoss kinda rolls one eye and grunts. 'Quick now,' shouts Jack—'Grab 'is tail while I hold 'is nose down. One—two!' Well luckily it was a mite downhill or we wouldn't have made it. As it was, what with me a-heaving and the black kinda feebly struggling we tipped him over. That cutbank's about twenty feet high and Sage Crick was running high. 'Plunk'—in he went harness and all. Out o' sight—I mean plumb out o' sight. 'The water cure for you,' says Jack with a kinda grin. It seemed like five minutes afore that ole' black bobbed up agin. Then he took to swimming round and round till the water cleared from his eyes and nose and he headed for the other side, which was low. 'Quick,' says Jack, 'if he gets away on us, bang goes a new breeching harness.' There's a log bridge right there at the buildings so we were able to get around about the time the black came out of his diving act. Jack grabbed the halter shank and we led him back up.

" 'Bring the stud,' he says. We hitch up the two of 'em again. Jack gives me the trip rope, and we scramble in the wagon box. 'Git up there,' Jack says kinda soft and just flicks snake eyes's flank with the rope. Well, dog me cats if those two hosses don't step out the yard and down the road as nice as me uncle's plow team in old Ontario.

"I allers say, it's patience what does it."

Talk would drift off. We'd crawl into our beds one by one. Someone would say "dowse the glim," and with darkness came sleep.

5

Winter was the time for visiting among the ranch families. It was the time when you could see something of your neighbors in their homes—and meet a few womenfolk.

Any rancher's daughter could have her pick of the cowboys, but, alas, far too many—so we thought—had an ambition to look for better prospects and took up teaching or some other profession; and what few young ladies there were in the ranch country mostly drifted off east to the brighter land of hot-water taps and electric light.

Few of them married ranch boys. The swing of the pendulum that had sent their parents a-pioneering now sent them in the opposite direction. Some of these young ladies did extremely well, and the majority achieved their ambitions of marrying "white-collar guys."

On their brief visits home they were apt to be a bit scornful of water carried in buckets and the pale gleam of coal-oil lamps. "Poor Momma," they'd say. But poor Momma was apt to meet such sympathy with a sniff.

6

Folks living in semi-isolation who see neighbors but rarely are apt to be extremely sensitive to supposed snubs and imaginary injuries.

It only needed a passing cowboy to compliment one lady on her plum cake for another lady to feel that *her* cake was not so good. A few carelessly spoken words carried by an irresponsible young fellow could sometimes cause the most bitter feeling.

Mrs. Manser, a Scotswoman, kept the local post office on her husband's ranch at McKay Creek, about seven miles downstream from Gow's ranch. Mrs. Gow, who had come years ago from Scotland, had brought with her a voluminous petticoat of black silk. Mrs. Gow liked to have a few geese around; never more than one pair, which annually raised a few fat goslings on the creek.

One winter's day a coyote carried off her gander which had had the temerity to leave the goose house on a warm January day. Mrs. Gow was at her wit's end. She was not the kind of woman to spend good money on another bird, so she bethought herself of the petticoat. She took me into her confidence—not, of course, to the extent of letting me see the garment. But she assured me it was of the finest silk—"and it has'na been worn—no, never since I spent good siller on it in the Edinbro' shop," and did I think Mrs. Manser—who had lots of geese—would trade her a gander for it? It would make over into a lovely dress. Next time I went for the mail I put it up to Mrs. Manser.

"Laddie," she said, "if that garment is as good as Mistress Gow says, tell her I'll take it and gie' her a bonny young gander."

Mrs. Gow was pleased. Riding for the mail again the next week I carried the "garment" well wrapped in brown paper and tied behind the saddle. I presented the parcel to Mrs. Manser who dodged quickly into the bedroom with it. When she reappeared she said, "I'll trade, whateffer," and took me to the chicken coop to pick out the gander. This creature was put in a gunny sack, and I had to take the heavy squirming thing across my lap, which put Buck in a bad humor.

However, I got it safely home and into the goose house, a low log hut on the creek bank. Mrs. Gow donned mitts and a heavy shawl and came out for inspection. She looked for all the world like some seeress peering into a cauldron. "Aye," she said at last, "'tis a bonny bird—a grand bird; and I'm that grateful to Mistress Manser belike I'll gie her a fat gosling in the fa'."

Shortly the old goose began to lay. I was supposed to get her egg every day for fear it would freeze—it was only March—and soon

almost a full clutch lay in a big bowl on the kitchen sideboard. Then
came the day I found *two* eggs in the nest. When I brought them in
Mrs. Gow said, "Losh, laddie, did ye no look yesterday?"

I said I had, but added, "I'm afraid that gander Mrs. Manser sent
you is a goose."

That did it. Mistress Manser, so Mrs. Gow declared, was a bad
woman. "Might the Lord forgive her, for she couldna'." A deceiving
body, that's what Mistress Manser was, a *licht quean.* Och aye, Mrs.
Gow didna care sae much for actual loss, but to be made a fu' of—and
she thocht Mistress Manser was her friend. But if she—Gow's wife—
had been made a gowk of, she could still hauld her tongue and gie
nae kind o' satisfaction to That Woman, etc., etc.

The climax came with the Reverend Mr. MacWhinnie's quarterly
visit. That gentleman was a devoted minister of the Presbyterian
Church. A dour lanky Scot, he made his headquarters at Medicine
Hat, from where he periodically visited the scattered ranches of a
parish as big as an English county.

He drove a team of shaggy ponies hitched to a top buggy. Sometimes
his team would stop on the trail, pushing sideways to crop the grass,
while the good man read one of the theological books in which he
could almost be said to live. Looking up, he would see the sun getting
low, pick up his loose lines, seize his whip and drive like Jehu to his
stopping place for that night. A rare and lovable type was the Reverend
James Hector MacWhinnie.

About a week after Mrs. Gow's gander suddenly became a goose,
we had a visit from this gentleman. It was the evening of the Sunday
before Easter, his invariable date for his spring visit to this part of
his parish. He usually got to Manser's on a Saturday night, held a
service and Sunday school for the Manser children on Sunday morning,
and in the afternoon drove down to Gow's where he had supper, held
prayers and slept before continuing across the bench to Faulkner's and
the wild horse country.

When not out on the range, it was my job to take Mrs. Gow to
those occasional services at Manser's. So this Sunday morning I har-
nessed the driving team and went to tell Mrs. Gow it was time to go.
"And ye hae nae need to tell me, laddie," she said, "I ken the day

and the hour. But ye can put the team awa'. I'm no for the sairvice the day."

About five in the afternoon Mr. MacWhinnie drove up. I put his team in the barn while he went to the house.

All through supper the minister was very quiet. Finally, when the meal was over, he pushed back his chair, slowly and deliberately took a pinch of snuff, passed the snuffbox to Mrs. Gow and said, "And noo, Mistress Gow, why were ye no to the sairvice the day?"

"I—ker-shoo!—I didnae care to gae, thank ye."

"Didnae care? Losh, woman, 'tis no a matter o' carin'. If ye were no ill, what ailed ye that ye wouldna go to the hoose o' God?"

Mrs. Gow sat very straight and looked the minister in the eye—"I'm a God-fearing woman, sir, and I ken me duty. I *wad* gang to the hoose o' God, sir—but I'll no gang to the hoose o' Manser!"

7

In those days a good many young gentlemen (and some not so young) from good British families were to be found "knocking about" (as they would say) the Western plains. Many of them received remittances (by check) from their people, for often, but not always, they had either been troublesome at home or had disgraced themselves in some way so that their relatives more or less "bribed" them to stay away from England. At worst, most of them were only misfits, like today's young people who "opt out." They did not work regularly but would help at anything in a pinch.

Our district had its share of remittance men about whom so many stories are told in the West. There is hardly a hill from Winnipeg to Calgary that is not claimed by those in its vicinity to be the very hill on which an Englishman hobbled his oxen to keep the wagon from running on them!

These gentlemen were charming and honorable individuals, and if they did not contribute much in the way of hard work to the country of their exile, they were much in demand as sources of advice in matters legal, matrimonial, and literary. While ranchers and cowboys poked fun at their accents, their manners, and their passion for soap and water, on the other hand they liked them and respected their facility in such things as letter writing.

The women folk liked them as much for their peerless manners as did the men for their sporting attitude towards hardships.

Most of them (the Englishmen) seemed to have aunts. (A few had uncles, but they were not quite the same.) These aunts felt very sorry for the poor boys out on that horrible prairie, building an empire. So checks always seemed to come just in time to thwart the proverbial wolf.

"By jove, old chap," one of them would say to his cowboy friend. "It's about time the Old Relation came through. Think I'll go to town for the mail." If the check had come through, everybody seemed to know it; and as the recipient hurried off to the bar the boys would tip their heads one to the other and presently quite a little crowd would push into the barroom as if by accident.

Most of these Englishmen loved horses and could ride, and that alone gave them a place among the cattle folk. Some acquired ranches for themselves. Others joined the Royal North West Mounted Police. And when the war came they enlisted to a man; and it would not be stretching it far to say they died to a man.

Tommy Waldron was one of those who had joined the Police. He fell in love with a rancher's daughter named Nancy. On his patrols he often stopped at the ranch, and in the evening he and his girl would go riding. Their favorite place to sit and talk was a bald butte. Here, on summer evenings, as the nighthawks zoomed overhead and the upland plovers piped their curlew notes, these two sat together. He would put the sweet prairie roses in her hair and a chain of harebells round her throat; and she would plait for him a soft wide ring of the fragrant sweet grass that the Indians say is holy. Then one day he rode away to war with Lord Strathcona's Horse. Nancy still rode to the butte.

She still saw the meadowlarks and the plovers, but they were silent these late summer days. The rose blooms had turned to hips and the harebells shrivelled in the heat. But the sweet grass still made fragrant the wind that sent the great white ships sailing overhead to become lost on the eastern horizon.

Her horse cropped the grass with a tinkling of bit chain, sometimes lifting his head to see his mistress sit so still, and follow her gaze away and away to the east, over the dappled grassland, over the great lakes and forests, over the restless moaning sea; her thoughts taking ship with the clouds—farther, farther to the mud and horror which the map called France. We sometimes saw her there, but rode no closer. Tommy was killed in action. His sweetheart lost herself in the Big City. The hill is still called Nancy's Butte.

8

We sometimes got a visit from the Indians. Mostly they were Assiniboins from Fort Peck Reservation across the Line. These "Stonies" had kinfolk away to the north and west at Morely and Rocky Mountain House.

Sometimes we were visited by Crees from the small reserve near Keely Springs. These people did a considerable amount of traveling and camping in the late summer. They would gather blueberries on the bench, chokecherries and saskatoons on the hillsides. And out on the plains they got the buffalo berries from the matted patches of prickly scrub that produced them.

They dried their fruit for keeping and easy transportation and used them in various ways; cooked with fish or meat or used like currants in bannock or biscuit. In the old days they were an important ingredient of pemmican.

When we butchered in the fall some Indians always came to camp on the creek for what they could get. They got the heads, feet, liver, and pluck, bearing them away in triumph.

"Them dirty Indians," some said. They were not. People in Europe eat all the parts we throw out, or give to Indians, or even to dogs. Hence, tripe, calf's-foot jelly, sausage casings, kidney stew, and a dozen other dishes rich in nourishment. The Indians washed everything in running water. Every foot of "guts" was used. It was cut in short lengths after washing, then dried and smoked. They were a pleasant, good-looking and smiling people who seemed to bear no ill will towards the whites who now occupied their hunting grounds. (Sad to say, things have changed since then, for the better for the white, for the worse for the Indian.)

The half-breeds mostly bore French or Scottish names and spoke English with a few added French and Indian words. Those who were not Scottish were descendants of the Burnt-Woods people—the Bois Brulés—and they had made and used the Red River carts (completely wooden, with neither bolt nor nail) that we occasionally still saw in use among the Indians, though they must then have been the very last of their kind. Once a proud and independent people based on the Red River (from whence they made their annual summer treks westward for the buffalo hunt), they had become squeezed by settlement and the modern way of life.

When Rupert's land was transferred from the rule of the Hudson's Bay Company to the new Dominion of Canada, there was unrest. Louis Riel and his métis followers tried to prevent the installation of the new governor. After this uprising failed, many of the half-breeds (both Scottish and French) left Red River for keeps. Their leader fled to the States, and Manitoba became a province; but most of these people hoped to relive something of the old life on the buffalo plains in what were the territories of Assiniboia and Saskatchewan.

This explains the presence, to this day, of the "French" settlements at Willow Bunch and on the Whitemud River. All the French-speaking métis were Catholics, very devout and partly educated by their priests. Among the women especially many spoke good French, did exquisite needlework, and carried themselves with quiet dignity; arts and graces that had been acquired in the Convent of St. Boniface in the far-off days.

They made their living by raising a few horses and cattle and by working for the ranchers and farmers at such jobs as riding, fencing, building with logs, or picking stones.

One man in particular—a sort of leader—not only excelled with an ax, but also broke horses, braided lariats, and made artistic and useful bridles and lines from horsehair, brilliantly dyed to rainbow color and cunningly interlaced and knotted. He had also learned tailoring at Deer Lodge it was said, but that was only rumor. Certainly he could put up log buildings with no tools but an ax, a crosscut saw, and a wood auger. He never used a square or a level. His eye was better, he said.

And he preferred to fasten two logs with a well-fitted wooden peg than a metal spike. Many years later it was this man, Barney Montour, who was commissioned to rebuild old Fort Walsh. And it was the same Barney who taught me how to use an ax, how to put up a log building or make a corral gate, all of which stood me in such good stead later in life.

Louis Dumont was a different type. Apart from being a good fiddler and having some knack with traps, he was shiftless and lazy—but utterly charming. Louis always said what he believed you wanted him to, even at the cost of truth.

"Seen any cattle round Egg Lake, Louis? You've been trapping rats there. Ought to be some."

Louis would smile and strive to please, "Sure, I guess mebbe some ole' cows down there. Mebbe over big hills *other* side! Seems lac I seen two, tree, mebbe more. Me, I'm pretty busy wid traps an' don' tak' much notice, but guess dere's some ole' cows, sure."

That way Louis didn't commit himself. He killed a bull snake one time with his rifle and showed it to me. It was Louis who had given me the bobcat, and we often talked natural history. This time I got his point of view on snakes. Louis said, "Dat ole' bull snake she's can be pretty bad when she's got liddle ones. My ole' fader he say, 'My son, you don' go too close to dose snake in de spring tam. Maybe she's got famalee, and more better you keep away. Maybe she's aint goin' bite or somting, but she's plenty power in de y'eye—an' one glance from dat h'eye is *certain death.*' "

The most noted hunter in that country was "Pinto Pete" Armstrong from up west. To him more than any other man goes the credit for finally cleaning out the last of the timber wolves. The last lobo he killed was an enormous eighty-pound, white brute, all of seven feet from nose to tail tip, credited with much cattle killing. Hector McRae killed a mountain lion near Battle Creek the same winter. It had probably wandered up from the Missouri breaks and it had killed several colts before it met its fate. It, too, was all of seven feet in length, perhaps a bit more.

Talking of wolves, it was considered fair sport to run down coyotes when the snow got deep and soft. A good "grained" horse could gallop along, but the coyote would sink deep with every jump. After a while he would play out. Then the rider would jump off and club the beast. A strong man would grab the prairie wolf by the tail, swing it high, and dash its head through the snow to the frozen ground beneath; in fact one of the Parsonaye boys killed coyotes this way right along.

All these people—Indians, breeds, ranchers, and policemen—were broad-minded, generous to a fault, and had a genuine love of the wide spaces and their way of life. They were held together by one common bond—they "belonged" to the plains and to one another. They became my friends and I became one of them.

The wolfer's horse and hound

9

The cattle ranchers did not like sheep on their range and were bitter in their denunciation of "stinking sheep men." But these sentiments were not really earnest, nor were they personal; and they could more easily endure the sight of the woolly bands than to see the newcomers who began to put the plow into their grasslands. For a new invasion of aliens was taking place.

The homesteaders were coming in. "Nesters," the ranchers called them. Men without a "way of life," without knowledge of or love for the country. Opportunists taking advantage of the Government's policy of homesteads—free land in meager blocks of one hundred and sixty acres.

These people were farmers. They did not understand sharing the country. They fenced it into tight little holdings. They had little tradition of freedom as we knew it. Where a plainsman spent his time riding over the grass and flowers of an empire in which two miles or fifty times two miles was all the same, these "grangers" knew and cared for only their minute acreage, tearing it up with plows, sending the dry, powdery dust across the land.

The "Wet Year" of 1915 had come. A year when even a few grains scattered along a road would sprout and yield a hundred fold; a year when the prairies bloomed in such a greenness, in such masses of flowers of every hue as we should not see again for many a year. A greenness that would remain as only a nostalgic memory when the dust storms of the thirties were to lay waste millions of acres of ground and countless human hearts, lured to their undoing in that wanton year of grace, 1915. A year that brought about disaster to many a stockman who saw his best springs and finest grasslands filed on and occupied. But they were occupied only to be later abandoned again to his lean cattle that wandered across the broken weed-choked fences back to their old range. There they found only a stinking mess of bones and mud when once they had slaked their thirst with sweet water.

And what, at the time, seemed worse still, the people who came to this area were not British or American "white" people, but European peasants, from central Europe and the unhappy Balkans.

A bare-footed people. Tanned as dark as Indians; but not living as well even as Indians. In their shabby clothes and in the bowed shoulders of the men and the stupid plain faces of the women could be read the legacy of oppression that had been theirs before their final migration. We did not understand this, then. It was not to be expected that the free and independent people of the plains could altogether know or even guess the latent possibilities, nor fairly assess the frugal peasant culture that suddenly confronted them. And language was a barrier. To the ranchers they were all "the Dutch" and "the Dutch have got us" began to be a sort of saying that implied the country was going to the dogs.

We would see them in the fall, harvesting their few acres of wheat.

We would see the women, with bare feet and head scarfs, up on top of the stacks laying the rows of sheaves by hand as the men forked them up. How could we know that within less than half a century the head scarf would be normal and becoming wear for ladies at all levels.

They came to the ranch sometimes. To beg a little flour or some coal oil—or to buy a horse. They were mortally afraid of a horse with spirit; and if shown such a one would say, "No *dobra,* meester—*niet, niet";* or, "dam bronco nix goot." They were settling, mostly, on the level plains north of the hills, but the tide of homesteading threatened the whole south country.

In spite of our feelings about these outsiders, it is not to be supposed that, within the limitation of different languages and opposite cultures, there did not very soon evolve a certain friendliness and mutual respect.

Scotty fed the men when they "pulled for the bush" in winter to cut their firewood. More than one rancher's child owed its life to the kindly ministrations of a Slovak midwife; and if the better-off ranchers gave the odd orphan foal or calf to a stockless settler as the nucleus of a little herd, his wife was not above accepting an occasional pound of sweet butter or some wild strawberry preserve that had been made in a mud-and-wattle shack. But they were still the "Dutch" who walked on foot along the prairies' trails that had known no other print than that of a hoof since the Indians first got horses.

Looking back, one is both amused and shocked at what we thought then. With a generosity that was no more than justice, we finally took these people to us; and they, forgetting past slights, worked steadily to send their young folk to school and university, welding their own values and cultures to ours; to the ultimate benefit of the nation.

Today, names queerly spelled and once thought impossible to pronounce are worn without comment in any group of those who are professionally great in the nation. So was the West built.

10

There would be a few dances or social evenings during the winter, usually held at some roomy ranch house, until later brand new little school houses would spring up in the "nester" settlements. The fun would go on till daylight. Cowboys came from miles around and the few girls would be almost danced off their feet.

Many were the good times on the Whitemud when the "French" put on a dance. The fiddler squealed and the moccasins of the dark-haired beauties thumped the floor to the jingle of their partners' spurs. Old Simon Pepin, the French rancher from south of the line, usually sent up a load of grub. Many of the younger "Frenchmen" worked for him in summer, and they all called him "Mon Oncle."

As the homesteaders got more settled in, some of their younger fry came—shyly at first, but with growing confidence; and the young cowboy who was brave enough to dosey-doe with a tow-haired Ruthenian girl was soon to find that she was lovable, too—and human. By the time Nap Ducharme's fiddle was finally put away, the young fellow was probably in love.

That summer more homesteaders came. Many were Germans who had left their homeland to avoid the Kaiser's conscription just before 1914. They had, many of them, worked for a year or two for farm families in Manitoba. I am afraid we felt that they symbolized the enemy, and we were not too welcoming.

Soon settlers' tar-paper shacks stood like little block-houses all over the once-lonesome prairies.

Blockhouses indeed they were, manned by brave men and women with little knowledge of what was before them, but feeling secure in the knowledge that they owned land. Blockhouses that were to be beseiged by overwhelming enemy forces—poverty, blizzard, drouth; wind, hail, and grasshoppers. The new railroad was operating and carpenters hammered noisily in the tiny hamlets that sprang up along the tracks—that bitter trail laid out so straight and shining to lure the feet of the optimistic.

The prairies had seen the hump-backed cattle of the red men turned to bleached bones. Now she saw progress rising over the horizon like the thunderheads that were to flail the new-sown crops; progress that was to whirl across the cattle ranges like the dust dervishes that danced across the Medicine Line, picking up, tossing high, and scattering the horsemen and the horses of a way of life.

Many of the nesters would leave in the next fifteen years. But not all, for some of the descendants of those German settlers, abandoning wheat for cows, are today among the respected cattlemen of the south country.

And so, although ranching became more restricted and the ranges had to be fenced, the cattlemen gradually took hope again. And the ranchers, substituting cattle for bison, did little harm—ecologically—to the country in any case.

Scotty was not as well situated as some of the ranchers who had acquired more deeded lands and larger leases. With the coming of the homesteaders, he decided to move to wider pastures. He had long had his eye on an area of open range to the south near the International Boundary and had applied for the lease of some twenty thousand acres.

He had had logs cut the previous winter by a bunch of 'breeds, and that summer I helped to freight them by wagon over the long trail that wound up over the high bench, crossed Battle Creek at Badger's ranch and skirted the east end of the Old-Man-on-His-Back.

Back and forth Gow's wagons shuttled, the good Clyde-bred horses eating up the twin wheel marks, the drivers nodding in the sun; or straining their eyes to the unattainable horizon that they might not see the violation of the grasslands that had been their playground by day and their bed by night.

11

The news from Europe was bad. The war had not been the short and successful one we had expected.

Canadians had retched and choked in the poison gas at Festubert and Givenchy while we had been enjoying the peace and plenty of the plains. Men without eyes, men without legs, and men without hope, were returning to their homeland. Recruiting was stepped up.

A friend from Moosomin wrote me: "They have lowered the height standard to five foot six. Come on down. Colonel Gillis is recruiting a battalion, and I reckon you can stretch that half inch."

Within twenty-four hours I was on my way, and within forty-eight I became Regimental Number 276119 and a member of the Canadian Expeditionary Force.

I never saw Scotty again. He died next spring from a heart attack.

Part II: WAR HORSES

War horses

CHAPTER NINE

1

Most of my friends had joined cavalry regiments such as the Strathconas or the Fort Garry Horse, or at least the Light Horse units and the Mounted Rifles. I fully expected to do the same, but alas! by the time I was accepted, the infantry were more in demand, so a footslogger I was obliged to become. Also, what men they took for Horse Artillery had to be a bit above my poor five foot five; and this was to be my curse later when it prevented me from joining the Mounted Police, in spite of the fact that in that attempt I had the backing of a certain inspector who said to the superintendent, "I'd take him on, sir. We have enough of those heavyweight *horse killers!*"

But I digress and must return to when I found myself an infantry officer in the mud and rain of northern France, always with an eye for any chance to straddle a horse.

As to the war, it has been written about plenty, so I'll skip most of it, although the memory of certain men, as well as horses, is green enough.

I think of Tomlinson and Paterson who were killed alongside me at Priez Farm, while I didn't get a scratch, but had to take over what was left of the company—which I couldn't have done without Sergeant Watts.

Right after that do, I was made acting transport officer. It's not a much favored job, and I was probably picked because I was from the West and my attestation papers had been marked *"ranch hand."*

However, it suited me. I rode a tall raw-boned hunter-type charger called "Major." He was a horse of iron nerves, and he took shellfire like a veteran.

I think he hated flies worse than whiz-bangs! He carried an Alberta brand, and had an old rope-burn on his off hind fetlock; I kept it softened up with axle grease, to the disgust of the brigade vet.

A lot of horses couldn't take the shock of high explosive shells, and we'd often find one dead after a bombardment, without a scratch on him. One early morning when I went to the transport horse lines I found the colonel's mount—a good horse, too—dead as mutton, and the nearest shell had exploded over a hundred yards away. I suppose his heart had just stopped with the fright.

Mules were much more phlegmatic. We used a lot of them, mostly tall, brown fellows from the United States midwest—from Iowa, Missouri, and Illinois. They were used for packing rations and ammunition up to the trenches.

The supply of these rugged animals began to run short before 1917, for hundreds died of some virus on the transports. This was due to the sabotage campaign of Franz von Papen, then German Ambassador to Washington whose agents "needled" hundreds of mules and horses in the stockyards or when they were en route after their purchase by the British Government. After that we used mules from Spain and the Argentine.

We would naturally go up under cover of darkness, and those rainy nights in France sure as hell *were* dark. We usually had one man to two mules, twisting about this way and that to avoid broken limbers, bits of half-caved trenches, and any number of shell holes. They followed each other more by sound than otherwise, and they would go where a horse couldn't—or wouldn't—and keep their feet where a horse would fall. And to fall flat in that knee-deep, churned-up muck was no fun for man or beast.

Often enough a mule would slide down into a deep shell crater with three to four feet of water, or rather thin slime, in the bottom. Then the party would have to stop and stumble about in the dark to try and get the poor beast out. Sometimes we did, sometimes we didn't, but at least we always tried.

A steady old mule won't panic too much or thrash around, so we had a fifty-fifty chance to save him if we could scrounge enough old planks or ammo boxes to throw down around him. The mule would work that stuff under his feet, and as a rule a few men on a rope would be able to help him as he clawed with his hooves at the slippery side of the crater.

On good going though, a mule can be contrary for no good reason, or some good reason known only to itself! Hence the ditty:

A thousand men once tried to pull a mule from off the track,
They pulled him just about a foot, and then he pulled them back!
Then someone did a silly thing, he must have been a fool,
He went and got a piece of straw, and he tried to tickle the mule!
Then he went travelling, yes he went travelling,
'way up in the air,
pieces everywhere, etc.

But you couldn't do much with a horse in the same fix. A horse would stamp and pump with his legs until he bogged deeper and deeper, and if you threw a plank down he would almost die of fright! Finally, he'd give up and just lie groaning, so, hard as it sounds, you couldn't waste much time with him.

2

The smell of dead horses hung around all the time. It got pretty rank on a hot day when we had to pull our wagons past German gun teams lying all bloated by the roadside. Poor devils!

Yet the smell of our own horses, live horses, always had a steadying effect on me. It seemed somehow to make a sense of sanity in a world otherwise quite mad. I'd often linger at the horse lines after evening "stables" just to talk to our wagon teams and get the mingled smell of horses and hay and oats as the nags munched away. Sometimes the transport sergeant would stick around, too. He had been a cowboy in Alberta, and we'd talk about horses, and it was he who said one night, as a star shell burst over the German lines, "Gee, don't that look like the shooting stars we used to watch on night herd!" ·

Another time I was reminded of roundup days was when we were watering horses and mules at the Somme River. It was a lovely summer's day, the Germans were retreating, and we had sent the transport drivers to water our horses and mules, with instructions to allow them a couple of hours of loose grazing.

It was a great sight to see the nags wade belly-deep into the stream;

good to see them clamber out one by one, to shake themselves, and
then enjoy a good grunting roll on the turf before scattering out on
the grassland to graze.

The whole scene, even to the rolling chalk lands, gave me the
impression of home.

3

It was shortly after this that we witnessed a cavalry charge. We were
the third line, lying in a sunken road. Our boys of the second line
had run into trouble ahead, on the high ground of Pierre St. Vaast
wood. Evidently, the Germans had let our first line led by tanks go
through but in retreating had left some hidden machine guns in the
wood. These were now harassing our second line.

Suddenly we heard a trumpet behind us, followed by a deep rumbling, and then, at full gallop and with drawn swords, came the Anzac
cavalry. They rode right through us, and I still have a vivid picture
in my mind of one young fellow, probably a stockrider from Queens-
land, who jumped his horse into the road and out again with a quick
change of feet, as coolly as if he were hunting the fox in England or
chasing a steer in Canada.

They galloped down the slight slope before us, about one hundred
feet apart, but keeping their dressing as if they were on parade, and
dodging the piles of wire and junk that our tanks had flattened, as
smartly as any cutting-horse working a cow herd.

Just as they started up towards the wood, a "sacrifice" German
battery got the range of them, and opened up. But they were a little
too late and not many horses fell.

The boys were close to their objective and traveling fast, and although they now came under the fire of the machine guns and more
horses and men went down, the Anzacs were soon on top of the
gunners. It wasn't long before we saw the boys, still with drawn swords,
herding a bunch of prisoners in our direction.

It was pitiful to see the loose horses wandering hither and thither,
lost and confused and whinnying loudly for their mates; but as soon
as they heard the "recall" they pricked up their ears, and by ones and

twos galloped towards the sound to rejoin the thinned ranks. Those cavalry horses knew every trumpet call just as well as their riders.

The way was now open to our infantry, and we soon moved forward, doing what we could for the cavalry casualties till the stretcher-bearers got into action. When a couple of our Canadian boys stopped to put a field dressing on one young chap, the only thing he said to them was, "Is my horse all right, mate?" They didn't know, but someone said, "He sure is, Digger."

4

As the fall days of 1918 shortened and the Jerry's retreat began to look like a rout, we captured literally hundreds of his transport horses. These were mostly the erstwhile property of the Czar that the Germans had captured when the Russians had folded up on the eastern front.

These nags were steppe-bred, pretty light, and rough looking. In a way they reminded me of our mustang-type ponies, but they were more thickset and not as good looking. They were obviously tough as whang-leather, and we used a few as replacements. But they didn't savvy English and had been used to a different kind of harness. What happened to them all eventually, I don't know, but I suspect that most of them were put into cans for the French and Belgians.

The last horse I rode in France was one of these. I called him Nicholas—Nick for short. He was a tough little chap, and I used him on several scouting parties.

There was an old monastery on a highish peak called Mont St. Aubert, right on the Belgian frontier, if I remember. It had been used as an observation post by the enemy, and my job was to take a small hastily mounted patrol and find out if any Germans were there.

We found it abandoned, and an old monk who seemed to be care-taker—the rest of the community having been removed—told me the coast was clear.

As I sat on that little Russian horse I could see over the plain to the east, and what a sight it was! German gun teams and wagon teams crowded the roads. Many of them, finding themselves so squeezed, had taken to the fields where they bogged down and had to be abandoned.

Infantry filled every possible space between the vehicles, looking like a moving mass of gray ants. The country was open, the maze of trenches were far to our rear, and it looked like a scene from *War and Peace*. I think if we had had enough cavalry then the war would have ended a month before it did. As it was, the Germans moved so fast that only our light planes were able to harass them.

5

The armistice came and I soon left France, but before I did I saw the last of the army horses under happier circumstances.

I was in Paris, part of a large crowd that thronged the sidewalks of the Champs-Élysées, watching a victory parade. It was made up of mixed French and British units. First came the French Dragoons, complete with red horsehair plumes on their helmets. Now came the Spahis, the Moroccan Colonial Cavalry, with their blue cloaks and white turbans, astride fiery little Arabs. Then came infantry and artillery, some of which were Canadian, and I thrilled with nostalgic pride for our country when the glossy gun teams passed and, knowing where to look, I picked out western brands, Bar C, Q, N Bar N, and many others I don't recall now.

Yet I hated to think how few of those gallant blacks and grays and bays would ever again run free on the good prairie grass; for their fate would be to pull dung carts for French peasants. Or, perhaps, it would be even worse . . .

By the spring of 1919 I was back in Saskatchewan, accompanied by a friend who had heard that there was good unoccupied cattle land west of Alexis Creek in the Chilcotin district of the B.C. interior.

So late summer saw us traveling west on the main line at special "returned soldier" rates.

Since the Calgary Stampede was just winding up, we decided to stop at that town and do some shopping and visiting. The place was full of cowboys from the States as well as local riders; and the second day I ran plumb into Frank Wolf, a horse rancher from Medicine Hat, whom I knew well.

We went into Riley and McCormick's saddlery shop on the main drag, chatting away as I tried on pair after pair of riding boots till I found a good fit. As we came out on the sidewalk Frank drew my attention to a group of men talking together on the street corner.

"See that stocky-built guy with the sash?" said Frank. "Well, that's Charlie Russell the cowboy artist from Montana. I heard he'd come up for the stampede. Ever meet him?"

I said, "No, but I'd like to."

"Well, here's your chance" said Frank, "I know him middlin' well—he used to knock around our part of the world down south. C'm on."

So I was introduced to the famous cowboy artist as a young Britisher who liked to draw horses.

He said a few words, mentioning that when he had been in England "years ago" he had never seen a poor horse in that land.

As I listened I noted his square face with a lock of loose hair escaping from beneath a neat Stetson, his well-fitted, neat riding boots, and, of course, his gay half-breed sash.

He sure looked like his own sketches of himself, and he could have stood out in any crowd, for there was something about him that let you know that he was an individual, a rare bird, his own man.

Our meeting was brief, as are most street-corner ones. Charlie had to go to Coutts, and we had to rejoin my friend who was taking on a few.

Frank told me that the previous year, when on a visit to his folks in Montana, he had shown one of my sketches to Charlie, who had said it "wasn't bad." I think this chance meeting had something to do with my increased efforts with the pencil, and I got to thinking how fine it would be if I could capture on paper the passing range days of Canada as Russell had done for Montana, so perhaps this book really stems from those thoughts.

Frank Wolf, by the way, had perhaps the best collection of my early day sketches—which I invariably gave away.

The last I heard of Frank he was living with a sister in Montana. I wrote to him, and the sister wrote to me when he died. She is dead now, and I have no notion where the sketches are.

Another man who had quite a collection was the late Vern McLean,

whom I write of as the "Wagon Boss." But he, too, is dead and no
one seems to know what happened to his scrapbooks.

As to the Chilcotin, we found it a lovely country, but since most
of the good grazing was taken up and most of the ranches employed
Indians for riding and haying, we returned to the prairies the next
spring with rather tight belts.

Since I have written a good deal about the Chilcotin in *Many Trails,*
I shall skip those months and go forward to 1920 and new jobs in
Saskatchewan.

Line Camp

Part III: HORSE PEDDLIN'

The Doctor's Team

CHAPTER TEN

The stud groom

1

All through the nineteen-twenties there was a brisk demand for horses to supply power to the new crop of homesteaders and settlers who were pushing north and west into the semibushlands around Turtleford and Meadow Lake and Elk Point and the Peace River country, as well as into those older areas where the change-over from oxen to horses was still going on.

This market was largely filled by ranchers from the short-grass plains of Saskatchewan and Alberta.

Horse prices had been good during the war years when thousands of animals had been sold for cavalry, artillery, and transport purposes. Since few of thòse horses came back to Canada (most were sold to French or Belgian farmers), horses were in short supply when hostilities ceased.

Some ranchers feared a general slump, but the impetus of settlement—largely by soldier-settlers—soon took up the slack, and after a few months horse prices were good again.

Moreover, cattle prices were poor; so a good many ranchers increased their horse herds, buying high-priced imported stallions of the draft breeds, to augment the limited supply of home-grown Clydesdales from the stud farms of Manitoba and eastern Saskatchewan. Farms with names like Kilmarnock and Bonnie Brae.

Thinking of those names, imported like the Clyde horses from the land of heather, reminds one that wherever you find cattle and horses you will find Scotsmen.

They were (and are) the great stockbreeders of Britain. They gave us the best Shorthorns, the Angus, the Ayrshires, the Galloways, as well as the feather-footed, high-stepping Clydesdales.

In Australia, New Zealand, Argentina, and Patagonia, as well as in the countries of South and East Africa and all over North America, you will find a list of ranchers and station owners running pretty well to Scots of every clan. If they are not MacLeans or MacRaes or MacDonalds or MacGregors, then they will be the Grahams or Lindsays or Sutherlands or Craigs. Most of the great British-American cattle companies from Texas to Wyoming had Scottish managers, such as MacBain of the Matador.

In those days most of the money spent by farmers was kept close to where it was made, rather than being drained off to the cities for combines, tractors, and forage harvesters to contribute to the urban sprawl. Hence the horse-sale dollars were plowed back into fine houses, roomy barns, and tall windmills, with all the materials and labor obtained from local sources, to the betterment of the community as a whole.

The ranchers bought their own stallions and their mares were bred on the range, loose. But a farmer with perhaps only two mares depended on the "traveling" stud in which he might have a share with perhaps twenty other farmers. To many farmers, the Scottish Clydesdale was the top draft animal, and many a classy stallion traveled the dirt roads from prairie farm to prairie farm to mate with the farmers' nondescript mares.

The "Big Horse" was cared for, as like as not, by a dour Scottish stud-groom, who led his charge (and his pride) from the seat of a two-wheeled cart (called a sulky). This was drawn by a gentle pony mare. And it was a sight to see this little procession approaching; the mare stepping daintily, the stallion prancing to one side, restrained by the pipe-smoking groom; while at every step the stallion's wide-mouthed drinking bucket clanged and swung from its hook beneath the axle. For these great brutes could not lower their muzzles into a bucket of ordinary dimensions.

It was a horse such as this, bought from J. D. MacGregor at Brandon, that it had been my job to feed and water when I began to work for Scotty Gow.

The agricultural journals of the 'teens and 'twenties had many pages of advertisements, with fine pictures, for every breed from Frank Collicut's Willow Springs Herefords to J. D. MacGregor's Clydes; as well as more pages of ranchers' brands, looking like hieroglyphics from some ancient Egyptian tomb.

2

Light-horse breeding had already begun to die down, owing to the demand for heavy work horses for the farms. Even the Indian Department, in the hope of encouraging their wards to cultivate grain, began to buy heavy draft stallions for use on the cayuse mares of the reserves. But the Indian is no farmer, and many of the offspring, awkward and big-headed, with heavy clumsy legs (for this was too violent a cross) were broken too early to saddle—perhaps as two-year-olds. A winter spent running down coyotes put a lot of them out of action, especially on one reserve I could name; and the end result was that before long (since the Department persuaded the Indians to emasculate their pony studs) a real clean-limbed Indian cayuse or mustang became hard to find. Unfortunately, we had no association to help preserve these fine, hardy, little horses. In Argentina, the Criollo Horse Association has been able to save a similar type of pampas horse, and in the States, too, I believe, there is a Mustang Association. But not in Canada.

Much the same applied to the good, light-weight brood mares of the ranches and farms. Under the influence of the broad percheron or hairy Clyde studs, the offspring became coarse and nondescript— good animals for the plow and binder, but no good for saddle. Even the Mounted Police were beginning to scour the country for remounts by 1928.

This was later to lead to the formation, by a few devoted enthusiasts, of the South Saskatchewan Light Horse Association, and it is to Colonel Greenly and others like him that we owe the final perpetuation of the hardy crossbred saddle horses that had already made a name for themselves on the battlefields of Europe, Palestine, and South Africa.

However, it takes several years on the range to breed large horses from mustang mares, and at this time most of the ranchers still had fairly small stuff with a good deal of hot blood, more (apparently) suited to cavalry or police work than to drawing a plow.

Yet they were good, no matter where you put them. These light-weights ("broncos" the farmers erroneously called them), brought less money than the heavies, but in the long run they did almost as much work on the plows and binders; for what they lacked in weight they made up for in willingness and fire—what we call "gimp"—and the fact that they ate a lot less hay and oats. In addition to which they were useful on the buggy or under the saddle.

One is reminded that the Irish farmers also used light horses for farm work, and in that country it is no uncommon thing to this day for a horse to be sold right "off the plow" for a gentleman's use in the hunting field.

These smaller horses made up the bulk of country sales. They came in all colors from pintos to roans, bays and blacks, and they were pretty wild.

Nevertheless, they brought prices from two hundred to three hundred dollars a pair, which looked pretty good when steers were worth only about thirty-five to forty-five dollars apiece.

What heavier stuff there was, if well broke and with age in their favor, might change hands at five hundred dollars a team or even more, and were in favor for city transport; for at this time horses were needed for coal and furniture delivery as well as for street maintenance. The cities and towns also took some middleweights for ice and milk and bread delivery, as well as some really good drivers for the professional men.

One feature of the larger city homes was the stable at the back of the lot, for the use of the fancy driving team. Those stables, or what few still stand, have now been remodeled to house the family motor car.

In the less affluent parts of the cities and towns a milk cow was often kept, and many towns had what was called the "town herd," in which all the urban cows were grazed by day somewhere on the outskirts. It was usually the job of one of the boys of the house to meet the family cow as she detached herself from her grazing friends when the lot were driven home by the herder. Quite a large "town herd" once grazed along Wascana Creek in Regina, not far from the Mounted Police Barracks. Many an old worn-out cowboy got a "town herd" job in his latter years.

3

Almost any light, free-trotting horses were used for driving; but the most favored were, of course, those of standard-bred or Hambletonian breeding, such as one sees in the trotting races of today. Most of them were lightweights, slim and absolutely clean-legged with long springy fetlocks. Most of them tended to be some shade of bay, although chestnuts were not uncommon.

These horses were naturally fast trotters and a matched pair on a light buggy or cutter could certainly eat up the miles.

Most livery and sales stables kept two or three such teams on hand for the use of customers, who might be most commonly government inspectors of some kind, or commercial travelers who needed to make visits into the countryside from the various rail points. These good teams could average at least ten miles an hour all day—better than that on a short journey.

At the same time a large number of professional men preferred to own their own driving teams, and this applied, especially, to small-town doctors whose patients might live anywhere from ten to thirty miles away. In those days doctors went to their patients, not the patient to his doctor; and, of course, few people went to the hospital except for a serious injury. Influenza and pneumonia were treated at home, and babies were born right on the farm or ranch.

The work of these country doctors during the flu epidemic of 1918, that spilled over into the next year, would fill many books.

We can imagine how many a settler's wife anxiously awaited the doctor's arrival in those days. We can see her peering out of the frosted window of a humble shack; looking for a speck in the far distance, a speck at last sighted, shrouded in fog and flying snow, the bells ringing out clear over the snowy plain, until at last the horses' heads take shape.

Nearer and nearer they come, their legs moving like pistons, their hooves throwing back snowballs, until they are at the door. A muffled "whoa" and the team stops as one, flanks heaving.

Out clambers the fur-coated doctor, his mustache hung with icicles, his black bag in hand, to hurry to the door thrown open for him.

One of the family unhitches the steaming team, all glittering with frost. They have not altered that fast gait for twenty miles but are still full of pep, shying sideways at the advance of the family dog, pausing as they are led to the stable to shake themselves and set the little bells into a wild clamor that shatters the frosty air.

And once tied in a stall, "well rugged" and facing a mangerful of sweet, mint-scented hay, they will rest themselves till needed for the return journey, or perhaps another visit in the district.

The doctors had little in their stock of medicines that was of much use to the fevered patients, but they always carried a supply of brandy, a thing hard to obtain in those prohibition days following the war. I have heard many a doctor say that the best he could prescribe was bed rest and brandy. And it is a fact that good brandy saved hundreds of people in that anxious year.

Time has dulled our memories, and many of these doctors have been forgotten—their names elude one, but I am sure they are writ large in heaven.

4

With horse sales in mind, many ranchers made drives of loose horses from the range country to the northern settlements. They would stop at various points on the way, selling here a team, there a saddle horse, to make trail money.

Another way was to engage an agent somewhere within striking distance of the demand, and ship carloads of horses on the railway, which he would sell on commission.

Watrous was such a point. The Allen Hills were settling up and many homesteaders wanted to substitute horses for oxen. A good team that could make the twenty miles to town in three or four hours looked enticing to a farmer used to driving for ten hours with a yoke of oxen to cover the same distance.

At this little town there was a butcher and cattle dealer who had a large pasture just east of Manitou Lake, with corrals and sheds. This man handled a good few carloads of horses, mostly branded C and Q—being from the ranches of C. C. Bowlen of Calgary.

His rider—most butchers hired a rider to bring in stock—was a former Q ranch cowboy named Charlie Wilson. Many old-timers will remember Charlie. He was a colorful character, but not in the rootin' tootin' way. He was as soft spoken as a Virginian, slim and graceful; sober and well broke; for he had a wife who had weaned him from the bunkhouse bunch.

They lived in a little white house on the edge of town, which was easy to find because one or the other (or both) of Charlie's saddle horses would be in plain sight grazing on a picket rope on one of the nearby vacant lots.

Charlie's job was to bring in butcher stuff to the slaughter house from the farms, to look after the cattle in the pasture, and to help gather and load market stuff on the cars for Winnipeg.

Over and above that, he had to unload any cars of horses that came, and maybe herd them a day or two till sale day. Meanwhile, he'd halter-break any green broncs that had forgotten a rope while in the cars. In the sales corral he'd be on hand to rope horses as they were sold and to help the new farmer-owner to halter them to take away.

He stood out among those bib-overalled farmers like a diamond in a coal scuttle. Lean, clean-shaven, dark as a Spaniard, he'd sit so casually in the saddle rolling his little Bull Durham cigarettes, that you'd think you were at the movies, and he was the hero all dressed up in a neat Stetson with riding cuffs and fringed chaps.

But he was no Hollywood cowboy. Only if you looked closely could you see his lariat hanging loose from his hand with a real small loop in it, as his horse moved quietly among the press of broncs shifting around in the corral.

The dealer would shout: "Now, boys, this is all good stuff. All halter-broke and most have been on a wagon." (He didn't add "once only!") "Look 'em over—there's plenty time. You kin match up a couple of them bay geldings or—look at them grays; like as twins!— Oh, one's a mare. All the better, you don't get no colts offen a gelding—he ain't got no more hope of posterity than a mule! So you gotta have something that'll raise a young one or you will be coming back to me for another, pretty soon.

"If it's a saddle hoss you want, why there's a choice; the little black or mebbe that pinto?

"Look 'em over; you'll find what you want if it's a single or a six-horse team, and say—any of them lookin' through a collar will look mighty good."

A murmur from the farmers. Two brothers with heads together. An older man, foot on the corral fence, turning his cud in his cheek and his eyes squinting in his creased face as he looked from horse to horse.

Snatches of conversation—"I'm looking for a mate for Billie."— "Yep, a fella could use that there sorrel."—"Wonder how well broke that black is . . ."—"Oh them dam broncs, you can waste a lot of time with them kind, and what you got? Broken wagon tongues and bust harness. No branded hosses for me . . ."—"Too small, why that'n' ain't over nine hundred pounds . . ."—"So what? I've seen them little rascals play out a big team—yep, and without no oats."—"They gets away from you, you gotta head for Montana afore you catch up!"—"Boy! That's a beauty, lookit that flossy mane!"—And so it went, and the dealer, who'd heard every word and seen every gesture, would say, "Charlie! Drop a loop on that sorrel, the gentleman wants a closer look," and Charlie, without moving anything but his eyes and hand

would send that rope to settle over the sorrel's head with the hiss of
a snake.

Charlie would snap his wrist back so the rope wouldn't settle too
low, turn his horse and say, "Who?"

"The big gent with the seegar," the dealer would say, and Charlie
would bring the horse alongside.

"How old?" the gent would ask.

"Old enough to vote!" some wag would yell.

But the big gent knew the answer, before he'd asked, and went on,
"How much?"

"A hundred twenty-five, he was told.

"Note?"

"Okay, go see the clerk."

Promissory notes were usually made out due at harvest time. Almost
three-quarters of these horses were sold on "notes." For things looked
good, and no one guessed there'd be a slim harvest that fall, and the
fall after; with dropping prices.

As a result, few promissory notes got paid up in full, banks refused
to take them as collateral, and a lot of ranchers—by the end of the
horse boom—were holding any amount of worthless "paper." It certainly was not worth the time and expense of repossessing the horses.
So the stockmen eventually went back to cattle, which at least had
a market price in cash.

5

By ones and twos and fours the horses would be sold. And for hours
after there would be a stream of wagons going home with half-broke
horses tied behind, fighting their halters, kicking and whinnying for
old comrades of the range; for horses have friends and relatives just
like humans.

Perhaps I should draw a veil over some of the barnyard scenes that
followed, as farmers and their men tried to tame down "them broncs."

However, there were usually some experienced men in a settlement
to lend a hand and show the others that it could be done. If you don't
know horses, it's a kind of a scary thing to go into a stall to feed or

water a beast that snorts and turns red eyes towards you, but these animals rarely kicked a fellow; they were too scared themselves. It's the half-tame colt, that has run free about the barnyard, who gets treacherous, for he lacks proper respect for man. A bronc will tuck in his tail, hump his back, and shiver, but he won't hurt you as a rule, and once used to your voice and hand he loses his fear, but never his respect; for the first thing that disciplined him was a rope, and he remembers that you are the stronger of the two.

To wagon-break a green bronc, nothing beat hitching him, with a steady work horse, to a set of bobsleighs. The bronc could be tied back by his halter shank to his mate's hame ring; or if he was really a tough customer, you could have a trip rope on one front foot, but a man other than the driver was required to operate it. With this rig the bronc could be put right off his feet if he bucked and stampeded too violently. After being pulled down on his nose a few times, a young horse learns to be more sedate.

Bucked off

The sleighs didn't rattle and run into the team as much as a wagon, and would not overturn as easily. The team could tear across the grassy prairie pretty safely, the wild one kicking and squalling; but the old stager would soon tire of that and start to slow down, checking the wild one's flight.

The green horse might kick his leg over a trace, or even the pole, and you'd let him crab along a ways like that till he'd skinned himself a bit, after which he wouldn't be likely to repeat that mistake.

Some settled down in two days, others took longer; but in a surprisingly short time four of these range horses would be pulling a plow as if they had never run loose for four or five years.

But you did not pussyfoot around them, or they'd get scary. You treated them as if they knew you were boss; and they'd believe it!

6

When a certain rancher sold out the Q brand to the boss of the Bar C, the deal was made in the Assiniboia Hotel in Medicine Hat, while the two sat drinking the awful 2 per cent beer that was all the government allowed in the early '20's. Of course you could sometimes get "washroom whiskey" or some other brand of red-eye that had never paid excise, but to explain all that I would have to go into the realm of moonshining!

Anyway the Q man said, "I'm getting ready to quit the horses, and my range has been cut down, so I'll sell you the lot."

The other fellow said, "How many?"

"Three—four hundred—range tally."

"Take twenty bucks a head—suckers to old shags? Say three fifty head?"

"Okay," said the Q. "I'll play fifty head each way. And you make the gather?"

"Okay, I'd best have the brand, too, outright."

"Can do. I'll drop a line to the brand inspector about the transfer."

"Good. That way I'm safe. But say, can I get some boys here? I'd like to get Charlie Wilson—you know him?—to ramrod the deal, but he'll need a few hands. And can you lend me a grubwagon, too?"

"I'll do better. I'll give you a wagon on the deal."

"Thanks. I'll be gathering in two weeks. When I get through I'll fix it up, eh?"

"Sure, that's fine by me."

Just two men's words. And that was the way plenty of deals were settled 'way back when . . .

Charlie and his boys made the gather that spring, mostly around Wild Horse and north to pretty near Egg Lake. They rounded up a little better than three hundred and fifty and finally got them corralled. Next day they started them over the Cypress Hills west bench, headed for the Hat.

There was a little old telephone line strung along the bench between Elkwater Lake and Battle Creek, for the use of the Forestry people. One pole was plumb down and the wire all sagged. The point rider hit this wire. He tried to signal the swing riders to head the bunch away to one side, but the loose horses were coming too fast. The leaders hit that wire real hard and a couple of them turned somersaults. The rest paid no heed but kept coming, the wire squealing for half a mile and poles coming down everywhere.

No men or horses were badly hurt, but the din and confusion was terrific and you could hardly see for dust. However, it slackened the pace, and order was soon restored.

Charlie said, "I bet those ranger fellows made the air blue when they come to fix their talk-line."

I like to remember Charlie riding free and handsome. But he's only a memory now; for while he was yet a young middle age he got caught in a blizzard with a bunch of cattle. It was in the hills south of Watrous, in early November, and it had been a warm day so Charlie wore only a Stetson and a light jacket. He stayed with the bunch and got to shelter in a shack; but he caught pneumonia, and in less than a week there was a graveyard ceremony for poor Charlie.

Too bad he hadn't stumbled on a moonshiner's place—there were plenty in the hills—for a good shot of White Mule would probably have saved his life. "Stills" made of copper with copper coils were all over the place since the bars had been closed in 1917—originally as a war measure. So the only way that a fellow could get a snort was either from a moonshiner or by doctor's prescription from a drug store. The druggists stocked liquor in eight-ounce bottles, and a group of would-be celebrants (but these would be townspeople) would gang together, and if they had enough "pull," they'd get enough booze for a good red-nosed evening. I think the whole thing got a bit scandalous, which is why the government finally allowed beer parlors and later sold liquor in their own stores which bore (and bear today) the delightfully anonymous name of "Outlets"!

But the still owners, the moonshiners (just as honest in their way as the men who work in "outlets" today) were sort of outlaws, and had to operate very secretly. Some made good stuff, some bad. I knew one little terrierlike Yorkshireman who boasted that he put his product through the still twice, and he'd pay fifty bucks to anyone who could find "one drop of fusil oil in a barrelful."

It kept the police busy, but I think it was to their credit that they only hit really hard at moonshiners who (a) made rot-gut, poisonous stuff, and (b) sold to minors. I knew of several "respectable" home-brew artists who made really good stuff, and sold only to responsible customers, including (so rumor had it) the local drug store whenever it had been drained dry by its ailing customers.

7

I was on several of those long horse drives in 1920. One drive was with Lee Bradford whom I had first met overseas. He had been with the Canadian Machine Gun Corps and had won a commission on the field.

We had to trail about seventy-five horses, mostly Bar Cees, to Turtleford for a dealer.

We started from near Davidson, to which town the nags had been shipped by rail. Driving them by day mostly by way of back trails, we always camped early wherever we could fine good grass, sometimes on vacant company (C.P.R. or C.N.R.) land of which there was quite a lot. Failing that we'd look for a fenced road allowance that had not been graded, which made night herding (in which we took shifts) very much easier. On a north-south road we would only have to guard the south side, because, of course, that was the direction the horses wanted

to take when the homing instinct got strong, which it often did. We
had two saddle horses apiece which we rode on alternate days.

We got to Sutherland in three days. This town, across the river from
Saskatoon, was then independent, but I believe it is now part of
Saskatoon City.

We night-herded the bunch on a stretch of railway land. All night
there were trains shunting around, but not close enough to bother the
stock, and when the sun rose it shone brightly on the new university
buildings which were just west of us.

Next day we crossed the bridge into Saskatoon and tried to slow
the nags to a walk and herd them around the east side of the city
into the open country.

Somewhere along the river bank (I doubt if I could find the place
now) was a nice residential district area—new houses, lawns, garages,
etc.—and we tried to herd the bunch by at a good trot so they wouldn't
be tempted to chaw on somebody's roses or tramp their grass.

Soon (with the open river bank on the right) we came to a tennis
court on the left, with young people in white flannels batting a ball
across the net. It woke memories of old England to hear "love all!"
ringing out.

We two cowboys sure felt out of place and off our stamping ground.
Everybody stared, for they never saw many cowboys in Saskatoon,
which was wheat country.

Then a ball suddenly skipped across the road, followed by a fellow
in white. You should have seen those nags scatter! About half of them
plunged down the steep river bank. I caught a glimpse of Lee riding
hell-bent up an alleyway after some others, while I plunged after the
water-rats, half of whom were swimming now.

Then the fellow yelled, "To me! Captain of the 10th!" He was joined
by another fellow. Down the bank they scrambled. They jumped into
a boat moored there and quickly rowed downstream to circle the
swimmers, shouting with glee as if they were in the hunting field.
"Tallyho! Forrard!"

The horses had never seen that kind of cowboy before and quickly
made for the bank to join the others. There was no time to stop and
talk, for the bunch was away on the high lope shying at everything
and dead set to get out of that mess.

But I had already recognized the first man by his voice and the second by that reference to the 10th Mounted Rifles. I had met them both at the Etaples Remount Station during the war, so I waved and shouted, "Thanks! 10th C.M.R.'s!" and dashed on leaving them grinning.

Lee told me after we got clear that there were some darn goodlooking gals in the tennis bunch, but how he had time to look 'em over I don't know, unless it was just his instinct at work!

This side of Borden we had to swim the North Branch. The CeePee bridge wasn't built yet, and the ferryman "didn't want no broncs on his barge." Anyways, he could only take a few at a time because the river was low and there were "plenty sand bars."

I was riding a horse of Lee's, called Bill, and he was supposed to be a good water horse, so I took off his bridle and shucked my chaps and pants and got him into the water just looking through a halter. I headed him for a sand bar that showed up midstream, and he only had to swim a few yards. I got to the bar and looked back to see the whole bunch taking to the water like seals, an old flea-bitten mare on the lead. By the time I'd blown my horse the first of them were coming out of the water, so I headed across the next channel—which was a bit deeper and faster—and landed a ways downstream.

There are few prettier sights than a horse herd swimming, strung out with just their heads above water; and I watched them land one by one, shaking spray all over the grass, and then finally Lee landed and we let the bunch graze around while we dried out in the hot sun.

We eventually made it to Turtleford where I herded the bunch on the rich grass beside the creek, while Lee rode into the town to locate the man we had to make delivery to.

Turtleford was booming then for the railway had come in, and every second sign along the rough plank sidewalk read SO-AND-SO REAL ESTATE.

The big end of the land close to town had been homesteaded, but a lot of settlers made it a jumping off place for Paradise Hill, Loon Lake, and Meadow Lake. With land prices booming, a lot of the older settlers wanted to unload their land and the real estate boys would swoop on any new arrival to offer them "the best farmland north of Battleford."

There were two livery and sales barns, jerry-built of rough lumber from the sawmills (there was plenty timber just north); both of them were crowded with teams, mules, and saddle horses. Someone had a bottle and there was a lot of going and coming to the barn office.

After the horses settled down I rode in, too, and found Lee with the "dry bunch" turning the dust in his throat to mud, which he said was easier to swallow. We fixed it with the barn boss to run the horses in his big corral as soon as they'd filled up.

Horse herd crossing the Saskatchewan

After we did that we went across to what was called the "Chink" Cafe, and just after the hot steaks came along, the man who was to take the bunch off our hands came looking for us.

Next day we were doing the sights of town, Lee with a wary eye for another bottle. A Mountie came up very affably and asked a few questions. Lee told him the owner had the bill of sale, so he said he'd check it against the horses, after which he jingled off towards the barn.

8

While this was going on a tall man strolled up. He wore a big black Stetson and good riding boots. As the policeman turned away he said, "You fellows want a job? I got a bunch of broncs the edge of town. I'm taking them up to my place at Meadow Lake. My brother hurt his ankle so I'm single-handed. 'Name's Jack Crow and our place is on the Beaver River. What do you say?"

Our time was our own by now, and a few extra dollars are always useful, so we finally settled at ten bucks apiece and grub and horse feed on the trip.

We set off next morning. It was raining. In fact, we found it was raining most days up there in June. The country around Turtleford was parky, with aspen bluffs and just the odd spruce; but by noon we were following a trail up the west side of Brightsand Lake in pretty heavy timber. This was the Boggy Creek trail, which headed across the Meadow Lake Forest Reserve to the new settlement north of the height-of-land.

This trail was notorious; bog holes and muskegs alternating with soft sandy ridges; all made worse by the heavy traffic and the present rains. The horse flies were scandalous—and hungry.

Crow's bunch were also from the south—not used to muskeg and timber. They had been shipped by rail from Moose Jaw to North Battleford.

They splashed and grunted ahead of us on a fast trot, and soon they were mud from muzzle to croup, with their long tails a mass of wet clay, and the faster they went the more those tails clubbed their hocks.

There were dozens of teams—horses and mules—plugging along, and we had to take to the brush to get around them. A few plodding oxen, too, but these didn't get into as much grief as the horses. But every few miles there'd be a wagon stuck in the muskeg, with horses mired to the belly and teamsters shouting and pulling, or unloading the gear in the muck, or bringing other teams to double up. There were some few women and kids, too, sitting in the wagons with the rain dripping off them. We couldn't stop to help or we'd have lost our bunch in the brush. We camped one night at Sealy's stopping house on Horsehead River where they fed us on out-of-season moose meat and fresh oven-biscuits and bottled saskatoons; and to hear Mrs. Sealy giving orders around was to hear the loudest voice you ever heard or ever will. The Indians called her "Almighty Voice," and they weren't lying.

Finally we got to Meadow Lake and then to Crow's ranch on the Beaver River hay flats.

Meadow Lake was just a log-shack village then and the head shogun was a Mr. Clarke who had a store, bought furs, and ran a bunch of cattle along the Beaver, not far from Crow's.

A little further west another rancher—Barnes—ran a pretty good herd of black Angus. He operated a homemade ferry on the Beaver and his place got to be known as Barnes's Crossing.

We spent a few days looking over the Beaver River meadow country. Lee liked it so well that he took a lease on some meadow land and proposed to get some cattle and run a spread of his own. But I didn't like the prospect of all that timber and muskeg—not to mention the flies and mosquitoes and what I was told of the floods that sometimes covered the meadow in haying time; so we parted company and I went south to Arm River to run a cow herd there.

It was a year or two later that Lee wrote me to say that swamp fever (equine infectious anemia) had hit the horses in the north, as well as the disease called strangles, and the bunch we had taken to Crow's had just about all cashed in. He mentioned a little pinto mare that he said was going strong and hadn't taken the sickness. I remembered her well because she was broke and I had ridden her several times when trailing this bunch north, to give Bill a rest. And that reminded me, too, of one of those times.

This pinto cayuse was really small, but quick as a cat. She wasn't a real pinto either, because the colors weren't right and didn't run in broad bands. She was white with a scattering of bluish blotches about a hand's-width wide and disposed evenly. Her eyes were blue and her nose pink—usually pretty scabby from the hot sun.

I'd ridden her most of one day, and that evening (it was somewhere on the sandy land near Langham) we found ourselves alongside a big fenced pasture.

Lee said, "I wonder who owns that land. There's plenty grass there, and we could sure do with a good night's sleep with the bunch safe."

Presently, we came on some shacks and sure enough the fellow living there owned the pasture, and said we could throw the herd inside the fence and camp the night with him.

So we did. He said that just now there was no stock in the pasture, which covered a whole school section.

I had put the little pinto on picket by a green slough, so as to have a wrangle horse for morning.

We didn't get up too early, so while our host was getting breakfast I thought I'd just chase the bunch into the corral opposite the shack.

I was in a hurry, and that's how I came to do a damn fool thing. I didn't bother to saddle the mare, but just bridled her, led her through the pasture gate and mounted. I couldn't see the bunch, but this was rolling country and that didn't bother me.

I thought, well, the bunch will be hanging by the south fence, for it's the way of range horses to fill up and then head for where they came from.

I got to where I could look along the fence, but not a sign of horses. I rode along a ways and darn if the fence wasn't down flat for a hundred yards or more, and it was easy to see where the bunch had crossed into the open.

Right there I made the second blunder. I should have remembered how far horses can go, especially if they start to move at dawn, which is usual. I should have gone back, eaten breakfast, picked up Lee, saddled the pinto and then gone after them.

Instead, I thought they wouldn't be all that far ahead, and since I was already a mile south of the shack, I dug old pinto and loped off on their track. I expected to see them every time I crossed a rise. Pretty soon we got on the trail we'd come. The sun got higher and hotter, and the pinto got sharper on the backbone, and she was hot, too. Presently, I became aware that the part of me that should have been sitting on leather was getting mighty sore!

I found the bunch about nine miles south, watering at a slough. By that time I felt I'd rather go foot slogging, but that wouldn't do or I'd be left miles behind.

I managed to get around the bunch and start them running on the back track, when about half-way I met Lee coming on the high lope. He'd had his breakfast and was grinning all over his face.

"You all right?" he shouted.

"Right as rain," I said. "You keep these nags going and I'll follow along—afoot!" Which I did, while Lee disappeared in the dust, whistling "Yankee Doodle."

By the time I got to the shack he had the bunch corralled and was drinking more coffee. He saw I'd walked up leading the pinto, and said, "Your mare played out or something?" But by then my mouth was too full of bacon to reply.

I begged some vaseline from our good friend, who said *he* didn't know that darn fence was down.

A few days later, when the scabs started to come off, I began to wonder why I'd ever wanted to be a cowboy. My legs sure ached, too—from standing in the stirrups!

Anyway, reading Lee's letter I was glad that the game little mare had survived and was having a fair easy time (as he said) as a kid's school pony.

I've said how range horses always headed for home when they had a chance; and I could tell of a team of grays that got away from a timber man called Ferguson at North Battleford, and landed up five months later on a ranch in the Cypress Hills. However, I'd have to guess how they traveled nearly two hundred miles, crossed two rivers, and avoided being hung up in fences or run into somebody's corral; for I don't know, and my guess could be wrong. So all I can say is that they *did* make it all those miles.

CHAPTER ELEVEN

Roany

1

I was looking after three to four hundred head of cattle at the head of the Arm River in an area of rough country made up of hills and sloughs; one of the best grazing areas I have known. The only drawback was that within a few miles there was unfenced crop lands, so that I had to be with the herd most of the time to keep them from straying all over the place. There was the best part of a township of this grazing land (and that's an area six miles by six miles), and had it been fenced it would have run twice the number.

The cattle had bedded down for noon in the green grass around the shining sloughs; lying comfortably, some blowing softly, others sleeping head to flank, others placidly chewing their cud and staring indifferently at the grassy hills with the big limestone rocks gleaming on their crests.

It was hot and still, and I was thirsty, so after making a circle I turned old Charlie's head for camp two miles away, reckoning to make a pot of tea and get back before the herd left the bed ground. "Camp" was a shack and corral by a spring on a piece of land I had filed on under the Homestead Act.

Just before dropping into the coulee where the shack and the corrals lay, I glanced over my shoulder and saw a cloud of dust approaching from the direction from which I had come.

Could something have stampeded the cattle?

In half a mind to turn back, I saw a point rider loping over the crest of a swell, not a quarter of a mile away. I turned to meet him and recognized Isadore Trottier, a métis cowboy I had known on the Whitemud.

"Hello, Isadore," I shouted; and "'ello, 'ello!" replied the rider.

"What takes you off your range?" I enquired.

"Horses, my fran'," he laughed, showing his white teeth below his black moustache. "*Oui!* Plenty horses—for sell or trade! From mon Oncle François! From Willow Bunch! You got grub, Charlie?"

"Sure," I answered. "Come along. You can turn your bunch in the corral. Let's go open the gate." We slid down the coulee bank, saddles squeaking in the heat.

We opened the big swing gate and then entered the oven-hot shack. I got the stove going and the kettle on.

"Dese sacre flies!" said Isadore, "better we wait outside."

"Did you see my cattle?" I asked as we squatted down against the wall outside to roll our smokes.

"*Oui* for sure! Dose cattle okay. We mighty scary for disturb, but I lead a circle 'way round dem an I don' see one get up. It's pretty hot by damn, an' I don' think dey move."

We rose as, with a swinging of ropes and a mighty swirl of dust, Isadore's three companions, two other Trottiers and Henri LaPlante, pushed the horse herd into the corral—about sixty head. The milling bunch looked like one of today's abstract paintings, for they were all colors, solid and broken. The riders pulled the heavy saddles off their wet steeds, and soon joined us.

The kettle boiled and I made a big pail of strong tea. I had enough salt beef and biscuits for the bunch, and as we lay in the narrow shade of the unpainted shack, we ate and chatted.

Isadore and his boys, it seems, had rounded up the horses on his uncle's place and were going shares all around on what they could make in sales and trade among the new crop of farmers in the Carrot River country.

"Sure, dey on de small side, but dey'll pull a plow," said Isadore; and I knew they would, for these little range horses have more git-up-and-go than most of the larger draft types.

After a little more discussion Isadore turned to me—"You want a cheap pony?" "How much?" I asked.

"You mak' de offer," he replied.

I strolled to the corrals and looked over the bunch. Some rangy mares with foals at their sides. They were long-maned and long-tailed and pretty snorty. I figured they were too old to break, and I didn't need any brood mares. Then maybe twenty good-looking geldings with foretops and tails trimmed—so they'd be halter broken anyway. About the same number of three-year-olds, too young to use yet. A few young mares, flighty-looking but they'd soon settle down, but I don't like riding mares. Half a dozen tired saddle horses that looked as if they must have had a run for it yesterday by the way the sweat runnels whitened their necks and flanks.

And a little cayuse that looked like nothing on earth at first glance. Just nothing.

He was thin and gaunted. He didn't weigh an ounce over seven hundred pounds—if that. No more than fourteen hands at his withers, about which a swarm of flies gathered, and from which a fearful stench reached me. I knew at once that he had a fistula—the worst kind of saddle sore.

I walked around him. He watched me, head up. I noticed his eyes. China eyes they were—walleyes some call them—blue as the sky and big as any Arab's; set well apart with long lashes. There was stamina, fearlessness, and spirit in those eyes.

I noticed his ears—real Arab ears (bless old Coronado!). They were pricked forward. Not too long, almost touching at their tips, and as beautifully curved as twin scimitars.

His neck was short. He was deep in the chest and high in the withers. His back was so short that I knew the skirts of my Riley and McCormick saddle would tickle his pin bones. His mane and tail were of short, fine hair—not too thick and real silky, gleaming like gold in the sun. Not a blemish on his neat legs and pasterns; his hooves small and neat like those of the Spahi horses I had seen in the war—and *they* had been Arabs of Arabs, and just as small as this fellow.

In color he was the pinkest strawberry-ice-cream-roan I ever saw, with a big blaze from foretop to nose, wide enough below the eyes to have given him those China ones (for China eyes—walleyes—must have white around them). And he had a white spot on his off flank big as a baseball, and by that and the turkey-egg speckling inside his hams I guessed that if his ma hadn't been a pinto, some other relative had.

As I walked around "Roany" (as I mentally called him), he turned, keeping his eyes on me. I came up pretty close and he twitched his ears back and forth and blew softly from the depth of his large round nostrils. I liked the looks of him, seeing in my mind's eye an extra one hundred and fifty pounds of flesh on him and that wither fistula healed. I knew I could fix that in two to three weeks.

"Can you catch him with a halter?" I asked. Isadore grinned as if that was a joke and went for his rope. He was making his loop as he climbed back over the corral from the top of which he made a half swing back and then forward. The rope settled nicely over Roany's head, and the little horse stepped up at once and blew at his captor, sending Isadore's black silk scarf to dancing.

"How much you give for heem?" Isadore queried. Well, you could buy a top horse those days for a hundred, a fair mount for fifty, a tired one for thirty and a sore-back for twenty. So I said, "Twenty bucks."

Isadore laughed. "My fran'—why you don' ask I geeve you? Well, we are ole' fran's and I like to geeve you somet'ing—an' for dat grub an' hay, too—so I *geeve* you! An' you can geeve me twenty bucks. Bote I don' *sell* him so cheap you bet!"

To ease his conscience—and mine—I gave him another thirty bucks for a pretty wild little mare that I reckoned might raise some good foals.

The money changed hands, and my friends departed at the high lope, whooping and laughing; their herd strung out nicely with one of the old long-tailed sisters in the lead. They reckoned to camp at Blackstrap Lake that night.

2

As for Roany and the mare, I put them in the branding pen for the time being, and forked them some hay before I rode back to the herd. I found them mostly on their legs and beginning to scatter out as the cool of evening started to fall. All around I heard them tearing the grass, circling the tufts with blue tongues, or making sucking sounds in the soft mud of the sloughs as they pulled up the green grass growing in the shallow water. No sight on earth is quite the same as the sight of cattle feeding on the prairie grasses, tails curled over their backs against the mosquitos; calves still lying in quiet groups; here a bunch working slowly up the side of a swelling down; there a group of three or four, flank to flank, ears forward, gazing at a moving bird, then, fears at rest, lowering their heads once more to the scented grass, so redolent of herbs and flowers. No neat farm crops, no trimmed orchard, no well-mowed garden could ever mean the same to me as red and white cattle feeding on a prairie unchanged by the hand of man since the brown buffalo made *their* trails and *their* wallows, and slaked *their* thirst at the same sloughs or lay in the shade of the same small shrubs of wolf willow and rose briers.

3

Looking back on the many horses I have ridden (and owned) over nearly half a century, there is not one that stands out in my mind like Roany.

Not Vinegar, the Bar C, good as he was; nor Blue Charlie, sure-footed and cow-wise; nor black Joe—rough as a camel but a stayer; nor chestnut Min of the flossy mane, sired by a blue blood from England and always ready to try and kick your head off; nor black

Monte, who hardly gave you time to grab the saddle horn before he was on the lope; nor Trig (acquired in trade from Chilcotin Charlie) who could scuttle down a mountain side like a tumbling creek; no, not one of the brave troop who now graze (I hope) in some grassy horse heaven.

Not one, for size and weight could hold a candle to little Roany. As I found after I had punctured and drained that fistula and turned him out for a six-week vacation on the curly prairie wool. That fistula had been caused by a broken tree saddle. The métis boys aren't particular about such things.

Roany wasn't young—about ten or twelve I'd say, but for over five years we worked together. Yet to the last Roany could only be caught with a rope, like so many of his kind. He just didn't care for oats, and he kept his head to himself, for he didn't understand why in hell a man wanted to put an arm around his neck unless he already had a loop around it.

Never would he eat oats. I'd put a handful or two in his box, but he'd just blow them out with one of his snorts, and go back to munching dry hay. He was the sort of cayuse the Canadian mounted troops took to South Africa, where grain was hard to come by and they had to graze the dry veldt; and no wonder a German cavalry observer in that war wrote to his superiors that those were the best mounts for a mobile war in open country.

I rode him (once) ninety miles in twenty-four hours. I'd off-saddle every two hours to rest for twenty minutes. He'd heave a great big sigh, have a roll, and graze steadily till I was ready to go on.

Never did he lose a trail on the darkest night.

Never did he push at me, nor step on my foot when being saddled. Never did he refuse a steep place or a boggy patch. Never once did he put a foot in a badger hole; and some of the knolls on that range were pocked like the lid of a pepper pot. To feel him change feet in the black dark to avoid a hole was to wonder how God made such an animal.

He could locate cattle by their smell. He could bite the tailbone of a steer that wouldn't turn to suit him. Yet bringing up a small calf, he was like a nursemaid, maybe just giving its behind a gentle shove with his knee.

Night or day, no matter the hurry or the need, he was always ready. Take him out on a dark, stormy night, after he had already done a day's stint, and Roany would step out cheerfully in any direction you turned his face.

And he'd lope easy or walk fast all day—no bone-racking trot, but a rocking chair gait so easy you'd nod off or could roll cigarettes as he ate up the miles. As to driving cattle, he could handle a bunch or a "singleton" better than plenty of young cowboys I've seen.

And you couldn't spoil him. He was as stand-offish as only a good horse can be. He no more cared for my petting than he cared to push me with his nose. Like two good men who think the world of each other and work together for years without showing it outwardly, never interfering with the other's privacy, so Roany and I were a team.

As he got older I gave him more and more free time, for I had plenty of mounts, and finally I gave him to a farmer's children for a school horse. The last time I saw the little fellow he was loping down a dirt trail packing two kids tandem without a saddle. He was sure packing them carefully—they wouldn't have spilled water out of a glass. How they caught him I don't know. Maybe they kept him on a trail rope all the time.

4

I called the little mare Buck, for she was a "sure enough" buckskin of the old-fashioned mustang type. There used to be a lot of them, but I haven't seen a real one for years.

Not that soft creamy color (or "amarillo"), nor yet a blue claybank (or "grulla"—which means "crane-colored"—that sheds out pretty dark and then fades to a bluish-purple with ochre lights); but the rich color of prairie grass in October; ochre, an artist would call it—dark ochre.

Her full mane and tail were jet-black and so were her legs, from the middle joint to the strong, dark hooves.

She had three to four zebra stripes above the joints, while down her back, from between her black-tipped ears to the root of her tail, was a very dark chocolate stripe (like a donkey's), crossed at the withers by a stripe leading down over both shoulders—the "sign of the cross." Her velvet-soft muzzle was of the same dark chocolate.

Her weak point—but only in the matter of looks—was her long sway-back. The same saddle that touched Roany's pin bones didn't come within a foot of hers. She looked as if she could carry two saddles between those high withers and that peaked rump!

I soon got her broke, and she proved a good ride, sure-footed, full of sense, and comfortable, but you sure felt foolish sitting down as if you were between the humps of a Bactrian camel.

She saved me from a nasty mess one dark night. Quite a few homesteaders were coming in (which finally caused me to pull out), and the old trails were being cut off by wire fences and bits of plowing.

On this particular night I was heading for a schoolhouse "hop," following a prairie wagon trail I'd been over only a week before. It was late in the year and overcast, and there was as yet no snow to brighten the ground.

Buck was loping along as free as the wind, and I hadn't a worry, although I couldn't even see her head, let alone the trail.

Then, all at once, whop! She stopped dead. I darn near went over her head.

"Buck, you idiot! What's into you?" I thought, and gave her a touch of the spur, thinking maybe she'd heard a badger or skunk rustle in the grass.

Buck didn't move, but just let out a long snort. So I crawled off and followed up her neck and felt around with one hand. "*Ting!*"—three strands of barbwire, as tight as a fiddle string, right across the trail!

Cursing all nesters I mounted, with a "thank you" to Buck for her sense, and followed that fence around, knowing there was a road allowance going my way somewhere to the left. I finally came to a corner and turned right again, but I knew that the road allowance was fenced on my left as well, and that there was a whopping big slough, a deep one, just ahead.

Pretty soon we came to it—slap across the road allowance. I felt Buck breaking through the reeds at the edge. The water soon deepened and first thing I knew Buck was swimming and breaking cat ice.

It was about one hundred and fifty yards across, and I was glad when I felt the rushes against Buck's flanks again. I hadn't reckoned on wetting her back that night and I was soaked to the waist—and *cold!* I got to a friend's shack. He was a married man and the two were just getting ready to go to the dance themselves. They pushed me into the bedroom with orders to throw out my pants and shirt, which I did.

I could hear the missus laughing as she washed off the mud and weeds. How they got them as dry as they were I don't know; but when they threw them back to me the pants were steamy hot with a real knife-edge crease—something they hadn't had for a year! They looked really smart, so I soon dressed, and after putting Buck in their barn I jumped in the buggy with them. As the schoolhouse was only just down the trail we were not late, for the fiddlers were just tuning up.

This particular "do" was what we called a "box social." It would be advertised as "Ladies bring baskets. Gents, $1.00" (or fifty cents, or whatever).

The idea was that the baskets (or boxes) made up by the ladies were often highly decorated with ribbons and so on, and contained all sorts of edibles. These boxes were bid for just about halfway through the dancing or other entertainment. You picked your box, hoping you had guessed the maker right, for you had the privilege or eating supper (from her box) with her.

This time I bid a dollar on a fancy pink-and-white contraption, but when I reached in my pants pocket for a bill my hand came out empty.

Whereat my Dorcas said, "Mercy me! I set them bills on the warming closet to dry!"

However the M.C. trusted me to pay later and I got my box, plus the girl who'd made it. Only she wasn't the one I *thought* had prettied it up, but a rather severe maiden lady of uncertain age. Oh well. After all, she turned out to be a real good sport and a whole lot of fun. We talked no end, for I wasn't as shy with her as I might have been with someone else. She reminded me a bit of an aunt of mine in the Old Country.

5

Which brings to my mind another box social. We had them once a month all through that long cold winter, meeting alternately in the school or in whatever house was big enough. They were great fun, and this one was a riot—for most of the folks anyway.

The same young couple had invited me to go with them. I turned up a couple of hours before the do, and found they had a visitor. It was a schoolmarm sister of the missus, who had never been in the district before.

Well, the girls cooked it up that I was to go as a girl, a friend of the schoolmarm's who'd come to visit with her. I was supposed to be fresh out from the Old Country.

I had to agree or show the white feather. Being short and slim—and at that time a pink-cheeked twenty-four—they were sure able to fix me up.

The schoolmarm sister had brought a wig (she was keen on theatricals)—a bright red one!

They made me shave twice and take off my military moustache; they creamed and powdered my face; they sprayed me with heliotrope or something.

They made me put on female unmentionables (they were big and roomy in those days), and they stuffed my bosom and my backside. They gave me long stockings, a green dress, and high-heeled shoes— luckily I have a small foot!

Then they pronounced me real elegant and dubbed me Miss Ella Bankhurst (or some such name) straight from London to see the Wild West—"and *don't* you forget—*Ella!*"

Off we went in the sleigh with the harness bells ringing, and me shivering in a woman's coat under a blanket. (Girls *must* be tough!)

The "social" was in quite a large farmhouse on the homestead of a fat and kindly German couple.

Little thinking of the consequences, I allowed myself to be ushered into the bedroom with my girl friends, and introduced to sundry ladies in various stages of dress and undress. I just guess my face was pink! Especially when they oh'd and ah'd over my "fresh English complexion!"

We sat on a big bed while ladies did various things for and to their squealing offspring.

As we waited for the "do" to commence, the good *hausfrau* bustled about seeing that everybody had what they needed. She stooped over me, breathing hard (she'd had garlic for supper!) and whispered loud and hoarse, "Das *pot* iss unter der bed, yet," at which my two companions nearly bust their stays, while I said in my best English, "Thanks awfully!"

Finally we all went into the main room to dance. There were about twice as many young bachelors as girls, so, of course, I had plenty of partners, all pretty well tongue-tied. But one American youth got real chummy; and when he later suggested we go behind the barn (I thought he had a bottle!) I perhaps stupidly consented.

In the porch he said something *real* nice and wanted to kiss me. Which made me back up and say, "Why—you—whippersnapper! I'm a *man!*" Understandably, this took the poor youth rather aback, but he had the good grace to laugh and so did I, and we joked together. But we'd been overheard, and of course that spoilt the whole show, so I took off that darned hot wig and had a good time till daylight.

6

A lot more of the ranch-bred horses I have been discussing landed up in my part of the country. That's how I got Min—a Q mare. A young English homesteader, Jack Reynolds, had bought her and he called her that because, he said, he had an Aunt Min in the Old Country who looked just like the mare for color and shape—or maybe it was the other way around, I forget.

Anyway, Min was a real red chestnut with a flossy mane, pretty tall, and a bit boney, so it wasn't hard to visualize Jack's "jolly old aunt."

She (the mare) had plenty of hot blood in her and was as nervous and restless as a cat before a storm. She was most expert with her heels, and Jack (who was afraid to work her) used to gather some of the young bachelors on a Sunday and lay bets that no one could throw a can at her heels without she'd kick it sky-high, one hoof or both!

I couldn't stand that; to see this fine mare all sweated and trembling with fright, tied up tight in a single stall and unable to get away.

So I traded Jack a big old plow horse for her.

I had a good mate for her, and they were about the fastest team on a buggy I ever saw. The neighbors called them the "two-fourteens'" (Trotting-horse jargon. A mile is two minutes, fourteen seconds.) Only

I had to jump on the buggy seat the second I picked up the lines, or they would be away down the trail.

I did have one nasty smash-up with them. But that was my fault. A neighbor's wife wanted to get to town, twenty-two miles away, in a hurry, so I gave her a lift.

The team was really raising the dust when a jack rabbit crossed the road ahead and made them jump. This lady got scared, screamed, and tried to grab the taunt lines! I tried to fend her off with my elbow but she reached ahead and grabbed *one* line and threw her weight on it. I'd had them well in hand, but that did it. The horses crabbed off at right angles, upsetting the rig in the ditch. The eveners and pole broke, and when I came to the buggy was on top of me, the wheels still turning dolefully in the empty air, the team was only a dust cloud a mile up the trail, and my passenger (unhurt) was standing hands on hips, giving me some plain talk in a broad Yorkshire accent, in which I heard the words "crazy loon" and "taking a risk with yon *wild beasts!*"

I guess we were both sore, but I was the sorest, for I had a bump on my head like an orange. That team ran the remaining eight miles to town, ran right through it, and were eventually found hung up in the corner of a farmer's fence. Luckily, they were unhurt.

As Mr. Finlay, the blacksmith, said, as he hammered out a new buggy "circle" on his anvil, "It don't never do to take another man's wife for a buggy ride—remember that, young fellah!"

7

About the same time I heard of another homesteader who had a mare that had turned outlaw. She was a medium-weight black with a good head, and she packed the −C brand. This fellow had got her at a sale and had tried to break her. But he couldn't do a thing with her, he told me, as she just squalled and kicked. Finally he got in a runaway with her on the disc harrows. All four horses piled up but she kicked herself loose and took off with bits of harness dangling. She had cut her off foreleg on the discs, just above the coronet, and was pouring blood. No one could catch her now (no farmer, that is), and she ran all fall in the neighbors' crops.

Several attempts were made to round her up, but she'd take off at the sight of a rider, and she couldn't be followed for she would jump any fence in the country.

That winter she was rustling out by herself—she wouldn't stick around with a farm bunch—and was having a rough time, as her injured fetlock was swelled up terribly, and it wasn't easy for her to paw.

I noticed her a few times as I rode back and forth, and I could see she was getting thinner all the time. So I went to see her owner and asked what he'd take for her. He laughed and said, "You'd never catch the bitch anyway. I was going to knock her over with my rifle before she gits me into more trouble with the neighbors on account no fence will hold her."

So I offered him ten bucks and guaranteed she'd not trouble him any more. He accepted.

A couple of days later I managed to get close enough in deep snow to rope her. As she was halter broke I had no trouble getting her home.

I put her in the barn and fed her good. I could see she was going to lose that hoof, but hoped she'd grow another, just as a man grows a new thumbnail after a bash with a hammer. But I noticed something else, something that I had suspected. She was in-foal.

Spring was just around the corner, so I kept her hoof well daubed with pine tar, and as soon as the grass greened up I turned her into the pasture.

In a week or two her hoof fell off. She seemed plumb content on three legs, and just grazed and loafed around, but at the sight of a rider she'd make for a hilltop and stand snorting. So whenever I ran in a bunch of saddle stock I'd leave her, and I thought if she ever did get better she'd be a hard one to run in.

She had her foal in June, a dandy little black, and by then her new hoof was showing and she was fattening up and shedding out well and beginning to look pretty.

By fall her hoof had grown out, but it didn't favor her looks. It was like a stump—or a mule's hoof—straight up and down, and heavy looking. I had to catch her and throw her down to trim it. Nevertheless, she hardly limped at all; and pretty soon I was using her for light work. I called her Belle.

But she hadn't forgotten her former owner, as I found out the next
winter when I kept her up with a blaze-faced sorrel, for I knew that
to winter out again would be too hard on her. I used this team to
haul hay and do other winter chores.

One evening I was milking the cow in the barn, and by the light
of the lantern I could see the team's rumps across the alleyway as they
chomped their hay.

It was pretty frosty, and I heard the squeak of a saddle horse on

The club-footed mare

the hard-packed snow outside, and presently a muffled figure pushed the door and came in.

The two horses raised their heads and stopped munching, the way horses do.

The visitor was Belle's former owner, and he began to talk about something in his loud, harsh voice. I heard a snort and a thud and saw Belle almost hit the roof and crowd up to the manager. Her head was turned and I could see her eye burn red in the lantern light.

"What you got here?" shouted my guest. "Why, if it ain't that son-of-a-bitch of a bronco mare!" And he made a step towards her, peering into the gloom cast by his own dark shadow.

I yelled, "Keep away!" and was almost too late, for Belle had lashed out with both hind feet; close enough to make the fellow flinch and whiten under his scruffy whiskers.

Turning, he grabbed a pitchfork, shouting, "I'd kill a bitch like that and enjoy it!"

"Put down that fork!" I said. "That's my horse, not yours." He hesitated and, "Well," I said, "seems like she'd echo that t'other way round!"

But he had already left and I heard him cursing as he mounted and rode on to wherever he was headed.

I went into Belle's stall. She was dripping cold sweat, but lowered her head with all the red murder gone from her big eye, as if to say, "You know, friend—a fellow can only stand *so* much."

8

Most cowboys were real good to their horses; but there was always the odd coward, and a coward is always a bully. It's a sort of law of nature.

I remember driving a bunch of broncs on a long trail with the help of one of that kind. He was big, and he was a good rider, but there it ended. I'll call him Butch, though that wasn't his name.

We were short of saddle stock and it was hot. One night we were able to put the bunch in an old corral by the trail.

Next morning as we were loading our beds on the pack horse I said,

"Wonder if we couldn't catch up a couple of those broncs to give our saddle horses a day off. They shouldn't buck much, for they'll want to follow the bunch."

"Good idee," said Butch.

He took his rope and caught a little mare. Of course she wasn't halter broke, but he snubbed her up and went along the rope to put on a hackamore.

"She looks pretty young," I remarked.

"We'll soon know," he answered; and grabbed her by the lips to look at her front teeth. She didn't like that and jerked her head away.

"You little b—!" he shouted, and hit her hard with his clenched fist right on the soft part of the nose. The little mare, quick as a flash, came up with a front hoof and hit *him* in the mouth, knocking out a couple of teeth.

Butch stamped and swore, but didn't dare hit her again. And at least she knew how old *he* was!

The upshot was we turned her loose because she still had two milk teeth in front.

We caught a couple more and managed to blindfold and saddle them. I opened the corral gate and as the bunch streamed out and luckily headed the right way (it was by a fenced road), we mounted. Butch's nag gave a couple of bucks when he pulled the blindfold, but mine didn't waste time because he wasn't going to be left behind by the bunch he'd run with so long.

We were both hard on the heels of the drag and were thankful they kept up the pace because a running horse doesn't usually buck. The old-stagers we'd been riding, came along behind, keeping out of the dust. We didn't dare stop at noon and made a good many miles before dusk, by which time the bunch began to scatter out to graze.

We two daren't dismount to unsaddle for fear our mounts might jerk away, taking all our gear with them, so we had to undo our takaberries (cinch buckles), then reach forward to unbuckle our throat lashes; and then throw ourselves off, bridle in the left hand and saddle horn in the right. That way we unloaded ourselves and our gear in one sideways slither. The broncs (pretty tired now) trotted a little way, had a good grunting, thumping roll, heaved themselves up, shook off the dust, and started right in to graze. The next day we got to our destination riding our old-stagers again; and we could truthfully tell the fellow that bought the bunch that "them two with the sweat crust" were good saddle stuff that would follow a bunch anywhere!

9

Like horses, cattle can sometimes become outlaws, and these are difficult to handle.

On the range an outlaw steer is an animal that has got in the habit of dodging away from the other cattle during a roundup. At that stage he is called a "bunch-quitter." One or more cowboys could usually head such an animal back, but if they were not successful in about half a mile, he'd have the better of them and lose himself in brush or badlands. The cowboys could, of course, follow him, but this usually resulted in very hard running in bad going. Anyway, the steer, now determined and completely riled up by his dodging and weaving and swimming creeks and climbing around hills, would become very hot and mad. So even if he were overtaken and turned back at last, he could become a total loss, as he might suddenly collapse and die.

So rather than risk that, the cowboys, after a short run, would leave him for next year's gather. Of course, by next year the steer was more than ready for a repetition of his first escape; and he had to be recognized and watched with an eagle eye. One of the cowboys would probably have his lariat ready, and if this steer broke, would get "onto his tail" and rope him. Then with a quick turn of his horse he would "bust" (In busting a steer, if it's caught by the horns, the cowboy flips his rope over the animal's back and turns his horse sideways, which jerks the animal down) the critter, and probably leave him hog-tied for a while.

That usually sobered up the steer, and he'd be glad to stay with the bunch. But if he did manage to escape a second time, he usually became a real outlaw, feeding always on the edge of a bunch, practically alone, and always watchful and ready to take off at the first sight of a horseman.

At this stage the steer was just a nuisance, and the wagon boss would usually give orders for someone to hunt it down with a rifle and shoot it for campmeat.

Such animals are not common in a farm herd, but occasionally there was one who had learned to break through or jump over fences; critters like these were the cause of a lot of trouble.

Farmers were not usually riders; they rarely had a good saddle horse, and were always busy on the land. Therefore, if cattle got into trouble among a standing crop they usually sent some kid to bring them home; perhaps on a clumsy horse, and accompanied by the farm dog.

Incidentally, there is nothing a cowboy hates around cattle as much as a dog. Range cattle will invariably turn on a dog, and this of course upsets the whole herd and scatters them.

Since I grazed cattle from a good many different farmers (themselves short of pasture), I naturally got *all* the bad ones they did not want at home. So I had several steers and even cows who through bad handling and ill-kept fences had become very close to being outlaws.

10

Among the "spooky" cattle in my herd of about four hundred and fifty head was a rangy two-year-old steer that I called "Blue," from his color, which showed him to be a crossbred Shorthorn-Angus.

I soon realized that Blue had spent his short life living in crops in summer and on haystacks in winter for no wire fence would hold him, and on the drive to summer quarters he had been in and out of fences all along the way.

I soon noticed his love for grazing alone, and often saw him standing on a knoll sniffing the breeze this way and that. Twice I headed him back after he had started off by himself at a fast, purposeful walk, in the direction of a few acres of fenced crop about two miles away.

I guessed his intention each time and hustled him back to the bunch with a few pretty good cuts of my stock whip, at the same time shouting "Blue" (with a few additions) at the top of my lungs.

On one of these occasions I was riding Ruby, a small blood mare from Nebraska. Ruby always kept right up against any critter she was handling, and she would get her teeth into the tailbone of a reluctant one and hang on like a bulldog.

Well, Blue got to have a pretty good respect for me, and for Ruby, too.

When we brought the cattle each night into the corral, old Blue would usually try to sneak off, but I was watching for that, and had warned Fred, my helper, to do the same; so on whatever side the steer looked for a break, he was usually headed back with shouts of "Blue" and the crack of a whip.

Blue soon got foxy the other way; I mean that he took to keeping well in the middle of the herd when being driven, and hardly showing himself.

I suppose we had gradually relaxed our lookout, for one day, circle-riding the bunch towards evening, I missed Blue. I counted all the "markers," that is, old lead cows and distinctly marked steers and heifers, and found them all; but no Blue.

Telling Fred to start the rest off for the corral, I made a big circle which brought me close to the piece of crop I have mentioned. It was the middle of August and crops had been ripening fast, but I was surprised to find this ten-acre patch had already been cut and stooked, for we had not heard a binder working. True, the wind had blown strongly from the southwest for days, and this field was to the northeast.

The fence looked pretty shabby, and some of the stooks were almost up against it; real bait for cattle, for they could put their heads between the wires and get a taste. One of the most irritating things a farmer can do is plow and seed right up to a fence, for the binder will throw the sheaves right against it, and the stookers rarely bothered to carry them back to a safe distance.

Oxen, proverbially, have tremendous strength in their necks, and if a cattle beast once has reason to stick his head through a fence he doesn't have to push very hard before he loosens the wire staples and pushes the rest of himself through. A few farmers, and *all* ranchers, would rather leave a rod or two of land uncultivated along a fence line; for this greatly reduces what we call "fence crawling."

It is not a question of "rights." Of course a man has a *right* to use all his land; but it's sometimes better to forget rights and do the sensible thing that will keep the peace.

Thus thinking, I rode a bit further along the fence and found several posts broken and the wire down, and worse still, cattle tracks and fresh manure.

I raised my eyes to the field beyond, and horror of horrors, I saw that several stooks had been pushed over and a lot of sheaves lay scattered with the heads chewed off.

I rode all over the field but found no cattle, but what I did find was the fence down on the *north* side, and tracks that showed me that not only a few head of cattle but also a big-footed horse and a dog had passed through. The dung was fresh, barely an hour or so old.

At once I realized that the farmer had driven my cattle to the pound.

11

Now, I must explain that in this municipality, herd law was in force. The few newly arrived settlers—mostly Scandinavians by way of Minnesota—were good farmers, neat farmers, but they did not like horned stock or people who kept horned stock, whom they thought lazy if not shiftless. Apart from a few placid milch cows, they kept none. True, there were a few old-timers around, stockmen who had used the grass for years. But the new settlers were dedicated wheat farmers, and they now formed a majority.

So they asked the municipal authorities for herd law, which meant no cattle could run at large without a herder who would be responsible; for under this law a farmer was not even obliged to fence his crop. It was the stock that must be fenced in or herded—one or the other. The only reason I had a considerable range at my disposal was that the area I grazed had so far been by-passed by homesteaders because it was so hilly and rough. (But that would not be for long.)

Naturally the farmers won the issue when it came to a vote, and following their success a pound was set up in each division of the municipality, and any cattle or horses found "astray," from May to November, could by law be rounded up and impounded, whether they had done any damage or not. The owner had to be notified by the poundkeeper, and could take his stock home on payment of so much a head for driving them to pound, and so much for their keep. If these fees were not paid within thirty days the law provided that the stock could be sold by auction, the various fees and indemnities paid to the poundkeeper, and any balance then went to the original owner.

It is not hard to see how such a system could be abused by anyone with a grudge against his neighbor, for it has actually happened that an unscrupulous man has taken cattle out of a pasture by night and driven them to pound on the charge that the said cattle were in *his* crop.

In this case I knew the poundkeeper to be the father of the young man who owned the crop where Blue and his companions had strayed.

The father was a sort of elder of the Lutheran sect to which these folk belonged. They had a small church of their own, and rarely neighbored with the old-time Canadians around.

The son did not live on his homestead—where the field in question was—but under the provisions of the Act was allowed to live with his father for whom he chiefly worked.

I guessed at once that the son had ridden over that day to stook his crop, followed by his dog. About late afternoon he must have finished the job and about the same time the cattle broke in. While he could have driven the cattle out the way they came, he preferred to "dog" them through the fence nearest his home and so to the pound.

12

It was almost dark by the time I had finished my look-about, so I headed for the ranch, but not before I had jotted down with a pencil stub the number of sheaves that the cattle had spoiled.

According to my reckoning, and the price of wheat, the damage came to about ten dollars for the grain and five for the fence.

I calculated as my pony loped along that there would be charges of a dollar a head for driving the cattle to pound—plus another dollar a day for their feed while in the poundkeeper's care.

When I got back Fred was frying eggs for supper. He pointed to a rather grubby note lying on the table, and turned back to his culinary duties.

The note said: "I have taken in 7 head of your cattles today. My son drove them here. They have been eating his crop on section 12 and have been raising hell. It looks like they been in many days. The charges against you is—

> 7 head cattles to pound $1.00 each is $7.00.
> To damage to crop is $100.00.
> To feeding hay and water to seven cattles at $1.00 each for day is $7.00. It will cost you that each day till you come.
>> Total is with dam. to fence at $10.00 for repair is $124.00.
>> Come right away."

This was followed by the poundkeeper's signature. I read it out to Fred, who grinned. He had evidently already got it by word of mouth from the kid who had brought the note. (Which is another irritation. These fellows hardly ever come face to face with you. They always send a kid.)

I said, "Fred, you'll have to take out the herd in the morning. I'm riding early to the pound. Say—did we have that Blue steer this morning, and yesterday, and the day before?"

"We sure did," said Fred, "and I'll swear to it if need be."

I left early and got to the poundkeeper's place about eight o'clock. The farmer and his son were both cutting wheat about half a mile south of the buildings, which were out of sight behind a rise of ground. It was hilly country even here.

I rode up to the farmer, a tall grizzled man. I did not know him well, for these people were not very friendly and kept themselves apart, speaking only Norwegian when at home.

When I rode up the farmer reluctantly stopped his horses, and waved to his son, who was on the leading binder, to go on.

I told him I would count the stock and see what condition they were in and that they actually were mine. If all was satisfactory I would take them home. But I added that the damage claim was excessive and that I would contest it.

No, he said, if I wanted to take the stock I would have to pay the full damage and contest the charges later, quoting from a tattered copy of the *Pound Act* which he took from the hip pocket of his overalls.

Seeing he would not budge I said all right, and rode on to the pound,

The blue steer's bunch in the oatfield

which he told me was in the corner of the pasture behind the barn. I located it—a very poorly made corral of only four strands of wire, with no apparent facilities for water, and no signs of feed on the ground.

It was completely empty, and I soon saw why.

The rotten fence was flat on the ground on one side, and cattle tracks led north to a slough where it was quite evident that the beasts had slaked their thirst.

Several tufts of blue-gray hair on the wire pointed to Blue as having been the leader of the escape exercise.

Trust old Blue, I thought, you'd be a good headache for any pound-keeper!

When I did find the bunch—Blue and six yearlings—they were having a party in a field of stooked oats, to which they had gained access by the simple expedient of pushing down the pasture fence, at the cost of a few more tufts of hair.

Looking back I could not see the farmhouse, and realized that the farmer's wife must have thought that the cattle were still safe behind the barn; all owing again to the rolling nature of the land.

I waited for a while and rolled a smoke as Ruby herself began to worry a fallen sheaf with great gusto. I rather enjoyed the zeal with which the steers plundered their breakfast stooks, knocking over far more than they plucked at. All this was no longer my responsibility and so I was in no frantic hurry, and anyway I had no authority to do anything about my own cattle until the poundkeeper gave me permission. They had apparently not been on the loose too long, but since they had not been fed (as they should have been), they were hungry and had already done several times more damage to the oats than they had done yesterday to the wheat.

13

Finally, I rode back at an easy pace to where the farmer was. Again he stopped his horses at my approach. Again the lead binder continued on its way, dropping its sheaves like eggs.

"Vell?" said the poundkeeper.

"Well?" said I. "There are no cattle in the pound."

"You mean you let dem oudt?" he shouted.

"No," I said. "There are no cattle in the pound. But I *did* find a bunch in an oat field beyond your pasture. One blue steer—a big fellow—and six yearlings. They sure are knocking over the stooks."

"Vat!" he shouted. "Vy you didn' drive dem oudt? Eh? To let dem do so damage."

"I couldn't," I said.

"Vy not?" he shot back.

"Because it's none of my business if some cattle are in a crop."

"But dey are *your* cattles," he yelled.

"If they are mine, they must be the ones you impounded yesterday," I explained, "and according to that Act—if you'll read it— you'll find I have no authority whatsoever to drive or do anything else with cattle that are in your legal possession as poundkeeper.

"It's up to you to fix the pound—it'll only take a day unless you have to go to town for decent posts—and then it's your job to drive those cattle in and haul a barrel of water and some feed to them."

The man almost exploded. You could see he was torn two ways. Pound fees were "money for jam," but the harvest season is short, and this was a perfect day for cutting.

After a short struggle he groaned and said in a short of wheedling way, "*Mein Gott,* I can't do that. I have to cut de grain yet—it could rain tomorrow. And Villy is in de same fix, ve can't hold up de harvest for yust a few cattles!"

"You—or rather Willy—didn't mind holding up harvest to drive cattle yesterday," I replied, "and while you are looking over your Pound Act you'll see that you, and only you, are responsible for the safe keeping of stock brought to you. And furthermore," I went on remorselessly, "for feed and water and general care of the same, as well as any damage done."

"Look," said the poundkeeper, "please look, mister, I got no saddle horse, and dose cattles got to be moved. That's *my* oat crop and I'll need it all. You and your cattles are a big troubles. Take dem avay so gvick you can, and yust pay to me damage—no pound fee."

About then I could hear a dog barking away back by the buildings. We looked that way and saw his wife hurrying across the stubble.

I think we both had the same thought, for the poundkeeper repeated, "By gollys take dem damn cattles avay—I said only damage do I charge, to Villy's veat crop."

"Now listen to me for a change," I said. "In the first place, the Act doesn't *oblige* you to take the stock to pound, so long as you know the owner. You know me well enough, and you also know I'd be willing to pay any damage.

"Your son could have driven those cattle to my place, or even turned them my way and I would have taken charge of them. Then we could have agreed on the damage. But you, you old skinflint, were going to squeeze every dollar you could. I've been running this herd for three years, and this is the first damage claim I've had.

"In the second place, your son used a dog on those cattle and that caused half the knocked-over stooks. In the third place, you did not provide what the Pound Act calls "an adequate corral or other place of detention"—in fact, you were too tight to spend a dollar to make a dollar.

"In the fourth place, you did not water those cattle as you are obliged to." Here he interrupted with, "I vas going to vater them"—but I cut him short. "Going to but didn't does not fulfill the regulations, mister. And it's a hot dry August day.

"And in the fifth place, they are now out of your control and even if I give you the money for damages and fees, you cannot deliver those cattle to me. If your claim had been reasonable in the first place, I'd have paid it and taken the stock. Twenty bucks would have been plenty. And furthermore, you'll pay for any animal that dies of bloat from feeding on those green oats."

At this juncture his wife arrived breathless. A short conversation in sing-song Norwegian ensued, during which I could see, out of the corner of my eye, the seven culprits trotting south through the wheat crop, gamboling playfully among the sheaves, with a black-and-white dog in pursuit.

Evidently the wife had gone to see that the cattle were safe, and finding them in the oat stooks had set the dog on them.

The conversation between the two came to an abrupt end as Willy drove his binder towards us, shouting, "Papa, papa! Look! Already the cattles go!"

Turing, the poundkeeper saw what I had seen. He nearly jumped on his hat!

"Yah!" he shouted, "take dem home, take dem home—I don't charge noting! Take dem (some Norse expletives) home!"

"Okay," I said, "just cancel this note you sent to my place yesterday. Here's a pencil."

He scrawled across it, and I wheeled Ruby and soon had the cattle on the homeward trail.

That was the last trouble I had with pounds. And I don't want to damn all poundkeepers. Most of them were decent enough chaps, but it was not a popular job, so often it was a fellow who only wanted easy money who applied for it.

Part IV: BIG DRY

A young métis cowboy

CHAPTER TWELVE

Left afoot

1

Of course, in running this herd I had to have some property rights or I might have met with opposition. My little shack and barn and corral was on a quarter section I had homesteaded. There was a good spring on it. The adjoining quarter I held under lease, so I fenced the two (making a pasture of 320 acres) as a wrangle field for my horses. But after three years I realized that it would not be long before I would have to give up this little ranch in the hills. Already some of my lease (I had four sections leased from the government) had been cancelled for settlement, and more and more land was being homesteaded. The last fairly big cattleman, with headquarters far to the east, had recently killed himself on a hill while driving a new Ford Model-T stink-wagon, which he should never have bought. He, who had ridden wild horses all his days, could not control the contraption, which had turned upside down, with him underneath.

He had just been winding up his ranch operations anyway; and I decided to do the same. I formally abandoned the homestead so as to keep my settlers rights, and sold most of my gear. As far as the shack and corral were concerned, well, the hooves went with the hide.

In the meantime, I had managed to get a job as Provincial Game Guardian, to be stationed in the Battleford district. So that fall, as soon as they were well fleshed, I sold out what cattle I had of my own, having already delivered the "boarders" to their various owners.

Herd law did not yet apply in winter, so I turned my seven or eight saddle horses on the range, but got a friend, Archie Laird, to take care of my favorite, Ruby, the daughter of the mare of the same name I have mentioned. Old Ruby had been pensioned off with friends.

I then went to Battleford to arrange quarters and other details. Once settled, I returned in early spring with my saddle, to take my horses north, as I should have work for them.

I had no trouble with Ruby, now a five-year-old. My neighbor had ridden her a few times and she was gentle. Her mother, the little Nebraska mare, had been mated to a standard-bred horse, and young Ruby looked more like a good driver than a saddle horse, yet she was, nevertheless, a good ride.

I scoured the country in vain for the rest of my saddle stock, until one day I ran head-on into Ponto, a buckskin claybank. He was pounding down the trail pulling a buggy!

I stopped the outfit, and making sure the horse *was* Ponto, I asked the driver, a butcher whom I knew, where he had got him.

"Oh," he said, "from So-and-so. Yes, I knew he had been yours, but So-and-so said you'd left the country and given him some horses for a debt you owed. I hope there is no trouble?"

"I think it looks like a lot of trouble," I replied. "I know So-and-so as well as you do, and we both know him for a saddle tramp and a crook. I certainly never owed him anything, or did I give him any horses. Did he give you a bill of sale?"

"No," said the butcher, slowly, "I guess I should have asked. I took it for granted . . ."

"Well, if you take fellows like So-and-so for granted, you'll soon go broke," I replied, "and I'll have to trouble you for that horse."

"Just because I didn't happen to tell So-and-so where I was going and for how long, he must have made a rotten guess on the basis that the wicked flee where no man pursueth."

"Pardon?" said the butcher.

"Never mind," I said. "But that horse is mine, he's branded Q, I have a bill of sale for him from Charlie Wilson. So I want him back."

The butcher, with bad grace, agreed; but added that he had to get home and would I pick up Ponto at his place next day? Naturally I couldn't leave him afoot.

That evening I had a talk with my friend. He agreed with me that So-and-so must have taken all my horses—as well be hung for a sheep as a goat—and that probably the rest of the nags were away to hell and gone by now and would hardly be worth wasting money to try to locate.

He also added that So-and-so had not been seen since January, and that he also would likely be hard to find. In fact, a good many people would like to see him!

I must explain that the expression "left the country" always carried the hint that whoever had done so was in trouble with the sheriff or the police, or was dodging a debt. To have it said of you was hard to live down.

That is why it is wise to tell all and sundry where you are going and why, to stop the rumors that are otherwise bound to fly around in a mixed settlement. Actually, of course, it was So-and-so who had "left the country"—with my horses!

Well, it was no use worrying.

I went to the butcher's next day, but he said, in wheedling tones, "Say, mister, I paid fifty bucks cash for that critter. I hate to lose that much. Want to be a sport and match who takes him?" I agreed.

He won the toss, but he was decent enough to give me twenty bucks, which I had a place for. I gave him a bill of sale on Ponto.

Next morning I started northwest on Ruby, cutting all the country I could.

2

Soon I had reason to be pretty mad with young Ruby. I'd stopped on the Dundurn Indian Reserve for lunch. It was all unfenced open country.

I put Ruby on picket and had eaten the sandwiches out of my saddlebags when, looking up, I noticed Ruby was not where I had left her, but a hundred yards further south, heading for home.

I saw that she had broken her picket rope somehow, and was dragging about twenty feet of it.

Hastily I grabbed my bridle—I had picketed her with a bowline on her neck—and walked towards her. She walked on. I stepped faster. So did she, looking back at me. Then she stopped to pick at some grass and I gained. I got just to where I could reach the end of the trailing rope, and made a lunge for it.

But the little devil just gave a flick of her head and twitched it away so that I came up with only a handful of grass.

She did this for the next three miles, and it was hot, as it sometimes is in April. At least twenty times I stooped for that rope's end, and each time she jerked it away and kept a-going.

I was pretty mad when I finally caught her, after she had got hung up in a fence. If it hadn't been for that blessed obstruction, I might have had to walk all the way back to where she had wintered.

Hot and sweating, I bridled her and mounted, thankful there had been no witnesses to the sight of a cowboy afoot.

After that I always checked any old picket rope to make sure no mice had been at it!

3

Arriving west of Saskatoon, I stayed at a friend's farm on the edge of the Pike Lake sand hills. He offered me an unbroken mare, slightly lame and about seven years old; I could have her for the taking, he said, for she was too wild to work, and anyway he was short of pasture and thinking of getting a tractor.

She looked pretty good, and I reckoned she'd raise some colts, so I accepted her with thanks.

Next day, with the mare in tow, I made it to Spinny Hill on the old Battleford trail that runs along the foot of the Eagle Hills south of the north branch of the Saskatchewan.

Here I stopped with a small rancher who took a liking to the mare. He wanted a few more brood mares, he said, after I told him she was about seven years old and not broke. So he offered to trade me another saddle horse for her. He showed me a bay gelding in the barn that looked somewhat familiar, even in the gloom of the log building.

When he led the animal out, I'll be darned if it wasn't an unbranded horse I had acquired the year before, one I called "Sonny." So I put a few questions to the man. It seems the same Mr. So-and-so had pulled into his place in March with several horses in tow, tied head and tail. He'd traded Sonny for a big work horse, aged.

The man told me further that he believed So-and-so had gone southwest, because a friend of his in Loverna (on the Alberta border) had said in the course of a letter that a horse trader had been at the livery barn there, and he described a big man on a sorrel horse that sure sounded like So-and-so.

Well, I didn't want to say too much to this man, but I liked Sonny and was glad to see him, so I traded the mare, and from there on spelled my two mounts off, riding Ruby in the morning and Sonny in the afternoon.

As soon as I got to Battleford I wrote to the police at Loverna. I didn't get much satisfaction. The Royal North West Mounted Police had recently become the Royal Canadian Mounted Police, and they were only handling excise work and so on, while other police work was in charge of the newly formed Saskatchewan Provincial Police.* Of course they had no jurisdiction outside of their own province, which made it a bit awkward, as my man had evidently crossed into Alberta.

However, I did find out that two horses traded to the liveryman in Loverna fitted the description of two of mine, but unfortunately this

---

*The Saskatchewan Provincial Police were a short-lived force, for within a few years the R.C.M.P. again took over the policing of the Province. A good many ex-S.P.P. joined that force.

liveryman had sold out a month before and was believed to be at Grande Prairie, Alberta.

The police boys likewise told me that it would be an expensive job to track the horses down, and the cost would hardly be worthwhile at the present price of horses.

So I let the whole thing drop. I reckoned my horses would likely be spoilt by now anyway.

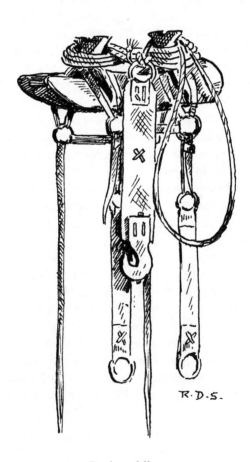

Pack saddle

4

From Battleford I made my first patrol to the west as a "game guardian," by way of Triple Lakes—the route used by Colonel Otter in 1885—and across Poundmaker's Reserve to the west side of Little Pine.

It was a beautiful ride. From Battleford to Triple Lakes, the old trail winds through flowery sand hills and you have the Battle River to your right with the wooden escarpment of its north bank hiding the uplands. I thought of that fateful first day of May in 1885 when, on little pretext, Colonel Otter and his four hundred men marched over this trail to confront Chief Poundmaker's almost starving and impoverished band of Cree.

Poundmaker's camp was just near where Cutknife Creek joins the Battle River. Otter gave the Cree no time to parley but attacked, only to be driven back. His losses would have been great had it not been for the chief himself, who by the strength of his personality held his people back and allowed Otter to withdraw his forces back to Battleford. "What a pity," I thought, as I surveyed today's peaceful scene, the only reminder of that bloody day being the Government Cairn in memory of the "Battle of Cutknife Hill." From where I rode, I could see it etched against the evening sky. "What a pity Otter had not sent a wagon train of grub. He would then have had no difficulty arresting those three malcontents who were responsible for the murder of Payne and Fremont. A pound of beef would have been worth more than a bandolier of cartridges."

I wanted to raise a foal from Ruby, so I knew I would need another horse, and there were several horse ranchers out in that hilly country through which the Battle River runs.

The chief of these was A. D. Smith whose ranch was in the rolling sand hills south of Maidstone; the other was Fail Murphey, tucked in between Little Pine's Reserve and the south bank of the river.

I got to Murphey's first. He greeted me with great hospitality and showed me quite a few horses. One striking mare was solid black with a white mane and tail. She was a beautiful animal, but I don't really like riding mares, and anyway she was far *too* striking, that is to say, far too easily recognized at a distance for my sort of work, which would often involve a certain element of surprise.

Fail showed me a most ingenious way of breaking horses to harness.

In the center of a strong corral, round in shape and built of heavy logs, he had set a strong post so engaged into another big post, that was set into the ground about five feet, that it would revolve like a wheel on an axle.

From this upright another stout pole stuck out laterally about three and a half feet from the ground. It was about twelve feet long. Its outer end terminated in an axle upon which was a single wagon wheel. Just inside the wheel was a pair of shafts, complete with a whippletree, much as one would find on a buggy, but very much stouter.

Fail would harness a young horse, put him in the shafts, and fasten the traces. The horse's halter was joined to the upright post by a rope long enough for him to face directly forward, but short enough to prevent him from plunging outwards to his right (or wheel) side.

Just behind the shafts was attached an old plow seat. On this Fail would sit, holding the lines from the animal's bridle.

It didn't matter if the horse reared and plunged, or jumped forward or backed up, or even threw himself; he was unable to run away and unable to break anything, as the heavy wheel would adapt itself to whatever moves the colt made.

In fact, Fail could, if he wished, dismount and leave the horse to more or less break himself and get used to the noise of the trace chains and the rumbling of the wheel; and it would soon be going quite happily in a circle.

The accompanying sketch will illustrate the contraption, which certainly impressed me after seeing so many wagons kicked to bits and harness broken in the taming down of the wild ones.

The genial Irishman told me that he was afraid he would soon be out of business as his range was being settled. What's more, in the rough country along the hills the poplar and willow scrub was taking over, since the Indian Department was stopping the Indians from setting spring fires—which they had done for years to make more grass for their ponies.

I did buy a fine little horse called "Billy" from Fail. This horse was hot-blooded and very keen. He was to carry me for hundreds of miles

Fail's breaking ring

in the next few years and got to know every trail, every livery barn, every spring, bog hole, and creek in my district, which covered a large piece of country, from near Prince Albert to the Alberta border and north into the Meadow Lake forest.

By night or day I could depend on him. A prick of an ear this way or that, a soft blow from his nostrils or a whinny, would tell me who and what was about on a dark night when beaver poachers might be operating. A man is never alone with a good horse, for his four-legged partner is much more than a machine to take him from A to B. His horse is also the rider's watchdog, his companion, his gager of water depth and swiftness of current, his foreteller of weather, his pathfinder in storms.

I have carried a live bear cub on Billy, a cub that whimpered and scratched. I have packed bloody hides on him, joints of moose, bags of illegal fish, and once an injured man who could not sit in the saddle, and Billy, the perfect gentleman, never did worse than blow disapproval through his well-bred and fastidious nostrils.

Like so many of my top horses, he was retired in a few years, for he was nine years old when I got him. He became a children's pet; and the last time I saw this gallant and handsome animal, he was standing in a barnyard eating oats from the hand of a three-year-old girl, while three other children sat on his back without benefit of saddle or bridle. And this was the horse that had been called "That Devil" by a poacher who had threatened to drag me from the saddle, but had not dared to approach those bared teeth to do so.

Today I treasure a water-color sketch I made of Billy, standing on the banks of the Saskatchewan—his glossy bay coat matching the fall shrubbery.

5

Sonny did not suit me for patrol work. He was strictly a cow pony, and he hated the heavy bush. So I sold him and began to look around for another.

A friend of mine told me that he knew a fellow, an old-timer called Southwick, who was raising some real good saddle stock, and advised me to try him. He said Southwick farmed about fifty miles west, just north of the Battle River.

He said, "You can't miss the place. It's the only two-story white house with a big log barn on the road south from Lashburn."

I located the Southwick's place about noon, a big white house and a big red-roofed barn above the river breaks. I rode in by the big gate, dismounted, and knocked at the door. Mrs. Southwick came to the door. I announced myself and asked for "the boss."

"He's at the barn," she said, and pointed. Mr. Southwick was feeding a team, but he put down the hay fork and came to meet me.

"Ain't you the game warden?" he said. I admitted that I was.

"Yes," he went on, "I knew you by your hoss. I raised him as a colt and sold him to Nelson at Battleford, and he told me he'd sold it again to the game warden. Well, what can I do for you?"

I told him.

"Well, young fellow," he said, "I've got two or three colts you could pick from. Fours and fives and maybe a six-year-old. You'll have to break him yourself. I'm asking a hundred and seventy-five each. But say, it's most dinner time, so put your hoss in and I'll slip to the house and tell the missus you'll be here to dinner. I'm as hungry as a coyote, and we can go through the colts after. They're down the pasture about a mile—'long the river." He went to the house.

I unsaddled Billy and fed him hay—he was too warm for grain, and I didn't want to founder him. A foundered horse goes stiff in the front legs and is useless. Then I followed him.

Mrs. Southwick indicated washbowl and towel, and I noticed that the table was not set in the kitchen, which is usual on a weekday for farmfolk.

They led the way to the dining room, complete with one of the then popular "congoleum" rugs; heavy furniture, lace curtains, and big oval photographs of an elder generation. Beneath one was a black coffin plate bearing a name and the words "Mother at rest" in gilt. Evidently, I was company.

The meal was delicious, and the homemade bread showed a master's—or should I say mistress'—hand. Conversation was stilted. Southwick was not a talking man, although he was a very good eating one.

Mrs. Southwick asked a few polite questions. I knew her at once for a type which, while the salt of the earth, was just so narrow that you felt they saw sin in all around them. The kind that mentions certain animals by such deceptive names as Gentlemen cows and Big horses, and only when mention is unavoidable. I felt sure she kept away from the barnyard, and would not even venture there for the hens' eggs. When the meal was finished, I felt for tobacco and papers.

"May I smoke, Mrs. Southwick?" I asked in my best company tones.

"Indeed you may not!" she replied. "*None* of my family have ever contaminated themselves with tobacco. Besides, it smokes up the curtains—"

I thought Mr. Southwick choked, but he recovered quickly. "And furthermore, young man," she went on, "I hope you do not carry spiritous liquors with you. *None* of my family even know the taste of rum. My father and my grandfather devoted themselves to the cause of temperance and fought Vice and Sin to their lives' end."

She looked at me severely. She was a handsome woman and her white hair gleamed like silver. I assured her I did not carry any rum with me and added I was sure her parents were to be congratulated. Could I, however, smoke on the porch? She bowed gracious consent, and I sat on the porch steps with my smoke.

Presently Mr. Southwick came out. "Let's go see them colts." We went to the barn. He saddled his horse and I mine. He said, "Before we go I must show you the sire of them colts." He led me to the gloomy back quarters of the barn, where, in a roomy box stall a fine stallion whinnied softly.

Mr. Southwick let down the bar and we entered. He told me the horse's pedigree with some pride. I patted the animal's neck and talked to him. Mr. Southwick had disappeared. "Hello?" I said in surprise. "Coming up!" was the reply.

I turned. Just rising from his knees in the far corner was Mr. Southwick. In one hand he held a bottle, in the other a plug of chewing tobacco. He came across the straw to me. He pulled the cork from the bottle, took a good swig, passed the palm of his hand over the bottle's neck to render it sanitary, and held it toward me. "Don't be afraid of it, young feller," he said, "it's White Horse—best in the West."

I took a swig, complied with the local sanitary precautions, and passed it back. He took another and offered the bottle again. "Enough for me, thanks," said I.

"Okay," said he, "have a chaw?" offering me the plug of black MacDonald with the tin heart still embedded in its side.

"I'd rather smoke," I said, "but I'll wait till we get outside."

He held a pawkish finger to his nose, and, "Beware of fire," he said, "hell or otherwise, hah!" He replaced his booty in a hollowed out log.

We mounted and he steered me across a field to the pasture gate; not a word was said.

At the gate, being the younger, I dismounted and held the barb-wire-and-post contraption to one side for him.

As he rode by he checked his horse slightly and, stooping over the saddle horn, he spoke huskily in my ear, "Young fellow—remember; what the wimminfolk don't know don't hurt them." With a sly wink he clucked to his horse.

We looked over the colts and I chose one. We made a deal right there, but I got the animal for a hundred and fifty dollars—perhaps he forgot that he had said a hundred and seventy-five—or perhaps the whiskey had mellowed him.

As I said good-by I could not forbear one question.

"Mr. Southwick," I said, "what about the smell when you go in the house?"

He grinned, "Oh that? . . . horse medicine!"

6

Buck, as I called this horse, soon broke out to be a good mount. But he did have one weakness. He simply hated dogs. Billy had never paid much heed to barking curs, but Buck would fret and dance and get all in a sweat if attacked, and I had a job to hold him.

There was one particular area of settlement north and east of Battleford where most of the people were newcomers from the Ukraine. At that time we usually called these people Galicians or Ruthenians in a loose sort of way, because that is how they spoke of themselves. I rarely heard one say he was Ukrainian. "Me Galician," they'd say. I think the reason they rarely (if ever) used the word Ukrainian was that their country had been so chopped up between Russia, Poland, and Austria-Hungary, that they had, in part, lost their sense of identity.

Some called themselves Polacks, but most were from the Austrian Empire (at least in the settlement I speak of) and so used the terms I have mentioned. A great many were from what they called the Hora

Caparthe, which would be that area in the Carpathians where Poland, Russia, and Austria met.

Many have told me they came from "Bukovina-Austria," but "Ruthenian" seemed their favorite title for themselves. For some reason few cared to call themselves Russian. However, since the downfall of the Austrian Empire in 1918 and of Poland in the 1940s all these people in Canada seem to have agreed on being Ukrainian, as we rarely hear them mention Bukovina or Ruthenia today.

These folk lived in small shacks of log and mud, scattered more or less through the bush. These shacks were mostly on higher ground and pretty well back from the trail, which gave them a wide view. I soon found out why.

A great number of them made home-brew whiskey from barley or potatoes, which was strictly against the law. So they liked to be able to see everyone who passed, in order to spot policemen on the prowl. They also kept their wire gates shut so as to delay any stranger. In addition, these folk all kept regular packs of the most vicious curs. These brutes would always leave the yard with a loud chorus of yips and barks at the sight of anyone passing, and then chase after him like wolves! This would give the occupants of the shack time to dispose of any illicit spirits.

I remember once working my way through such a pack to make an enquiry at a house.

Several sheep-skinned men sat around smoking impassively, and not one got up to call the dogs off.

I made my enquiry and was answered in broken English. "Dogs no *dobra!*" I said, "no good," but no one seemed to notice the remarks.

Then I saw a kerchiefed figure poking about in the little vegetable garden at the back. It was well fenced with tightly woven willows, a typical feature of such dwelling places. I could barely see over the fence, but I could tell it was an old woman, and she appeared to be burying something.

The men began to rise and move together in a leisurely sort of way, evidently attempting to block my view. I suddenly realized what was up and said, more or less as a joke, "You can tell granny she doesn't need to waste the booze—I'm not looking for that."

At this the men stared at me, and then began to move forward, looking black as thunder. Then, as if my words had finally penetrated, they all paused and broke into rich, deep Russian laughter, slapping their thighs! I joined in the laugh and we parted on good terms.

It was a fact that some old grandfather or mother was always involved in any seizures and arrests made by the police. It was one of them who always came forward and took the blame; the idea being that such an old creature could not do much farm work and could best be spared as a sacrifice for the sins of the whole family, and a trip to the "pen" at Prince Albert didn't seem to bother the victims. I have heard an ancient crone tell of the warm quarters and good food provided for free by the kind authorities!

7

But I was writing about dogs and must return to them.

As I said, Buck would go almost loco when a pack of dogs raced around him, nipping at his heels, jumping at his head, and barking, yelping, and growling alternately. I tried shouting at them, cursing at them and jumping Buck into their midst, but all to no avail. It only made them attack more vigorously.

So next time I took that particular trail I carried a good fourteen-foot stock whip, and I laid about with that, slashing them over the backs with the popping lash.

That was even worse; they went almost mad and kept up the attack for a good quarter of a mile, with Buck in a blue funk.

This, I thought, is plumb nonsense! I'd have to try something else. If curses and whip-lashing didn't work, thought I, what about coaxing?

I made a point of riding that way once more a few days later. I slowed up when the pack made their usual rush, controlling Buck as well as I could. Then I gently slapped my leg and began to call in dulcet tones, "*Good* dogs! Nice dogs! Come on then, Bowser! Come on, pup! Come and be petted! Here—(whistle)—etc.! *Dobra, dobra!*" (wishing I knew Russian for "I love you").

The effect was electric! Those curs stopped in their tracks looking very foolishly from one to another; then, with dropped hackles and with their tails between their legs, they one by one slunk back to the house, looking completely crestfallen and ashamed.

It had worked. When they thought I wanted to steal them with soft words, oh no, they were not going to be caught that way!

From then on I had no trouble with dogs. I could send the worst growling brute off simply by asking him if I could pat his bootiful fur, then!

I must add that these people eventually did well, for they were hard workers. They sent their children to school, and the younger generation gave up the traditional still tending in favor of business and professional jobs, and if one of these has a dog today, it's probably a pedigreed animal of a known breed!

CHAPTER THIRTEEN

Me and the horses

1

With the 1930s the Big Dry—which had more or less tried its wings in the twenties—really got into action with day after day of hot winds and blowing dust.

With the general drought came the beginning of the end of the horse bonanza.

Not that the ranchers fully realized it. "Shucks," they said, "when it starts to rain again the farmers'll need horses. There's lots more land to break, and them new-fangled stink-things won't be no good in brush and rough country."

Many settlers in the north were now experimenting with brushcutters made by local blacksmiths out of heavy railroad steel. It took eight head of horses to pull one of those things, and the users began to think that big powerful tractors (the "stink-things") would look good.

In the meantime, the southern ranges were becoming so dry they'd scarce feed a grasshopper, and in order to save breeding stock, both horses and cattle, the ranchers went to the Provincial Government for aid.

The Department of Agriculture appointed several men to assist the stockmen in finding feed and range in the northern settlements for both cattle and horses. The man for this job in my district was Hooper Coles, who is still living not very far from me.

In some cases municipalities were prepared to lease out areas of rough grazing, such as the sand hills north of Battle River. These were used mostly for cattle, the cowmen obtaining winter feed by way of what straw and grain they could get from farmers.

In other cases, established settlers who had plenty of pasture and hay took so many head of horses to graze. Horses, of course, could stay out all the year provided there was plenty of grass; although the odd weak one was supposed to be cared for in the barnyard.

These settlers did not necessarily own all the land used by the horses. Most of it was unoccupied C.P.R. or Crown lands, which lay adjacent to their private holdings. On these vacant lands they turned the horses and were responsible for them, at a price paid by the government.

Certainly a few farmers in the south were still able to hang on to a team and even a milch cow or two, by dint of mowing the dense growth of Russian thistle that had taken over so much of the scoured and drifted land that now lay uncropped. And a blessing in disguise that prickly weed proved, for in those years it was the only thing that held together what was left of the topsoil. It was not the best of feed, but it kept a few scarecrows on their feet.

The picture was better in north-central Saskatchewan where there was still some grass, some big hay sloughs, and plenty of brushland in which coarse grass and vetches flourished. Most of the farmers and stockmen here had some slough hay as well as strawstacks. My district was, on the whole, a paradise compared to the plains in the south. A good many people came trekking up with bands of horses, and it was Mr. Coles's job to make arrangements for them, as well as to make periodic visits to see how the stock was faring. Since our districts practically coincided, I met him quite often on my rounds, usually driving a pretty good team.

Among those older settlers who took horses from the south were the Waldron boys from north of Lashburn. They were surrounded by several sections of "wild" land in the rugged hills around Pike's Peak, on the other side of which the artist Gus Kenderdine had his ranch. These hills grew a dense crop of prairie wool, interspersed with quite heavy poplar on the north slopes, and there were also plenty of deep sloughs full of water.

Farther west was Vivian Foster who also took some horses. Quite a lot of stock was taken care of around Battle River, where the Reid boys boarded a cattleman from Swift Current who'd brought up about two hundred cattle to run in the sand hills on the north side of that river. There was a good lot of straw on the Lilydale flats (on the south side) at that time.

Near Freemont was another stretch of sloughs and grass hills near Toby Nollet's ranch (he was later minister of agriculture in Douglas' government). A French-Canadian fellow called Phygim Quillette (if I've got his name right) had a place there; he was a wild, happy cowboy character, and he ran a bunch of south country stuff for a while; as did the Eaton boys at Red Pheasant, who ran their bunch on the Indian reserve. There were plenty more, especially across the river at Onion Lake and around Fort Pitt.

2

One die-hard horseman of the independent sort was Bill Greathouse, and his story could be repeated over and over by swapping names—all but the ending perhaps.

There was Bill McRae down at Egg Lake—but that would be rambling far-afield, and I'll get back to Greathouse.

Bill had owned a horse ranch at Sounding Lake, Alberta, when the Dry hit; so, lacking the only two things he needed—grass and water—he saddled a horse, packed his turkey on another, rounded up his two hundred-odd horses, and headed north and east by stages, allowing them to scatter out whenever he found a little grass. It sure hurt those old-timers who'd known grassland from Manitoba to the Rockies to have to hunt for grazing like a dog looking for a lost bone. Some people boasted how for twenty-odd years they had turned the grass wrong side down; but not men like Bill. *They* would rather boast that in spite of all temptation to make a dollar, they'd never done *that*.

At night he would try to find a fenced road allowance where he could camp to the south (or west) of his bunch so as to hold them from turning back.

In this slow way Bill came in about a year to the Maidstone district. And now this once well-to-do rancher had become a herder as nomadic as any Mongolian of the Steppes.

I often ran into him on my patrols. Sometimes in the sand hills, sometimes along the Saskatchewan River bank, or along Cooper Creek in the Eagle Hills. If I saw a scattering of horses on a piece of unfenced land, I knew I should soon spot a thin spiral of smoke rising from some slough or creek side; and there would be Bill's saddled horse grazing along with the little pack mare that carried his bed.

Bill would be squatting or lying, eating some cold grub, or perhaps hunkered over his little chip-fire with a baking-powder bannock browning in the little frying pan that always hung from his pack and clanked against the smoked-up tea pail that completed his cooking gear.

In summer he slept out at all times with not so much as a tent, just his blankets and tarp.

Bill himself was a big grizzled man in his sixties; a bachelor by long preference whose only love was horses. His clothes were darned and patched; and I often saw a shirt or a pair of socks drying on the bushes, so I knew he kept clean.

Anyone not knowing him might have taken him for a hobo; but his good fawn Stetson, bright neckerchief, neat riding boots, and silver

inlaid spurs, together with his assured manner and total lack of sub-
servience or air of inferiority soon gave the lie to any assumption that
he was a foot tramp—though saddle tramp he might have been, and
that means several things, not all of them degrading.

He rode a good center-fire saddle on a visalia tree made by a famous
saddlery firm—Hambley and Company of Pendleton, Oregon, and his
bit was a costly Crockett—silver inlaid and hand-forged. His headstall
was a braided work of art, and from his Navajo saddle blanket to his
coiled riata, Bill's outfit would be called tops from the Rio Grande
to the Peace River.

Bill had never worked for anyone but himself since he left his dad's
ranch in Idaho; and although he could have had a stockman's job
anytime, he'd have scorned an offer. He was a range man, and he'd
take the ups and downs without altering his philosophy of "be be-
holden to no man."

Nothing could shake Bill's conviction that "hosses would come
back." So, although he was often offered a fair price (for those times)
for a saddle horse or a team, he'd always turn the offer down. "What?"
he'd say, "fifty bucks for that there blaze-face? Why, he's worth a
hundred fifty! Take or leave, that's my price."

I only once knew him sell a horse, and that was to get some salt
and canned beef at a little store. And the fellow who bought it only
did so because he was afraid Bill would starve; and Bill wouldn't take
a loan he couldn't repay.

He must have had at least fifty head of promising geldings that had
never even been halter broke. Some of these were seven to eight years
old, and they should have been put to work at five. They were just
getting old on idle time, and each year they'd be harder to handle.
He had a couple of studs with the bunch, so naturally the increase
more than made up for any old ones that might winter-kill each year.

Some of the settlers got to complaining about Bill wandering around
with "them no-good hay-burners," adding "there ought to be a law";
but old Bill, when he heard the complaints, just quietly moved on.

Finally, he crossed the river and ran his bunch along the southern
boundary of the Meadow Lake Forest Reserve; mostly around Birch
Lake and Midnight Lake and west to the Turtle River.

In winter he would sometimes shack up with a 'breed or bachelor white man, but with the first breath of spring he would desert mankind and it would be "me and the hosses" again.

He never grumbled, nor was he talkative, but I knew he pined for the high plains and the purple horizons, the broken buttes, and the tang of sagebrush; and being among the wet marshes and somber spruce groves of the north depressed him in mind and body.

But for the horses' sakes he stayed with them until one cold November day he was found stiff and dead in his bedroll—with only one of his precious nags no longer with the bunch; the one he had betrayed that he might eat.

Bill Greathouse was one of a type. One of many who thought that the good horse days would go on forever; who thought that the stench of gasoline was but a passing evil, who thought the new bonanza was on the horizon—if he could hang on for a few more years. But he was to find it elsewhere than in this ever-changing world.

He was the dedicated kind that some people may laugh at. He knew, as many of us know, that no twelve-foot combine, no turbojet motor, no wonder of technology could ever inspire its operator to such self-sacrifice and devotion as an owner would feel for his horses.

The coroner's verdict was "Death by misadventure," and when he was buried by the municipal authorities, there was a sum of money found on Bill, with a note under the rubber band reading, "Kase i kick the bukett fix thngs up."

CHAPTER FOURTEEN

Settlers pulling for the north

1

About the last thing a lot of south-country horses did was pull the groaning wagons of those who left the denuded prairies for the greener northland. With their poplar groves and lakes, the northern fringes of the parkland prairies looked inviting, even though the brush soon became heavy and merged into the evergreen forests of the timber belt.

Although the best homesteads had been already taken, there were still many to be had along the Carrot River, in the Nipawin and White Fox districts, along the Beaver River and around Loon Lake in Saskatchewan, as well as at Elk Point, and at High Prairie and Dawson Creek in the Peace Country.

Families by the hundreds left southern Saskatchewan and Alberta as the drought increased. Hitching their thin horses to wagons and buggies and hayracks, loading high their household goods, they set out onto the roads to join the stream of trekkers whose goal was the "Green Belt," or "On to Peace River or Bust."

They had only two choices. To move and try to save their only possessions; or stay and starve. The world-wide depression that coincided with the Big Dry did not allow for a welfare state—something which most of these people would have felt uneasy about, anyway, for it was an age in which self-help and self-respect might be a man's only capital.

Few looked back at the weathered, unpainted buildings; to the little house where they had laid on the hot nights listening to the gritty sound of what had been good field dirt pattering like rain on the windows.

The raggedy children kicked up the dust with their bare feet. Father sat on the wagon seat looking into the bleak distance with that far-away gaze of the hopeful pioneer. Mother knitted and fretted over her precious things. Or sometimes she "walked a ways" with the children, or picked pretty dry-land flowers like golden rod or blazing star in the same vague way as she picked at her thoughts. But then she realized with a pang that water was scarce and her vases packed, and so dropped the wilting blooms in the dust.

2

The best the horses could do was only a few miles each day, then camp had to be made, and the beasts would stumble among the dirt drifts of the roadside, or around the edge of some slough where willows and sparse grass tufts might give them a bite; or perhaps, nearing the green belt, go to gnawing on the bark of such straggly poplars as had survived.

Then into harness again, the wagon wheels making a moaning sound, time kept by the slip-slap of unshod hooves, as the heartbreakingly slow procession again dragged itself north.

Only the sound of children's voices enlivened the dust-bedevilled exodus. The older people faced what they had to in tight-lipped, gray-faced silence, hardly caring to look at each other; the men almost afraid to say a word of comfort to their women for fear of starting a tear which they could not bear to see, perhaps thinking, "This was the girl I loved and promised to provide for."

But the children were on an adventure, and in all that parched land the only bloom was on their cheeks, the only music was in their voices, the only moisture was the dew of youth upon their brows.

Yet the hearts of all began to lighten as more and more poplar groves came in view, or perhaps a small lake, fringed with lush grass. The sight of ducks on the water, the sound of mud hens calling or of pipits caroling overhead was a balm that soothed the anxious thoughts and even brought a smile.

The groves were at least green, except where grasshoppers had passed in their hungry, heartless thousands. The water might be foul smelling and stagnant, but at least it was water, which would remove the dust from their clothes and cool their wind-cracked cheeks.

And in the shelter of the trees, the hot, dry winds would drop to a pattering breeze, restful to tired bodies. There would be brittle twigs for cooking, and after the meal would be a chance to rest.

Looking from her sleeping children to her dozing man, the mother could take a little heart and perhaps, even hum a few bars of a hymn they had sung together—how long ago?—in the parlor of the big house at Weyburn or Kerrobert.

And the man would think sleepily, "Only another hundred miles and them nags can fill up and git that bad blood out of them." That thin blood that was the best that Russian thistle and dry weeds could make in the land where hay and oats were now no more than words.

"And Rosie, the cow, could be bred, and that would lead to a little herd again, and the kids could have milk and there'd be butter for the bread . . ." and he would drop off to sleep with the memory of golden pats in his mouth; while Rosie tore at the slough grass in company with the one young heifer they had saved. Yes, and they had saved one steer, too, but he could not have walked north. So after his meat had been shared with a neighbor, the rest of him now lay, cut-up, in the brine barrel; pretty lean meat at that, but at least it made soup.

3

If such a family, having started out in early summer, reached their homestead before freeze-up, they were lucky. They might have time to mow a little wild hay, and put up a shack of crooked logs; painfully and with many a blemish, for the wheat farmers of the bald prairies had never made much use of axes except perhaps to split kindling wood. Water might be scarce, in which case it would have to be hauled in barrels, but at least there would be plenty in winter when they would be able to melt snow for themselves and their beasts.

Those who did not "make it" before the big cold would be in harder shape. But people who are hard-up are always generous, and many a family would be invited to "double up" with a more fortunate one that had perhaps "located" the previous year. But this was thought little of. The women and children shared the bed, while the menfolk slept on the floor, and meals had to be eaten in relays. But it was just part of the life and up to twelve people in a cabin 12' x 15' was not uncommon.

There was little feed in some places, even in the green belt, for the Big Dry was spreading, and some families found themselves little better off. But at least there was some rough grazing in the bush, and there was poplar bark and willow brouse, and wild rose berries to be plucked (which are strong feed), and the thin cattle and thinner horses now had a fifty-fifty chance—and perhaps it would rain next spring.

Only one team of horses to a household could be "kept up" for winter on hay that was perhaps a mixture of tall wheat grasses and pea vine, cut with a scythe—clumsily—among the trees and stumps. All the others had to take their chances, rustling for what they could find under the snow, and before spring broke the howling of wolves might be heard all too often. And when the snow melted a few scattered bones gleaming white among the willow clumps would be all that was left of faithful Glen or Dick or Bessie.

So weak were most of the horses—that first winter—that sometimes they could not even make the trip to the little log-shack "town" for necessities; and the man of the house would prefer to make the trip on foot; to count out—reluctantly—the few crumpled bills or the dwindling silver coins for what small groceries he could afford.

Meanwhile, at home, his wife stitched the carefully saved and carefully washed flour sacks as fast as they were emptied. Children's underwear or nightwear, even her own petticoats, took shape under her busy fingers, and she felt thankful to the Five Roses and the Ogilvie mills for having put up their products in good cotton bags; for "yard stuff" was dear.

Next year would be better, she would tell herself. She and the children could make a garden and pick wild berries for bottling, while Father broke a little land until fall. Then he could leave his plow for the rifle and perhaps get them a moose, or at least a deer.

And all the time the few precious horses would be their only power. They must nurture them, work them short hours, even go without if need be. Father had already put his pipe aside, for the money that his tobacco would cost would buy a few oat sheaves from some more fortunate and older-established neighbor. And yet, thought they, how lucky they were to have horses rather than a tractor, for gasoline was cash—and there was no cash and no way to earn it, for the times bore as hard on the townspeople and the old-time big farmers as it did on the newcomers.

Those gallant horses! Mere racks of bones, scarred from the un-accustomed brush, the "poverty lines" deeply incised on their once glossy haunches.

At the words "git up there" they would push into their collars and lean forward until their weight started the wagon wheels arolling, and step out—clip clop—hesitating at rough places.

Or, swaying a little, but still game, drive in the rusty plow with a tearing sound that might have come from their own hearts, while slowly—oh so slowly—a furrow began to turn and fall, to make a dark ribbon behind the hunched plowman, at which he would glance over his shoulder with the first trace of a smile around his grim mouth.

It was hard. It was slow. Dead slow when willow clumps barred the way, and the man had to hack at the tough purple roots with his ax. In the bigger clumps those roots were interlocked like fat serpents, and they yielded grudgingly, rebounding like living things at every blow.

Dead slow when heavy sod underlaid by softer soil let the share drive too deep. Dead slow when the sun was hot in the breathless bushlands, when mosquitoes gathered like a gray dust cloud, to settle on the beasts' wet necks and flanks.

Dead slow, too, because two hours in the cool of early morning and two hours in the afternoon was all the horses could take.

Between whiles there would be harness to mend, for the years and the drought had taken their toll on equipment, too, and half-rotted or brittle-dry leather could take only so much strain among the stubborn stumps. And there were plowshares to be laid. The man who had brought an anvil and knew how to use the blacksmith's hammer was lucky. Everyone else had to come for him to have their shares beaten-out in exchange, perhaps, for a few eggs or some cabbages—or, perhaps, for nothing; for nothing can give nothing.

4

However, of those horses that survived, many did finally flesh up from the better grazing, and some mares did have foals, for nature is generous.

And the colts grew up lusty and strong, as did the children, and by the time of the Big Betrayal—when tractors finally took over—a healthy horse population had developed; many of which would never fulfill their true destiny, but would land up at the Edmonton Horse Cannery, or be turned out to idleness in the bush.

All this I saw and, in a sense, was part of, and my admiration for man's four-legged partner increased more and more.

I know that in today's technocratic society there is many a man in a sumptous office, many a woman in a carpeted and centrally heated home, whose fondest memories are of those faithful and beloved horses that had shared their parents' famine years, that had lightened their parents' poverty, and that had been their own childhood companions.

Bessie and Brownie, Dick and Silver, Ben and Blackie—they are not, could not be, forgotten.

They took the trail of scarceness, they hauled the logs for home, they plowed the good land and drew the sheaves to the barn. Their ordure went on the garden and sprouted into beets and carrots and corn, they packed the moose meat from the dark, silent bush, they

went for the doctor as fast as lean muscles would take them, and they
hauled the sleigh loads of laughing boys and girls and old folk to the
schoolhouse dance, where for a short time the battle of life could be
forgotten by the oldsters; where the young, by the alchemy of music,
lights, and laughter, could make for themselves a brief fairy tale to
be relived on the sleepy homeward road.

It was in 1935 that the "sleeping sickness" struck. It was called
"equine enciphalomyelitis," but it affected quite a few people as well
as many horses. Some recovered and the Animal Health Branch of
the Saskatchewan Department of Agriculture tackled the research work
in spite of almost non-existent funds. But in 1938 it broke out worse
than ever, causing the loss of 15,000 horses. These outbreaks certainly
hastened the change from horses to tractors for farm and ranch work.

5

In the middle thirties I found myself at a Ranger Station on the
Carrot River, sixty miles west of The Pas, and almost due south of
Cumberland House. This was a land of heavy forest, quite unsettled
on the Saskatchewan side, and although I kept a saddle horse and
a team—which were also pack horses—I used them only on the Pasquia
Mountain, most of my patrols being by canoe or dog team, according
to the season.

Yet even here I did one job of "cowboying" which brought back
a touch of the old life. A man called Mitchell (a good Scots name!)
ran about sixty head of good Angus cattle on the meadows fifteen miles
west of the town of The Pas, which was my nearest mailing point. These
cattle lived mostly in the bush all summer. Mitchell, though a good
cattleman, had not adopted western ways, and had no saddle horse.

He put up plenty of hay on the meadows, which he fed to the cattle
during winter. Every morning he called them to the feed by voice,
and they would come one by one from their beds in the willows. He
did the same in summer, whenever he took salt blocks to them, and
so, in short, if for any reason he wanted to check them over, this was
his way of gathering them.

But Mitchell sold the whole bunch to the proprietor of one of the hotels in The Pas. This man had once ranched in the Moose Jaw district, and still felt a little lost without cattle. So he had obtained a lease on some land near Reserve, south of the Hudson Bay railway line, which he now proposed to stock with cattle well acclimatized to the north and accustomed to bushland grazing.

Bruce, the hotel man, also had some good saddle horses; and being anxious to get these cattle moved, he asked me to lend him a hand. He said; "It will take a couple of good cowboys to drive those beggars into the stockyards at The Pas, so's I can ship them on the railway down to Reserve. You know, those critters have never seen a man on a horse, and they have never been driven. Mitchell says they'll come to him if he calls, but I'm sure they wouldn't follow him, at least not 'way off their home range. And none of the breeds and Indians 'round here have ever had anything to do with driving cattle—nor any of those lumberjacks that work for the mill."

I agreed, thinking the department would hardly object to my doing a job "beyond the bounds of duty," seeing it was a weekend and I hadn't even had a Sunday off for months.

So I saddled Jack, my big, useful bay, and met Bruce by appointment. He was mounted on a fine sorrel, which he said was used to the bush. Mitchell had the cattle gathered around a salt block on the open meadow by The Pas trail. Sure enough, we managed to herd that bunch east to about the limit of their range, and then the fun began.

6

I won't describe the brush-popping that followed, except to say that by some miracle and after being almost unhorsed a dozen times by the spreading limbs of spruce, we finally got the cattle together, but only by the expedient of roping one of the old lead cows and tying her to a tree (where she almost choked herself). She formed a rallying point for the rest, who stood in a circle staring at her as she struggled and bawled. All we lost was one spooky little heifer that swam the river and eventually landed up back at Mitchell's.

Without giving the herd time to rest, we loosed the cow, and started off again, pushing them pretty hard along the dirt trail, giving them no chance to break off.

Our horses were pretty well played-out when we were met by a lad bringing two more of Bruce's horses. Quickly we changed saddles, turned over our sweated mounts to the lad, and pushed on. Soon we left the heaviest bush behind and were crossing the wide open meadow with its big hay stacks which everyone who has been to The Pas must know. That gave us a lot more room to maneuver.

We relaxed a little and grinned at each other, and I guess we did look a pair of tramps. It was a hot September day, and our faces were streaked with sweat, all mixed with blood from the many scratches that the wiry brush had inflicted. The toes of our boots were about scuffed to pieces on the trees (we had no tapederos) and our knees sadly bumped. Bruce's jacket had been well-nigh torn from his back, one eye was closed from the bash of a springy sapling, and his horse had a spruce twig stuck in one ear which made him shake his head until I reached out and removed it. I was not in much better state, having lost my hat and the lariat strap from my saddle.

We managed to cross the bridge at the Pasquia River, near the breed settlement we called Moccasin Flats, and then came to the edge of The Pas itself.

"We'll head 'em up along the railway fence," said Bruce, "that way they'll turn easy into the stockyards. I told the section men to have a gate open and watch for us, so's they can stand beyond the gate and give 'em a boost in."

Alas, the best laid plans . . .

The cattle followed the fence in good order, the elder cows stepping out in the lead. But just before they reached the stockyard gate we saw the lead cow jump off to the left—the bush side—her tail straight up. Then came a chorus of barks and savage howls, mixed with the high-pitched bellowing of frightened cattle, and within seconds the whole bunch was milling madly, splitting into groups, *sauve qui peut*. In seconds they had disappeared into the heavy bush, closely engaged by about a dozen gaunt sleigh dogs!

The brutes had come from goodness knows where—probably from Moccasin Flats—and must have been just scrounging around. We cursed, we spurred, we beat at the dogs with the heavy hondas of our ropes, all to no purpose, for the whole caboodle—cattle and dogs—went whichever way they chose in a regular stampede.

Two or three squaws and an old buck Indian who were passing, stopped to see the fun, and they grinned broadly at the white man's predicament. We tried to work our way through the heavy timber and brush, but it was slow work, and as the bellows, the yells, the howls, and the crashing of branches faded into a sort of uncanny silence, Bruce called to me, "Well, that's that. Let's go up town and have a drink!"

I left the North shortly after that, but Bruce wrote me to say that all the cattle landed back at Mitchell's, and that the two of them got them to The Pas after the snow was deep, by baiting them along behind a load of hay! Which is how it should have been planned in the first place, of course. But then neither we nor the dogs would have had all that fun!

Looking for a way

Part V: ON THE BENCH

Looking for stock on the bench

CHAPTER FIFTEEN

Winter feed ground

1

When I left the North, it was to be posted to the West Block of the Cypress Hills with headquarters at Battle Creek.

It was good to be back once more on my early range, and to find that many of my old acquaintances were still in the saddle, though somewhat aging and getting ready to turn their holdings over to a younger generation. I had been younger than most of them, but I was now older than their sons and daughters who were now running the ranches and raising their own sons and daughters.

The previous ranger had used his own horses and had taken them with him, so I was once more in need of two good mounts. With this in mind I called on Walter Boyd of the Six Mile ranch, which lay at the foot of the hill at the east boundary of the Forest Reserve. To reach this ranch it was necessary to ascend the steep hill just east of the Ranger Station, then cross the high bench to the wide valley of the Six Mile (called the "Gap"), below the pine-clad slopes of which lay Boyd's holdings.

The word "bench" may not be familiar to all my readers, so I should explain that this is western parlance for plateau. This particular high plateau, or bench, extends for many miles as the roof-tree of the Cypress Hills, although frequently broken by the heads of the coulees that carry the snow water in spring to swell the numerous creeks. The bench extends some sixty miles east and west; the greater part lies in Saskatchewan and the rest—west of Battle Creek—in Alberta. This part is usually spoken of as the "West Bench."

The bench itself is almost flat and mainly open grassland, much beset with the small bushes we call buckbrush, but properly known as shrubby cinquefoil. Many cattle graze here in summer, and some hay is cut. The view from this high, windswept plain is magnificent. You can see south 'way into Montana, and north almost to the South Saskatchewan River.

2

Arriving at Boyd's, I was greeted with the usual *"Put your horse in!"* in a voice accustomed to shouting against the wind.

"Well," he said, when I'd told him my errand, "there aren't too many good saddle hosses for sale right now. Most of us just raise what horses we need for ourselves, and if a horse is a *good* horse, then he's not for sale, anyway. I know the Mounted Police find it hard to get replacements."

This didn't sound encouraging, and I said so.

"Tell you what," Boyd went on. "How about I lend you old Darky till you get time to look around? He's old and he's a bit stiff, but he knows the country and you can sure depend on him. He's out on the range now, but I'll pick him up next week and you can have a look at him. It won't cost you nothing, for I'd never sell him nor let him out for rent. He was my first real top horse. He's in good shape, too, for I don't use him much any more."

I agreed to this thankfully, and the next week I rode him over the bench to the Ranger Station.

Within a week we had a horse roundup. My job as ranger was to tally all stock brought in or taken out of the reserve, which was fenced and contained close on a township.

The weather was good for early winter, with a chinook blowing from the southwest day after day, and with temperatures up to the sixties. After the wet and chilly north it was wonderful to be able to ride in ordinary gear in early December; fine to see the haze of golden dust as we gathered bunch after bunch of nags during the short days. So fine and autumnal was the weather that we actually heard an elk bugling, although the hunting season was long over.

It was on this roundup that I first met "Goldie" McCallum of the P.F.R.A., the government organization which was then well into its good work of rehabilitating the dried-out country by digging stock-watering dams and seeding abandoned land to grass.

Goldie was staying with George Naismith who had a big ranch just north of the hills, and who ran a big herd of horses. George was a great horseman—one of the best—but even he had come somewhat under the spell of mechanization, without realizing that by doing so he was helping to make his own good horses out-of-date.

I remember one day seeing him talking to some other big-hatted ranchers on the sidewalks of Maple Creek. It was haying time, and George was holding forth about the merits and convenience of a new power mower he had bought, powered of course by a tractor. "Yeh!" he was saying, "I can cut as much hay with that as with two horse mowers."

Well it happened that just before that I had been talking to some farmers who were themselves getting ready for the haying season, and they had asked me if I had seen Mr. Naismith, as they wanted to buy some horses for mowing. I said, "Yes, I think he's somewhere around," and left them for other business. And it also so happened that as I listened to George's enthusiastic comments about his new machine, three of these farmers strode up.

Being polite and not wishing to interrupt the speaker, they stood quietly to one side till they had an opportunity to speak. They were unnoticed by George, but for their part they drank in every word he said. Finally, George did notice them. "Anything you fellows want?" he asked the farmers.

"No," said one, "we was just putting in time," and off they strolled in the direction of the International Harvester Company's dealer!

3

Right after the roundup the weather changed its mind. The wind switched to the northwest and it "snowed and blowed" for three days.

The bench was under a foot and a half of snow, while the heads of the narrow coulees were plugged from bank to bank. In good daylight you could tell where the coulees were by the tops of the straggly pines, which became shorter and shorter as the coulees played out on the bench. But at night it was a different story, and for your horse to stumble into one could be bad, for he would sink into anything up to ten feet of soft snow.

As soon as the storm died down I started across the bench for Boyd's, for I had to get my reports posted, and he usually took the mail to Maple Creek on his weekly trips by motor car, as the trail through "the Gap" was good.

It was cold, and there was still enough wind to make a bit of a "ground blizzard" as the snow scudded along. The journey was of the steady plug-plug kind, which anyone who has ridden in deepish snow will remember as tiring, slow, and monotonous.

I stayed at Boyd's for supper, and it was suggested I stay overnight, but I wanted to get home, for they had brought my mail, and I felt I should get to work on it. I felt sure I could make it, I said, and declined.

"Oh sure," said Boyd, "old Darky knows the bench like his own stable. He'll take you."

I said goodnight and bridled Darky. He didn't seem too keen, but riding up the Six-Mile coulee with the dark pines on either side, I could see the trail pretty well. But as soon as I came out on the open bench it was a very different story. Not wind or snow, but something worse—a real thick woolly bench fog in which I couldn't even see Darky's head.

There was a Forestry telephone line linking Battle Creek with the Six-Mile and by luck I could hear the wire drumming overhead in the frosty fog. I thought for a second that I could see a pole, and putting out my mittened hand I could feel it. Darky stepped straight on till I passed a second pole, and then a third. Good, I thought, all the old horse has to do is keep on along the line and we'll get home easy.

Then, somehow, there were no more poles, nor could I hear the humming of the wire any more. I could have sworn that Darky hadn't swerved to right or left. All I could do now was sit tight and leave it to him. He stepped along quite confidently and I thought, "a blessing on a wise old horse who knows his way without seeing it."

That seven miles across the bench seemed like twenty before at last I felt we were going downhill. This should be Battle Creek and the Ranger Station could not be far. After a quarter of a mile, however, I began to feel uneasy. This hill seemed too steep; and then all at once we were in heavy timber, the pine branches brushing against my shoulders. Something was wrong, for the west slope of Battle Creek valley was open grassland with only a few straggling poplar groves.

"Damn you, Darky," I muttered, "where in hell are you taking me?"

Darky just plugged along, but gradually began to lengthen his stride, and as we suddenly broke from the timber onto level ground, I saw a light ahead. "Darn you," I said again, "where have you taken me?"

It couldn't be the Ranger Station, surely, unless we had come a real roundabout way.

We were getting closer to the light when all at once a large building loomed up and I heard a muffled nicker. Darky turned the corner of the building, stopped, heaved a big sigh, and turned his head around to nuzzle my foot, saying as plain as day, "Here we are, boss, you can dismount."

Just then a flood of light came from the house from which the light had glimmered. A man stood in the open door, and shouted, "*Put your horse in!*"

It was Walter Boyd.

He came out with a stable lantern, by the light of which I could see we were at his stable door.

"Thought you'd be back." He grinned. "Old Darky has played that trick before. I didn't want you to start out, for I reckoned there'd be a real old fog, but when you were so determined I says to myself, 'This fellah must have forgot what the hills are like, and it'll be a good thing for him to see he's not all that smart!'

"I knew dang well Darky 'ud make a big circle and bring you home by the back way—that's why I kept the lamp lit!"

4

It was some years before this that "Dad" Gaff had divided his ranch holdings between his son and his daughter and retired from active work.

Dad had come to Saskatchewan in the early days from the Nebraska sand hills, driving his cattle and horse herds overland. His household goods occupied several wagons, and a surrey drawn by two horses brought his wife and family. His son, Bub, was then only fifteen, and the year after they settled in the Cypress Hills, he was sent back to Nebraska on horseback to trail up another troop of brood mares. Many of them had foals, including his favorite saddle pony, which he wanted to ride back.

This caused him some embarrassment for, in his own words, "Whenever I left the bunch to graze outside a town, so's I could ride in to get a change of grub at an eatin' house, as sure as shootin' I'd meet a bunch of gals, and that darn foal would git in front to stop my pony, and then start to take some refreshment, smackin' its lips and drooling. Then the gals would laugh and giggle and I'd feel myself getting red in the face. I used to try to kick that darn little critter away with one foot and spur the mare into a lope with the other, but she'd give a whicker and he'd answer and run in front agin."

(There is a similar story in B. M. Bower's *Chip of the Flying U,* and Bub always swore that this episode was based on his ride from Nebraska; for Dad had met the author when she was gathering material for her book.)

Anyway, when he came to retire, Dad's folks persuaded him that he should return to his home state rather than tough it out any longer in Canada. From then on the story of his doings have become history, losing little in the telling. The most popular version is as follows:

Dad said he'd go and stay with a sister in Hastings, Nebraska. Bub was to drive him by sleigh to a small town on the new railway line between the ranch and the border.

It was about thirty miles to this town, and it was about thirty degrees below all that day. Dad planned to stay in the town that night and then take the morning train.

Bub dropped his dad off at the little raw lumber hotel, and took the team around to the barn.

Dad was a tall, lean man, with the droopy "Texas" moustache of his generation (and curiously, is now to be seen again in the younger generation!) When he strode into the building a few men were sitting around the front office, which was heated by one of the (then) new-fangled oil-burning stoves. Dad went up to it, threw down his driving mitts and cap, opened his big fur coat and stood, legs apart, pulling the long icicles from his moustache.

Very soon he began to fumble with the front of the stove, pushing and pulling this way and that with one hand, while with the other he felt about for a poker.

The proprietor, who stood behind the desk, was new to the country. He had put up the little hotel more or less on spec., but business had not been good and he was an irritable chap at the best. (He'd come to Canada from Michigan on spec. He was short, with a beer belly, and seldom without an unlit cigar which he rolled from side to side. Pale and flabby, he was in marked contrast to the weathered range men who patronized his premises.)

Seeing that Dad evidently thought that the stove was a regular coal burner, and guessing his intent, the owner called across the room, "Hey! old man—that ain't no coal stove! It's a space heater. It ain't no good to stand over it, 'cos it circulates the heat, and it's just as warm by the wall as it is on top of it. Anyhow, it's seventy degrees in this here place right now!"

Dad straightened his long legs. His eyes flashed beneath his bushy brows, and he roared in the voice he used when giving orders to his men on a windy day—"How in hell do *I* know it's warm, 'less I *see* the fire! What in hell did you want to get a contraption like this for?"

"Old man," retorted the proprietor, nettled, "if you don't like it, you kin go some'eres else."

"I can, eh?" barked Dad. "Well, I do reckon to stay, see? Who are you, anyway?"

"I own this establishment," said the man at the desk.

"Oh, you do, eh?" answered Dad. "So what'll you take for the joint?" and with that he started to haul out his check book and stepped up to the desk.

A seedy-looking fellow, with the air of a broken-down cowboy, who'd been sitting near the desk, now woke up from his doze and began to look interested.

Meanwhile the hotelkeeper said, "Look, this place ain't no joint. It cost me three thousand to build, let alone fixin's and good will; so by the looks of you I'll be keepin' it awhile," and with that he picked up the *Maple Creek News* as if all conversation was at an end.

But Dad was now at the desk with his check book out. "Take four thousand?" he demanded.

The proprietor stared at him. Just then the broken-down cowboy got up, tipped back his shabby hat, shot a stream of tobacco juice dead center of the spitoon, and ambled around to the back of the desk, crooking a finger at the boss. No one heard what he said, but it produced a sudden change in the proprietor. He straightened up, laid down the paper and said, with a smile, "Well, Mister Gaff, four thousand don't hardly cover the fixin's and all. Say five thousand—cash deal?"

"Four thousand and five cents," said Dad, "not a cent more."

"Okay" said the hotelman. "Lookit, I wouldn't *be* selling the place, only this country don't suit my hay fever. Too dry."

"Very good," said Dad, "here's your check—Bank of Montreal, Maple Crick. You can give 'em a ring if you want. And if there's a lawyer around we'll make out the papers later. Meantime—*I'm* the boss now. Want to stay till the train goes? What room are you in?"

"Well, I'm in number four," was the reply, "but it'll take time to pack . . ."

"Hell," said the old rancher, "the boys'll help you in the morning. Don't worry—I won't charge you for one night!

"Now," he continued, turning to the cowboy, "what are *you* doing here—aren't you the fellow I fired a couple of years ago?"

"Oh," that worthy replied with a happy grin, "I'm the general roustabout and nightman here. You didn't never fire me—I just left 'cos it rained all that roundup!"

"You are, eh? You did, eh? Well, first off, you go across to the hardware store, see? You're working for me now, rain or no rain. And you git the biggest, pot-belliedest coal stove they got—and a coal bucket and a poker. Charge it to me. Then you go across to the livery barn and tell that drayman to shove four ton of coal in the basement here. Tell him who it's for, see?

"Now, git going. I aim to have this joint hotter'n a branding iron before tomorrow! Yes—and take that dang-blasted new-fangled sewing machine or whatever it is to hell outta here. Chuck it down a coulee or anywhere so's I don't see it.

"That's all—git going."

That was the end of Dad Gaff's trip to the States. He ran that hotel till he died (about six years later, I think), and to anyone coming in on a cold day he'd shout (from *his* chair behind the desk—"Just grab that poker and open up the stove door so's you can warm up, eh? Ain't no sense freezing when you're under cover!"

As for the general roustabout, he sold that space heater to a woman friend for more money (taken in trade) than he would make in two months' wages.

CHAPTER SIXTEEN

1

I was able to return Darky to his owner before spring, since by January I had picked up a team, two saddle horses, a brood mare and some colts. I would need the team for cutting hay in the summer, but for the rest of the winter I hauled wood with them. Also, after each storm or big fog I had to use them to cross the bench for the purpose of keeping the telephone line repaired.

The big winds often knocked the poles over, and during a fog the ice would gather inches deep on the wire, which would sometimes break under the weight. Hence my many cold, slow trips following the line, with the horses plugging for miles through the deep, often crusted snow. The line went across several shallow coulees. When they were plugged full of snow, I had to make a detour around them, which took a lot of extra time.

It was cold work and the horses hated it, especially as they often had to stand still while I climbed a pole or joined a wire, or perhaps propped up a broken pole by making a tripod; for, of course, one could not dig the frozen ground.

The bench is high, and exposed, for the timber stops dead at the top of the north slope, and if the chill fog lifted, the wind usually blew, threatening frostbite to cheeks and nose. What's more, it filled in your tracks so completely that during the short days it was wise to start for home before it got too dark, or chance being lost.

One man from the Alberta side was lost on this bench for hours. He had started from his place south of the hills and landed up twenty-four hours later at Percy Drury's ranch northeast of my station.

Another time, Percy (who'd been a rider for the 76 in an earlier day) told me he'd been looking for a horse on the bench after a night when the snow had been blowing pretty badly.

Nell and her foal at Battle Creek

It was just daylight when he got to the Bull slough, and he ran into some sleigh tracks, pretty well packed down, but partly blown in. He wondered how come, for not many crossed the hills in winter. There was just enough fog that he couldn't see the edge of the bench.

Percy followed the track for a bit and noticed that it gradually began to edge away as if making a big circle. Then he saw a weary team plugging along *behind* him, with the driver muffled up and apparently half asleep. So Percy turned back and accosted the man, whom he recognized as a new settler who had recently come to Merryflat, south of the hills.

"Where are you headin'?" said Percy.

"Maple Crick, of course," replied the man. "But say, I had a rough time in the ground storm; the horses kept plunging and I couldn't see a thing, and it got dark on me after I'd been on the bench a spell. Thought I, I'll never git to the other side, and dang if I could tell when the hosses went down the hill. Then after a bit I knew I was on a better trail, and thinks I, I'm getting towards the settlement, for the trail's well broke out, so I reckon I can't be too far from town now."

"As to that," said Percy, "Maple Creek's near thirty miles away yet—you're still on the bench! And that old team of yours must have made a circle till they hit their own track, and they've been following it all night. They look pretty well tuckered out, so you'd best come on down to the ranch—it's only four miles—and get yourself a good feed and rest them horses!"

2

There was an awful lot of snow that winter, and very little was gone from the bench by mid-April, although the plains north and south had bared off already, and everyone was using wagons.

That was how it came to pass that Reg, the ranger from the east end—about thirty miles away—came to the Six-Mile in a buggy on some errand that would take him to Battle Creek.

He stayed overnight with Boyd, and next morning started up the Six-Mile coulee to cross the bench. Boyd had warned him there would still be some deep snow and bad drifts "up top," but Reg thought it would be soft enough for his buggy wheels to cut through them.

The trail up the coulee is pretty steep, and it sticks to the gravelly bottom between hills which get steeper and steeper and closer together until near the top the trail is so narrow that turning is impossible. The water-worn pebbles and small stones give good footing for horses, and enough water had already rushed down on the first warm days to expose them. The coulee sides are pretty well timbered to within a hundred yards of the top, leaving only a few stunted junipers and pines as a sort of fringe just below the edge of the bench.

There was still a trickle of water running between the stones, but not much, because the night had been cold. Reg hurried, however, for it was now windless and the sun was beginning to get hot. The banks at the top were clear of snow, but as he came close enough to the crest of the hill to see the blue sky ahead, he noticed a tremendous V-shaped overhang of snow at the very head of the coulee which extended to right and left along the brim. He reckoned, telling it afterwards, that it was like a white wall seven feet high.

He halted the team and climbed the sidehill to investigate. As far as he could see the bench was still white and the snow looked deep. He plunged through a narrow part of the crest drift, and found that he sank to the bottom, for there was a foot of water underneath the snow. Only a rim of ice formed by the night frost held it from cascading down the hill.

He realized that he would get nowhere with the bench in this state; he would have to unhitch and try to turn the buggy around, or else just leave it there, while he took the horses back to the Six-Mile. But just as he came to this decision he heard a muffled and long-drawn "swoosh!" and he saw the whole surface of the bench snow sink about a foot.

In a couple of jumps he was down the bank. He knew the only hope for his team now was for him to turn them loose to scramble up the bank. But before he could reach them he saw the big drift at the head of the coulee collapse, and a mass of suddenly released water came charging down the narrow cleft.

Reg was just able to get a death grip on a stout juniper when the flood hit him like a millrace. He clung there fighting to keep his head above water as the flood surged around and over him. After a quarter of an hour he realized that the worst was over and ventured to relax his grip enough to look below.

He could not see his horses nor the buggy. When the flood finally subsided enough for him to investigate he found both horses drowned, just beyond the first bend. The buggy, of course, was matchwood. But Reg managed to scramble down through the timber to get back, exhausted, to Boyd's in his dripping clothes.

3

The high water of that spring remained a hazard for the next week or so. Many a rancher risked his life crossing the swollen creeks to attend calving cows.

There was no bridge at the Ranger Station itself, for here Battle Creek was wide and shallow and everyone used the ford. However, one day the water, already high, suddenly deepened as the result of a spring thunder storm that exploded over Graburn butte. Just about the time the rain stopped pouring I heard a shout from across the creek, and saw a neighbor from the West Bench standing in a wagon looking at the water. He was driving a big, strong team of work horses, and they kept looking at the flood with arched necks, blowing through their nostrils in distaste.

"Reckon I can cross?" called the driver.

"Wait till I get a saddle horse," I shouted above the roar of water. I was back soon with Jack and a lariat; but it was too late. The neighbor had already put his team into the creek and there wasn't much of them showing. They were well upstream, however, and with luck the current wouldn't take them down past the fairly level approach to the ford. However, just below this crossing place was quite a steep bank with some big willow bushes at the base; their tops, all filled with trash, were only just showing above the water.

The team had to swim, but only a yard or two, and I saw them feel bottom with their feet as they passed the halfway mark, but when the wagon hit the deep water, the wagon box began to rise off the bunks (for, of course, the box is separate from the running gear and is simply held onto the bunk by pegs at the side).

Just as the team got into shallower water—only up to their bellies— and the danger seemed to be over, a raft of sticks and trash swept down right in front of their noses, and they hesitated just long enough for the current to get the better of them. One went to his knees and dragged the other horse with him. They were swept down into willows.

Meanwhile the wagon was swept down at right angles to the team. My neighbor yelled for the rope, which I threw. He caught the loop and fastened it to the step-iron. Luckily the box was a fairly tight one or it would have filled and sunk at once. Already its hind end was afloat, only the driver's weight keeping it on the front bunk. I stepped up Jack who took the strain and held the outfit where it was.

One horse now found some footing on the bank and gave a heave which brought his mate to his feet. Then my neighbor gave an unholy whoop, Jack put all his weight on the rope, and the team heaved themselves up the bank; but there they teetered, in danger of falling back. Quick as a flash the driver reached down and pulled out the draw pin. He shouted again, and the team, suddenly freed from the wagon's weight, scrambled to the top, where they stood dripping and heaving.

The front wheels of the wagon were now well stuck among the willows, but the lurch had caused the wagon box to leave the front bunks. Now it was afloat, but in the wild river it was rapidly sinking, with my friend on board. I rode quickly downstream beyond the team, and by urging Jack to the utmost, managed to get to the strange boat and draw it and its occupant to the edge of the bank. My friend grabbed a willow and jumped ashore. We tied the lariat firmly to a willow, and saw the wagon box slowly sink.

It was quite a few days later that the flood went down sufficiently for us to get a chain, first on the running gear of the wagon, and then on the box, and draw them both from their watery bed with the big team.

"Oh well," said my neighbor, when he realized he'd have to camp with me for a day or two till the creek went down, "Sadie won't worry, and I'd just as soon visit with you for a day or two." In this way he accepted the inevitable with the good grace so well suited to a country where it didn't pay to be in a hurry, and you didn't fret, because there is always another day coming.

Your modern businessman would, under such circumstances, be apt to bite his nails or contract an ulcer, or do both; but that attitude would never have settled the West.

4

By spring I had acquired yet another horse. She was a pretty wild little mare called Birdie; a buckskin with black points and as smart as paint.

A settler from beyond the Four-Mile had been using her to haul wood. I took a liking to her, and hated to see her on such a hard job. So I bought her quite cheaply, and led her home by the trail that winds around the base of the range of high bare knolls which we called the Four-Mile hills, about ten miles northeast.

At the weekend I turned her out into the pasture with the rest of the bunch, which included a big sorrel work mare called Nell, who was due to foal almost any day. The snow was all gone locally, and there was plenty of old grass in this pasture, which lay just across the creek from the barnyard. The water was fairly high all right, but the bunch got across without mishap.

On Monday morning I needed the team. I also wanted to check up on Nell. I hadn't seen any of the horses since I had turned them out, for most of this hillside pasture was out of sight due to a hogsback that curved down to a bend in the creek. All I had in the barn was a four-year-old filly called Julie that I was breaking.

The water was too high for wading, so I crossed over on a big log which straddled the creek north of the barn. But search the pasture as I might, I saw neither hair nor hide of the bunch. I heard Julie stamping and whinnying from the barn, for she was lonely; but I heard no answering greeting from the bunch, which was unusual.

I finally got to the east fence—half way up to the bench—and found some posts pushed over, the wire down, and a plain horse track going uphill to the northeast.

"Confound it," I thought, "that darn Birdie has headed for home taking the bunch with her, and leaving me afoot. She'll never stop till she gets to the Four-Mile gate and that's eight miles or more."

There was nothing for it but to ride Julie, and it wasn't the right kind of a job for a green horse.

Julie was getting in a panic. She knew her mates were gone, and she alternately whinnied and pawed the floor of her stall, twisting this way and that. She fought me so hard that I had to blindfold her to get the saddle on, and then a hackamore, because I didn't want to use a bit. In the ordinary course I would have ridden her a few times in the corral to get her settled down and bridle-wise, but now I reckoned she'd probably follow the scent of the bunch anyway.

I got her into the creek, headed the right way, and then flicked off the blindfold. She humped up as if about to buck, but changed her mind and bucketed across the creek instead. Up the bank we went with me keeping a good hold on the hackamore rope. She circled the pasture pretty fast, whinnying and putting her nose close to the ground every few yards till she got the scent of the bunch. This took her to the Gap and she swung out of the pasture and up the hill at a lope. Her high whinnies sure shook me in the saddle and blasted my ears.

She was a bit winded when we got on the level, but her nose never left the scent, even in places where the horses had scattered briefly to graze, and she always hit the track again. I couldn't steer her worth a damn, but I finally relaxed and she took me like a bird over the bench, across the coulees, and down through the timber to the plain below, wallowing through the Four-Mile Creek so that I was pretty wet. We rounded the corner of the hills, and there, quite close to the gate, was my bunch, all placidly grazing—except for Birdie who stood with her head over the fence staring in the direction of her old home.

Julie, on the high lope, let out a shrill whinny, and was answered by a general roar of greeting as the bunch gathered up. I noticed then that the big mare, Nell, was absent.

Julie galloped right up among the bunch and stopped dead to blow noses with Jack. I slipped off with my rope, got it around Jack's neck and then transferred my saddle and hackamore to this more trusty mount. After a quick circle around in which I failed to find Nell, I decided she'd stayed behind somewhere to have her foal.

So I rounded up the bunch and started for home. I had a little trouble with Birdie, but after I had smartened her up a bit with the end of my rope she gave in and followed.

All the way I kept my eyes skinned for any sign of Nell, looking into every little valley and nook, but didn't have any luck. Wherever she was I knew she'd eventually land up at home with her foal, but out of natural curiosity I sure wanted to see what she had produced.

I wasn't worrying, of course. It's very seldom a range mare has foaling trouble, and if she does, it's apt to be so bad that there's nothing you can do about it.

When we got to the home creek the horses went down into it, jumping and kicking and squealing in tune with the glorious spring day.

They hit the water in a cloud of spray, and as the leaders began to haul themselves out on the other side, I heard a long and piercing whicker from behind. Turning I saw big Nell thundering along, her big feet at a flying trot, her mane streaming behind, and her handsome old face showing hysterical concern at being left behind! And to my joy, running at her flank was a day-old foal, a lively little chestnut with his mother's blazed face, and an umbilical cord still unshriveled!

"Hold it!" I yelled, reining Jack about. I didn't want the foal to get mixed up with that scramble in the creek, with the current boiling like a tea kettle.

But old Nell dodged me and plunged straight into the creek on the heels of the stragglers. My heart was in my mouth for the foal, but the little fellow clung close to his mother's flank on the upstream side, and swam like a seal, his head well up, his lip wrinkled at the spray, and his nostrils flared out like a little merry-go-round horse.

Up the other bank scrambled Nell, big hooves slipping and sliding on the wet ground and her wet tail dragging, with the foal keeping pace and lifting its baby hooves like a toy horse, as if crossing swollen creeks was the best of fun. (I called him "Sea Horse" later.)

5

Through bad luck, I did lose a foal the next spring. And it was a good one, from the Birdie mare that had caused me all the trouble.

I had put her with three other brood mares into the lower hay field, which had the creek as its east boundary. The home pasture adjoined this on the north, and since I turned my team of geldings in it on off days I didn't want the mares there, because old geldings get quite excited by foals. They want to run and play with them at any opportunity, and their play is apt to be pretty rough, and it worries the mares, so they all take to running.

This morning I'd crossed the creek and was halfway up to the bench, well above the valley. I heard the galloping of hooves and a couple of loud whinnies, and looking back, I saw below me the two geldings racing down the hay field towards the mares.

I turned back and galloped down to the creek, crossed it in a shower of spray and took off down the pasture. As I passed through the gate I saw that it had been opened and dragged to one side.

I rode fast, but not fast enough to get between those crazy geldings and the mares. The whole bunch was on the run, each mare trying to get away with her foal. Birdie made for the creek bank, running all out with her foal alongside. Old Blizzard, a gray gelding, was trying to get at the foal, but the mare kept herself between the two. This gradually forced the foal to the very brink of the bank, which is steep at this spot. And just as I drew near I saw the foal stumble, recover, stumble again as the edge of the bank gave way, and then turn turtle and land, legs up, in the deep, fast water below. Quickly I made a loop, but the willows were too thick for me to throw it, and by the time the current had taken the little fellow fifty yards, I could see that he was already drowned.

Poor Birdie grieved for her young one for days; running up and down the creek bank and whickering softly.

As to the gate, I never did find out who had left it open, or why.

So now the creek and I were even. One foal had made it with ease; but the other one never had a chance.

6

The best horse I had at that station bore the name of Jack. I bought him from Graham Parsonage, who ranched south of Fort Walsh.

The Light Horse Society, of which Graham was a member, had obtained a really top thoroughbred stud called Egremont for the use of its members, and Jack was a colt from that famous horse. Not a colt, of course, when I became his owner, for he was then about seven years old and a trained cow horse.

Jack was a strong horse of over fifteen hands, showing both his sire's good breeding and color—liver-chestnut with mane to match—and his dam's native toughness.

I rode that horse a great many miles and he never failed me. But he did have one disconcerting habit, and I had no idea how he had acquired it. He would be trotting or cantering along and then, without warning, he would fling up his hind feet with a squeal, and explode off to one side.

Trimmin' his hooves

I would pull him up, cuss him, and he'd be as good as ever. This happened perhaps once a week, and not just at the start of a ride, which would be understandable in a blooded animal feeling fresh and sassy. It was just as likely to happen during a long, steady ride, after perhaps twenty miles.

I wondered if he had been in rattlesnake country, for it takes only a twig or something that makes a rattling sound to stampede any horse who knows what snakes are. But there were no rattlesnakes nearer than Milk River, so far as I knew, and that was a good many miles away, in Alberta.

So one day I made a buzzing sound with something—I forget what—while Jack was in his stall, and sure enough, he just about jumped into his manger, snorting like an ox.

The next time I saw Graham I asked him about this habit. "Well," he said, "I did lend him to a fellah to ride on the Milk River ridge for a couple weeks, but he never said anything to me and I didn't ride him but a few times before I sold him to you. I know he did it with me once, anyway, but I didn't pay no heed—just thought a rabbit or something had scared him."

7

That fall we had a stock meeting, and the question of the Four-Mile hills came up. They were short-grass and good spring range, but the complaint was that the horses cropped them too close all spring and summer, and they looked pretty bleak and brown.

So it was decided that any member of the Cypress Hills Stockmen's Association, or the ranger himself, would have authority (if passing that way) to drive any horses seen there up onto the bench or beyond.

One day, as I rode Jack along the Four-Mile Creek, I saw quite a mess of horses—about forty head—scattered all over the hill, like flies on sticky paper. So I turned towards them, got them bunched-up and headed them through the timber, following the Bull trail that came out on the bench.

I knew the owner of these nags. He was a good friend of mine. The bunch consisted mostly of brood mares and foals—four or five slim, handsome, dapple-gray mares, some of his famous buckskins, clay-banks really, with black points, white faces like Hereford cattle, and white stockings, a mixed lot of two-year-olds and yearlings of every color under the sun, and three broadly marked pintos.

They started to stream across the bench, dodging clumps of buck-brush and shying at the prairie chickens they flushed from the heavy grass. I kept on their tails to take them across to the other slope, thinking what a wild and beautiful sight it was to see these, the noblest of the animal world, running free and wild over the roof of the prairies, the wind in their faces and their unshod hooves drumming like the beating of a great heart.

But my happy dream was interrupted most rudely by a high-pitched shout from behind me, and I turned to see the wife of the owner of this multi-colored troop thundering towards me on her blaze-faced sorrel, riding as well as any cowboy and swearing as freely!

I pulled up, and she met me with, "Who in hell do you think you are to go chasing our horses that way! I just rode to look 'em over and what do I see—*you!* And you must be stone deaf! I've been hollerin' for the past half hour! Dang blast your hide for a blankety-blank smart aleck! I've a good mine to take a quirt to your etc., etc. . . . !"

She was breathless when she got through with that lot.

I told her the result of the meeting, and how her husband had agreed; and suggested that if she didn't like the horses to be moved . . . And when I added that she'd best put her hair up under that big hat, or someone would think she was Buffalo Bill, she relaxed with a broad smile, and asked me would I like to come to dinner, if that same wasn't burnt to a frazzle by now.

So we rode back to the ranch together—talking about horse breeding, on which she was an expert.

She didn't say a word to her husband during the meal—that is, about horses being run—and taking my cue from her, I also remained silent on the subject.

She was a fine woman, and a splendid rider, and I had no blame for her actions, because she hadn't known the score; and I could only admire her for her loyalty to her ranch and her horses, as well as her ability to speak her mind in good salty language with no ifs and buts!

8

With the beginning of the 'forties and the return of the rain clouds, farming got into full swing again. But the horses did not make a comeback; and the careful carrying over of breeding stock showed itself to be love's labor lost, for now the gasoline tractor was to drive the "hayburners" from the land they had plowed and fertilized.

Farms had to be larger to pay for the great combines and heavy tillage implements, and the process of joining field to field was to create today's latifundia. The farm workers, too, would be driven to sitting in front of machines to make tractor parts, tightening the same two bolts hour after hour, day after day. They would breathe the foul air of city streets and tread the paved ways of our modern Babylons, and be told they had a higher standard of living; where football and beer took the place of the meadowlark's whistle, and potato chips replaced the crusty farm loaf.

Even my job was being mechanized and put under the hand of efficiency experts—which made me decide to go to the Peace River country and try to find a place to ranch. I knew there would still be horses in use there, and I was not to be disappointed.

Part VI: PEACE HORSES

Pack train

CHAPTER SEVENTEEN

1

I found a valley in country very like the Cypress Hills. It was towards the foothills, west and north of the little trading village of Fort St. John in British Columbia.

There I established my ranch. I've told its story in my book *The Broken Snare*. There was no proper road, and not a motor or a tractor within miles. The demand for packhorses was good; for survey parties were doing a good deal of prospecting in the mountains. The range was wide open and both horses and cattle thrived on the good grass and plentiful pea vine.

Many settlers had lately come by wagon from the dry prairies and homesteaded north and east of the little town, but up our way, towards the foothills, the land was too rough for farming, being mostly creek and river valleys with high ridges between. This meant that there were plenty of open side hills for spring grazing.

Some ranchers were already there, the dean of whom was Vern McLean, formerly of Manyberries, Alberta, and São Paulo, Brazil, where he had been range boss for a British outfit. He had a lot of horses on the range, and we always called him "the wagon boss."

North of us were Frank and Charlie Hudson with a good herd of cattle; 'way up Halfway River there was Bill Simpson and the Westergaard boys, and on the Graham River Teddy Green on the Federal ranch. These boys trailed their cattle over Indian pack trails to market at Dawson Creek, about one hundred and twenty miles away.

At the Big Hill on the Cameron River was a horse ranch founded by one Billy Hill; but it had been bought by Alex Gilchrist who also had a place on the Peace River. Alex, curiously enough, had been raised at Silton, Saskatchewan (where I now live). His father had been a Presbyterian minister.

Through the deadfall snags on Monte

Up there, we were back in the good old days of ranching with cowboys and horses. Almost all the younger fellows (as well as many of the old) were good riders and ropers, whether they were whites or half-breeds. The Beaver Indians, too, had a lot of cayuses, as they traveled by pack and saddle back and forth from their hunting territory in the mountains to the west. The whole country was crisscrossed with their pack trails, which wound up and over great gaunt ridges and down into brushy bottomlands. There were no bridges, of course. All the creeks and rivers had to be crossed at fords; and these often changed locations as water rose or fell or altered the course of the deep channels.

The country was like a menagerie, for game was everywhere—moose, deer, timber wolves, and black bears were common, with stone sheep (saddlebacks), mountain goats, and woodland caribou in the mountains to the west, as well as grizzly bears. And once in a while a silver-tip or a cougar would drift into our country, which didn't help our cattle herds.

2

Riding was rather a different job here from what it had been in Saskatchewan, but it certainly yielded plenty of excitement.

Horses brought from the prairies were shy of the heavy brush at first, but the native-bred stock, born and raised in the rough country, were perfectly at home among thickets and deadfall and steep creek banks, and would follow a steer anywhere.

One time I was trying to get a very wild cow with an even wilder calf to join a bunch we were gathering for branding. The wily old girl skittered and dodged in and out of the heavy willow brush, but Monte, my little black horse, kept right on her heels, looking for a chance to turn her.

Those clumps of brush and poplar trees were dotted pretty thickly, with patches of prairie between, but none of these openings were wide enough to give Monte a chance to get ahead of the cow, and she was working towards the brush all the time. She'd hide herself among the tall purple fireweed that grew so luxuriantly among the piles of fallen timber, and you'd wonder how any amimal could penetrate such a spiky fastness.

I'd got her out of one such place into a small opening, with Monte shoving on her shoulder, but she made a bound and went under a big leaning tree into a patch of tall willows set among a few heavily branched poplars. Monte had to dodge around the dead tree and his blood was up. I could see his flared nostrils glow red as he made a leap that would have cleared a five-bar gate, right through the tops of the tall brush which was slapping my face. Then I felt a jerk that seemed to tear my head off, and Monte went on, leaving me swinging from a tree like Absalom, my neck firmly clasped in a forked bough.

I reached the branch with one hand and got my head loose and dropped ten feet to the ground among the spikes, dizzy and hatless.

Monte, like the gentleman he was, stood waiting for me, looking like an Indian travois pony; for a long dry stick had somehow run up under the saddle skirt and was sticking up over his shoulder.

I did finally get that cow brute to the bunch, but it cost Monte a few rough scars where he'd been barked; while it cost me a skinned nose, a bloody ear, my lariat strap torn from the saddle—and my hat, which I never did find!

Except when they were in the mountains, or when it was icy, horses went unshod at all times, as they had done on the prairies. But here the ground was softer, and hooves became sadly overgrown, especially with loose range stock. We had to round up our horses at least once a year, and get to work with the hoof clippers and a rasp.

If we didn't keep their feet trimmed they would usually either crack or break off in chunks; and some of those old mares, especially, would come in with hooves that looked like skates. We hoof-trimmed our saddle stock about once a month; much more often than on the plains, where the harder, dryer ground usually kept a horse's hooves worn down evenly.

After a "frozen" chinook, when mushy snow turned to ice, we had to put "neverslip" shoes on our mounts. These shoes are fitted with round calks that screw in, obviating the necessity of heating shoes and welding on calks. This we called "cold shoeing," and we all had to be able to do this job, even if it meant throwing down a wild one, who'd only been ridden a few times, or possibly not at all. Few of the range brood mares had ever had their feet handled.

If deep snow came again after shoeing, those shoes would have to be pried off pronto, because the snow would "ball up" in them till a horse couldn't walk; or worse, a horse would "calk himself" when plunging through deep drifts, leaving an ugly wound.

And sometimes the snow *was* pretty deep, which makes for laborious riding. But although the grass would be covered, there was a lot of pea vine and dried willow herbs up on the ridges, which was where most of the old "burns" lay, and cattle would tend to work into those areas in late fall. And there they would stay, for they could get water in the open warm springs.

When we thought it time to start winter feeding, say, about mid-December, we'd have to find the stragglers that hadn't come in to the feeding ground. After a fresh snow we would make a big circle up-a-ways, and usually find their tracks. Then came the job of plodding and scrambling among the fallen logs and uprooted trees to round up the critters and start them for the home ranch. It was sometimes cold work and you had to keep your eyes peeled for snags and whipping branches.

We called this "brush-popping," and our sheepskin jackets needed many a stitch after a day or two spent at this, while the tapederos on our stirrups would be scuffed and ripped like a pair of old shoes. A harness needle, a ball of shoe thread and some cobbler's wax was a real necessity in that country.

Range horses, however, wandered at will throughout the year; even

Range horses rustling

into the streets of Fort St. John. Sometimes they raided gardens, from which the women folk evicted them with loud outcry and flourishing of brooms.

3

With the demand for packhorses and because of the size of the country with its deep creek valleys and coulees in which a rider could travel unseen for miles, there was naturally a certain amount of rustling. Even a steer that strayed off from a bunch was apt to "turn up missing"; for every rider carried a Winchester, ostensibly for wolves and bears, and a critter could be shot in a gulch and packed out by night on horses, after the meat had cooled and been cut in quarters. An odd shot, heard at a distance, excited little comment, because there were lots of cattle-killing predators.

Once in a while a couple of renegades would be in such a damn hurry that they would pack out the beef without waiting for it to cool. They usually regretted this, because the uncooled meat, wrapped in tarps and packed on a horse, would sour.

I once stopped at a log shack and was invited in to supper with a couple of boys who said they'd been cooking up a mess of moose meat. I was hungry and ate hearty. I pretty near cashed in next day! I had to lay around a day or two with tigers in me before I could do any work. So I wasn't too surprised a few weeks later when Slim, a rancher down by the river, told me he'd found some guts and an unbranded hide lying in a deep wooded coulee. He reckoned it was some stray homesteader's beast; and *I* reckoned that's where my bellyache had come from!

Loose horses were considerable bother to some of the homesteaders around Charlie Lake; and one fellow in particular got so mad at them that he took to peppering them with a scatter-gun. I bought one horse from Vern that looked pretty flea-bitten in the hind quarters. I dug a lot of shot out of that fellow.

It was a hard country in which to keep a fence up. I had a biggish wrangle field for saddle horses but was everlastingly fixing it, for some old moose would blunder into the wire and drag it (with broken-off posts) all in among the trees. There was plenty of bush, but there were also plenty of nice prairies, so horses had good grazing and good shelter, and could winter out in fair shape.

Booze was pretty free on that (then) frontier, whether of the liquor-store brand or the more potent home-brew kind; and at the annual rodeos most of the boys got a pretty good skinfull of Dutch courage before they made a ride—as did the poor Indians who used to set up their little tents in the bush behind the stampede corrals and lived on what hand-outs they could get. If they had any money, that went for booze because for both men and women that was preferred over something to eat. Their kids did pretty well on the candies the whites gave them.

4

On one of these occasions for celebration, the wagon boss acquired an interesting piece of live property. Vern had retired from ranching, although he still owned a bunch of "Pine Tree" horses up along Cache Creek. He and his missus had settled in a house just north of town, with a barn in the back yard, where he kept a saddle horse once in a while.

Things had got going pretty wild and high in the beer joint that night, and Vern was in top shape for any crazy thing. In comes a fellow called Carriere, who was the local "mortician" (among other things). He was leading a big scruffy old billy goat.

"Here, Vern," he said, "you are a stockman, but you must feel lonesome without critters about. Take a look at this animal—pure bred from horns to hocks! You can have him for twenty dollars!"

Vern was holding forth to the bunch, and without stopping to look around, reached in his pocket, peeled off four fives and absent-mindedly passed them over his shoulder.

"Here—take this," he said, "and don't bother me, I'm talking."

Carriere took the money, led the goat to Vern's place and shut it in the barn.

Next morning about daybreak the missus dug him in the ribs.

"Whatzematter?" he asked. "Leave me sleep."

"You better get up," she said, "and feed the stock."

"Haven't got any stock. I'm retired—remember?"

"That's what *you* think," his wife persisted. "You just go to the barn and take a look!"

Vern dressed—cowboy fashion, hat first—and staggered out. He threw open the barn door and there's old billy goat staring at him with yellow eyes from the gloom.

"My God," he moaned, "what was in that beer?"

Old billy stamped his foot and bleated. Vern slammed the door and fled back to the house. The missus was frying bacon, her hair in rats. "What damn fool put that stinking goat in my barn?" demanded Vern.

"Mr. Carriere, dear."

"Carriere? That idiot? Call him on the phone, Roberta, and tell him to take his goat away."

"It's not his goat, dear. It's yours."

"*My goat?* I never had a goat and never will. It *can't* be my goat! How come?"

"You bought it, dear—from Mr. Carriere. Last night. For twenty dollars—yes you did! So now we have a goat ranch and we're away up in sassiety. Take your medicine, Big Boy. If you will make a good fellow of yourself, how come you never gave me twenty?"

"Twenty bucks?" Vern went through his pockets. "Seems to me I *lent* somebody some bills . . ."

"You didn't lend nothing. You was in the market—come on now, sit in. Here's your breakfast."

The upshot was that Vern gave the beast to a homesteader who had a couple of nannies, and tried to pass off to the boys that he'd bought it to help a poor man out. But that story sure didn't wash, and once in a while after that you'd hear a soft bleat when Vern kept talking too long.

CHAPTER EIGHTEEN

1

Jackie was one of several brothers who'd been raised in that part of the country. They were all able and all reckless, there wasn't any kind of a jam they couldn't get out of and nothing they hesitated at from riding broncs to flying a plane—after those things became popular. Already Grant McConachie had been flying his bush planes in and out of Charlie Lake for years (and was well on his way to working up to the presidency of Canadian Pacific Airlines).

Jackie had been pretty badly shot-up in War Number Two and his nice wife was apt to excuse any little lapse from the path of teetotalism by saying, "No, but you see, Father had a bad time in the war!"

Anyway, Jackie left his ranch—which was a fair way west of us—to go guiding each fall with his brother who was an outfitter for rich big-game hunters from the States. He and the dude he was guiding were at a fly-camp (one that could only be reached by bush plane) on the Muskwa River, pretty far back in the mountains. It was late in October with just a skiff of snow, but pretty cold.

His dude already had a caribou and a stone ram and wanted to round out his trophies with a silver-tip, but only had a couple days left before the plane came for him. Jackie had spotted a grizzly through his glasses. It was on a mountainside 'way across the valley.

So they set off and just after noon he got his dude in range and told him to shoot, which he did. But he only wounded the bear, which spun around and disappeared into a heavy patch of bull pine.

Jackie said they'd best wait till next morning to give the bear time to stiffen up. According to what he had seen through his glass, Jackie reckoned it was a hip shot; but the dude thought it was hurt bad, and anyway it was too cold to camp out—they were twelve miles from the fly-camp—and he was dead set on following the bear up then so that he wouldn't miss the plane next day.

Mastheaded

Jackie finally agreed, so they mounted their nags and started up to where the bear had been, on a sort of wide ledge covered with that young pine growth. They followed a sheep trail that skirted the base of the cutbank below the ledge and then circled around to lead up to the right.

When they got near the bull pine—their horses puffing hard—they saw bear sign and blood just ahead.

Jackie said, "We'd best go slow," and just then the grizzly charged out of the bush. He was plenty mad and out for scalps. He reared up on the rump of Jackie's horse, and as his mount jumped forward, Jackie unloaded himself in the snow. He couldn't get at his rifle which was in the saddle scabbard. A guide doesn't use his rifle unless he must, and the dude had his own in the crook of his arm.

"Shoot, shoot," yelled Jackie.

Nothing happened, and he couldn't see the dude—only the two horses. To his left was the cutbank, steep as a cliff and a long way to the bottom.

The bear left the horse, which was kicking madly, with blood running from his rump, and started to paw at Jackie who was lying face down among the bull pine, expecting to hear a shot.

The grizzly got him by the upper arm and ribs and started chewing away, but Jackie's leather coat and chaps gave him some protection. Jackie was now trying to heave himself towards the edge of the cliff a foot or two away. The close growth of small pine saved him some, because it got in the bear's road as Jackie humped himself along, still on his face, to save his belly from those long claws. His hat came off and the bear gave him a swipe on the head which peeled his scalp way back.

Finally, Jack got a hand over the edge of the cliff and gave a mighty heave. He felt himself falling but in a second one leg was nearly jerked from his hip joint. The grizzly had grabbed him by one foot as he was almost clear. Now it was starting to drag him back up; but Jackie kicked like a mule and by great luck his moccasin rubber came off in the bear's paw, and he slid and bumped to the bottom. He landed pretty hard, but got up as quick as he could and looked for the dude.

That gentleman had unloaded off his horse at the first onslaught, and had run all-out down the steep trail, losing his rifle in the process! Now he was standing wringing his hands near the foot of the cliff.

"How are we going to get to camp?" he yelled. "The horses are up *there;*" and he pointed to where the nags had taken off, right up the mountain side.

"Walk, of course," said Jackie, pulling his scalp in place and tying it down with his neckerchief. "Come on."

"I can't walk that far!" cried the dude.

"Nevertheless you bloody-well will," grunted Jackie, feeling his chewed arm. He didn't even *want* to look at it then.

"And would you believe it?" he told me later, "that damn dude had to hang on to me all the way back or he'd have fallen down in the

cross-timber an' rocks; and I had to just about carry him acrost the
river—which was shallow but awful cold. We got to camp 'way after
dark. They'd lit a tremendous big fire so we didn't have no trouble
finding the tent.

"Garry took one look at my arm and says, 'You're for the plane
tomorrow.' "

" 'But that's *my* plane,' whimpers the New Yorker, 'and I got to be
back by the end of the week at the latest.'

" 'You'll get back to St. John when we do,' says Garry. 'You'll come
on down with the pack-string—only takes a week, so cheer up.'

"The dude grumbles but it don't do him no good. Anyways, Garry's
got to go back up next day after the horses and the dude's rifle.

"So they flew me out next morning and into the hospital at the Fort.
I was chewed up pretty bad and my scalp . . .

"So the nurse says, 'Bend over with your pants down; I gotta give
you a tetanus shot.'

"Which I does and gosh! she must have thought I was tough, for
I swear she backed up full length of the room and comes a-running
with her toad-stabber and plunk! It went to the hilt! It was a worse
than what the bear done to me—and anyway *he* weren't supposed to
know about love an' sympathy!

"They sewed my scalp back and told me I'd have to wait two weeks.
I says, 'What for?' and the doc says, 'To watch it an' take out the stitches
from your head an' arm.'

" 'Nothing doing,' I says. 'I'm for Upper Cache. My wife nursed me
after I was wounded, and she might as well earn her keep. She's a
hell of a good watcher, and she'll jerk out them stitches easy.

'I ain't sticking around here,' I says.

"So in a couple days I'm home and it's sure good.

"When Garry got back he told me he went up the mountain next
day. That old bear had stiffened up good and he shot it easy.

"Then he went up among the rocks for the hosses. They was just-
about on top of the mountain, cold and gaunted, and their bits froze
in their mouths. He got 'em down and threw them in the pack-string,
none the worse, barrin' their lips was skinned.

"That's dudes for you," he concluded. "The only thing good about
them is their bank roll."

CHAPTER NINETEEN

Shorty quits

1

Pete was a small rancher down along the Big Bend. He had come our way one winter's day looking for a steer he was missing.

Only a few days before, we had started to feed for we'd had a big snow and plenty of cold and most of the cattle had come in. At that time we'd noticed a blue steer in the bunch, which certainly was not ours. He wore his hair pretty long and was wild as a skunk, so we hadn't yet savvied what brand he carried, but we reckoned to run him in first chance we had, so we could clip him and find out who owned him.

Pete identified the steer as his, to our satisfaction, but since the days were short, and since it was already dark by the time we'd finished with the steer, we offered Pete an overnight bed in the bunkhouse.

He was a disagreeable sort of a chap, pretty "windy" and fond of boasting about what I suppose he considered to be his "manhood." He'd tell of barroom fights, and liked to sneer at anyone he considered to be "soft."

The wagon boss was staying with us for a few days, and after a while, as we sat chatting over coffee, the talk inevitably turned to horses. Vern set the ball rolling, "Say, Bob, how did that little black Monte horse of yours break out? I saw you riding in on him yesterday and by gollies he looks good to me. I hadn't seen him since you first picked him up to halter break."

"Just as good as he looks," I replied, "and the best thing about him, he'll go any place at all without hesitating. I'd likely have been in a mess but for him last branding time.

"We were bringing a bunch of cattle up from the big canyon, following the creek bottom on account—as you know—the cliffs are too steep to climb till you get to the forks. As usual, the beavers had been putting in new dams all over, and there were lots of big ponds.

"Anyway, we had a big steer in the bunch that was on the spooky side, and just as we got to the dam at the foot of the Big Slide, this critter cut off to the right across the dam; and before I could stop him, Monte was on his tail. We were tangled up in branches and kept breaking through the dam, which had already been mucked up by the steer. It was like walking a tightrope, but Monte changed feet so quick he never fell. The steer tried to turn right-handed when he'd crossed, but Monte was in the way—I couldn't hold him back, of course, or he'd have upset. So mister steer took to the slide. You know it's a hundred feet high and steeper than hell, with about twenty feet of water in the pond below. You ever got plunked in a beaver pond, Vern?"

"I sure have," said the wagon boss, looking up from the cigarette he was rolling, "and I darn near got my horse drowned, too. Banks too steep to get out."

"Right," I said, "so you'll guess I was a bit nervous. All I could do was sit tight with a slack rein. The steer made a high jump and the bank slid with him, but before he hit the water he jumped high again, the dirt sliding.

"Monte did the same. The cutbank was over a hundred yards wide, but it seemed like a quarter of a mile! If Monte hadn't had the balance and spring of a cougar, he'd never have kept out of that dark, deep water. I couldn't help him in any way but by freezing to the saddle. He'd make a jump six feet high and ten feet long, and the bank, which was fine shale, would simply bring him down to the level he started, and what kind of a grip he got with his hind hooves I don't know, but he'd give that great spring again. And so we traversed that cliff in a series of loops.

"The steer was doing as well, just ahead, but then a cattle beast can always navigate those places better, and he had no weight to carry—but it's a sure bet we'd both have upset if he hadn't been able to keep just out of my way. We got to the end among a bunch of deadfall, but that was nothing, and pretty soon we got back to the bunch."

"As to that," commented Vern, "I knew that little horse's ma, and you couldn't put *her* off her feet, neither!"

2

Pete refilled his coffee cup.

"Yep," he said, "a hoss has got to be willing or he ain't no good at all. Anything that takes a balky notion I could kill. I've seen some bad ones, too, freighting and packing. I've stuck 'em with pitchforks, I've lit fires under them—burnt up a wagon and rack once, too, but I hate to be beat.

"I mind a little roan mare I tried to pack when I was around Rocky Mountain House. I was with Shorty Anderson—you know him, kind of a soft fellah—and we was packing for a survey outfit.

"Well, this day we'd started up a pretty steep trail along by a canyon, and up near the top this dam' hoss just stood and wouldn't take another step. She hadn't been packed much, nor handled, so I reckoned it was time to educate her. I took a rope to her, but she'd just stand and flinch ever' time that hondoo hit her, and not a step would she take.

"Shorty says, 'Mebbe she's cinched a bit tight. I've seen that afore—wait'll I see.'

"'Stand back,' I says, 'ain't no hoss going to best me! An' if you don't want a taste of this, leave her alone.'

"Well dang it she finally lays down, so I says, 'Shorty, give me a hand,' but Shorty don't answer, an' I see he's up ahead fixin' a pack. So I don't ask him a second time, but I undoes the block cinch and takes off her pack but leaves the 'sawhorse' on. Then I takes the hobbles from off her neck and buckles them on good.

"The ground slopes to the canyon so it ain't no job to drag her by the head and then the tail and just topple her over the edge. She bounces and bumps some on the rocks and lands at the bottom—it ain't far. It was comical reely, to hear her grunt!

"Shorty helps me divide her pack—it's only bedding—atween the other nags and we're ready to go.

"I says, 'We'll leave the bitch there for a while. We're due at the camp up top this evening and we got to move camp tomorrow, so we ain't got no time to monkey.' Shorty don't say nuthin', and we starts out.

"It was pretty near a week afore we got back. I looked down the canyon, thinking old Sis should be ready to take the tit about now, for there ain't no water and dang little grass and she'd not have made it out the bottom among all them rocks, with hobbles on.

"I worked my way down, stepping from rock to rock and hanging on to the junipers; and there stands little Miss Muffet just a-whisking her tail.

"I goes up to her and she kinda stares at me, sulky as hell. She's ga'nted some and the flies have been a-working round her eyes and the edges of the cinch and on the scabbed-up places and around the hobbles. It was hot weather, you see.

"'Well,' I says, as I took down her rope, 'I reckon you're going to behave yourself now, but I'll git rid of you just the same.'

"Shorty he'd scrambled down, too. He says, 'I'll give you ten bucks for her and you keep the packsaddle,' he says.

"'What in hell d'you want a thing like that for?' I says.

"'Will you take ten bucks?' he says. Sure, a fool and his money is soon parted, thinks I, and he gives me a couple fives. He takes off the hobbles and loosens the cinch and coaxes her down the canyon back to the trail.

"Shorty quit that night, and rode off leading the roan. He's a mite short of sand, that fellow."

Pete stopped to take a gulp of coffee, looking around at the little company with a grin. But he didn't get much change.

The wagon boss looked up with a poker face and said, softly, "Must be getting hard of hearing. I couldn't understand what you were saying," and with that he started on another subject. But we all had our thoughts, you may be sure. The code of the range does not allow one man to criticize another's way with his horse, other than by silence.

Perhaps the reader will judge from this uncommon (thank God) story of brutality why I have already said that bad horses are made—not foaled.

3

I came out of those thoughts to hear Vern saying: ". . . the winter freight trail to Nig Creek, you know that's about one hundred and fifty miles north, and too much muskeg to use in summer. It passed close to my old place, and it was nothing to see a whole string of freight sleighs traveling north on that trail with supplies for the company.

"A year ago last winter I was coming from the barn after evening chores, and I could hear and dimly see a four-horse team going south, and I thought it must be Jim that has that place on Squaw Creek. I knew he'd taken a load of freight north a few weeks before, and I knew also that he traveled alone.

"He'd had the Indians cut him a set of barn logs up-a-ways, and this fellah that passed had on a load of logs, so I guessed it was Jim making his trip pay two ways.

"It was a bright night so I waved the lantern and yelled, and it was him all right. He yelled, 'Good night, Vern,' and pulled on. I looked at the thermometer before I opened the back door. Fifteen below, it said, and I thought, it will hit twenty before morning.

"That night old Frisky kept barking and barking. He woke me up by scratching at the door; but that's an old trick of his when he wants in. He had a good boxfull of straw with a tarp over it and he was used to sleeping out, so I paid no heed. Next time he barked, it sounded like he went a-ways from the house. I looked out but the frost-fog was pretty thick and I couldn't see anything. This kept on all night, but I reckoned mebbe there was a wolf around and figured I'd take a look-see, come morning.

"After I'd dressed and lit the stove I went out. There was just a hint of daylight in the southeast as I walked through the deep snow on Frisky's tracks. He was quite close to the road, and still barking. When he heard me plunging along he came back and nudged me and ran ahead again. 'There's something going on,' I said to myself and followed the dog as fast as I could.

"Then I thought I saw something down the trail, mebbe a quarter of a mile from my gate. Couldn't make it out for a bit, till it moved, and darn if it wasn't a horse's head—in fact, two horses' heads. They were just showing above a rise of ground beyond which was a dip in the road.

"Then, as I came over the swell I could see Jim's four horses standing perfectly quiet in the hollow; still hitched to that big load of logs. But where in hell was Jim? He wouldn't leave the horses even if his sleigh was broke down.

"When I got up close I heard a groan from the far side. I sashayed around and there was Jim, pinned under the front runner of the sleigh, which lay across his thigh. He was still holding the lines.

"I didn't waste no time, but first pulled the draw-pin in case the horses moved. Then I undid the chain on the load and took off the tightening pole—nice and easy so no logs would start to roll off. I could use that pole to pry up the front runner. When I got it in place I said, 'Jim, if I raise the runner can you pull yourself free? Hang on to my leg if that will help.' Jim nodded. I managed to pry up that runner just enough for him to pull himself clear. I managed to get first Jim, and then the team, to the house, and while the missus made coffee and hot cakes I put the horses in, and gave them a big feed. We had Jim on the couch, and when he could speak he told us that he'd been a bit sleepy, and when the sleigh hit the hollow he'd lost his balance so that when the team snatched up the slack again he'd fallen on to the eveners. Before he could say 'whoa' he slipped to the ground and the runner had caught him. Luckily it didn't go far, and most of the weight was on the hind end of the runner, but for the life of him he couldn't get clear. He darn't try to back up the team, because the hind runners were on higher ground, and as like as not the front runner would have turned on him and maybe smashed his ribs.

"He said he shouted for help, but only the dog answered. He still held the lines, and he had to lay all night and just keep talking to those restless, hungry horses, speaking to each by name and just touching the lines enough for them to know they were still hitched up and under control.

"Yes, old Jim told me he lay there just counting the stars overhead. He was getting awful cold but luckily had on his big old fur coat and felt boots and good mitts. He said old Frisky come once in a while to keep him company, while the horses stamped and jingled their harness.

"He said, 'I was scared to death I'd faint or go to sleep, but Frisky sure helped me to keep awake and I got to thinking, sure as shooting Vern will come soon. I could hear you call to him to shut up his barking, but I was beyond shouting by then.'

"Well, Jim's ears and cheeks were frozen some, but they recovered. But he lost four toes on his left foot and his hip was in bad shape for a while. Oh yes, and I think he lost a few fingers—three I guess—at the middle joint. But he came out of hospital in a couple weeks, and was as good as ever by spring.

"It just goes to show that hosses will treat us as we treat them, and Jim had always thought of his team afore himself, and I just bet he was glad to see them again, and them him.

"*I* wouldn't like to have to stand still all night at twenty below—and on an empty belly at that."

These accidents I tell of are not intended to give the impression that riding or driving horses was all that dangerous. Such mishaps were very much the exception rather than the rule, and rarely resulted in death. Today's toll of the road by way of cars, trucks, skidoos, and so on is a far more serious matter, chiefly because of the speed involved.

Injury from a horse itself was even more rare, because no horse will step or roll on a man if he can possibly help it.

Jackie (the fellow who had been hurt by the grizzly) lived not far from me. He palled up a good deal with a fellow I'll call Red.

This Red had a small spread of his own, but he hated batching it, so he spent a good deal of time with the neighbors, always ready to lend a hand for whatever was going on.

When he worked, he worked. Otherwise he played, mostly at break-ing-in the snuffy ones.

He always wanted to get a job done as fast as possible; so if he happened to help me with the hay, he darn near wore me out, for he'd be up at four in the morning and go till after dark. It didn't matter to Red too much *how* the hay was stacked so long as it was off the field. When he needed firewood he'd fell dry trees like a whirlwind, not even stopping for a smoke. Naturally, after such a spell he'd need a lay off, which he'd often spend hunting.

One day he came to our place. We were out of meat. This didn't suit Red, who planned to stay overnight and was looking for a better supper than dinner.

"Can't *understand* it!" he said, shaking his head. "'Lots of meat in the bush and you eatin' *macaroni and rice!*"

There was a big chinook blowing. Its arch hung over the mountains all dark and stormy, and the spruce by the house were swaying and creaking and you could hear big dry trees going down one after another on top of the ridge. That's the best hunting weather because the game doesn't hear you.

I saw Red riding up the big sidehill on his best horse, little Benny, who was plunging through the soft drifts.

It was late when he got back. He was dragging a big deer from the saddle horn. He was eating a piece of raw liver, and his chin stubble looked gory. As he coiled up his lariat and I started skinning, Red told me his adventure.

"You see," he said, "I had only one shell for my Winchester, so when I saw that buck I got pretty close for a sure shot. Just as I up and aimed, ole fool Benny shook his head, which put me off, so all I did was break its leg.

"He took off, going to beat hell on three, and headed into thick brush. I pushed him hard, but he didn't seem to want to play out, so when we got onto an open sidehill I got above him and drew alongside. Then I pulled my knife and transferred from the saddle to the buck's back. That slowed him up some, and grabbing an antler with one hand I let him have it a couple times in the neck. He folded up and I stepped off. But you know, it makes me mad not to make a clean shot. Gee! Just look at the fat on his rump. Here, I'll finish skinning him out and you take these side ribs to the house!"

4

Another time we'd had a roundup of horses on what we called the Big Bend country. This was a rolling prairie with plenty of sloughs and poplar bluffs, willow runs and the odd spruce clump.

The wild gray mare

One little gray mare got away on us twice and finally the wagon boss—Vern—said, "Let 'er go! She's a bunch-quitter anyways!"

That evening Red said, "Who owns that little gray—didn't see her brand?"

Vern said, "I did—she's a Pine Tree."

"Oh," said Red, "I was thinking I might run her down come winter, but I don't want to pay a lot for her."

"You won't need to," said the wagon boss. "If you can run down that little mare and get a rope on her, she's yours for free and I'll fix a bill of sale.

"I wouldn't," he said, "run a *good* horse into the ground for the sake of a cayuse like that'n. But as I said—you want her—you go get her."

Red waited till there was about two feet of snow on the ground. Then he rode over to Jackie's, which was the nearest house to the Big Bend. He wore chaps and a big coat, a fur hat and mitts, and behind the saddle he had a blanket in which was rolled some bannock and tea and a few quarts of oats for Benny.

Benny, by the way, was a real little hot-blood, bright bay, a good roper and a good stayer. He'd been well grained for some weeks and was in top shape. Red stayed overnight with Jackie, and started his hunt at daylight. The snow had just crust enough to make hard going for a wintering horse that had to paw for a living.

About noon Red ran onto sign, and soon after he spots the little mare. She was awful scary from having run alone since fall. She took off at sight of Red; who didn't hurry but just followed up easy. Every once in a while the bronc would stand for a moment on a knoll and look back at him. Then off she'd take to her heels, tail up, working in a big circle, so as not to be chased off her range.

Red stepped up his pace a little, not to give her too much chance to rest. By dark he was pretty close, and the mare was starting to tire. Her head wasn't so high, and she'd stumble once in a while in a drift.

There was no moon, so Red camped under a big spruce and turned Benny loose to paw for grass, after he had given him a couple handfuls of oats. He left the saddle on because it was real cold—about twenty-five degrees below zero. He knew the mare wouldn't travel till day light, for she would be hungry and have to feed.

Red spent most of that night hunkered over a fire, eating cold grub, listening to the hoot owls, and counting the stars.

He was moving by daylight and made some tea in his little billycan; then he mounted Benny. The little mare was in a willow run where she'd been rustling. He choused her out of that, and away they went again. By now Red thought he might get close enough to throw a rope on her, and so he could have, only she kept in the bush as much as possible.

She was tough all right, for she was still out of rope reach by the next evening.

So Red had to spend another night in another clump of spruce. His grub was about gone and Benny had cleaned up the last of his oats; but the little horse was game, for he still hadn't put on full speed.

Towards noon the mare's pace began to slacken and when she had to cross an open prairie, Red spoke to Benny and soon ran her down. He roped her and snubbed her up. He'd taken a fine rope for a war bridle, a quick-breaking device, and he soon got her halter-broke good enough so she'd have to follow. So he put on a stout new halter he'd brought, keeping out of the way of her front feet, which she couldn't use much anyway because of the deep snow.

He put a bowline in his lariat and left it on her, running it through the halter ring. Then he took a dally on the horn and started back to Jackie's place.

He got there at dusk. Jackie heard the corral gate squeak and called out from the door. "I'll lend you a hand, Red!" but Red said, "Okay! I'll manage! Go on with your supper and tell Bernice to keep some grub for me."

He was very cold and very hungry, and anxious to get to the house for supper; and I suppose that's why he made a fatal mistake. First he tied the mare to the rails. Then he unsaddled Benny over in a corner, and while he was having his roll, Red got a couple of oat bundles from the stack.

He threw one in the corner for Benny and the other in front of the gray, who jumped back and snorted.

Then he went to the house, and started to take on Bernice's good cooking. But halfway through the meal they heard a couple thuds and a scream from the corral.

They both ran out, Jackie stopping to light the stable lantern.

They found the little mare flat out at the end of her rope. Her neck was broken; and old Benny was munching on her oat bundle. Evidently he'd just snatched off the grain heads of his own bundle; and then, being "cock of the roost" on his home ground, he'd just naturally walked over to bully the little mare away from her supper. She—as was natural for a bronc—flew back and kinked her neck—and that was it.

Jackie, telling me of it, remarked, "You know, there isn't a guy in this neck of the woods would have the guts and the know-how to do what Red done—trailing that little outlaw! And there isn't a guy in this country—not even a green Englishman—would have been so crazy as to tie up the *wrong* horse. Anybody could ha' guessed that the ole broke nag'ud just naturally go for the newcomer!

"All that work—I'm sure sorry for ole Red."

5

On the same roundup on which that little mare got away, another incident happened to show how Red could adapt himself.

They were gathering a bunch onto a creek flat, and Red came pounding down a steep cutbank with a few mares and foals. One of the lettle fellows tripped on a juniper root and went head over heels, breaking its neck. Red cut its throat and then ran the rest of them into an old corral they'd fixed up to hold the bunch.

The grub-horses didn't show up, and everyone was hungry come dark. All at once Red saddles up and rides out. He came back pretty soon with a bunch of steaks. "What you got?" asked the boys.

"Horse steaks," said Red, "I ain't going hungry. It was clean butchered."

No one spoke for a bit while Red set a few steaks to broil. They smelt pretty good. After a while a couple more men tried it, too. They said it was good. But the others heaped scorn and abuse of the eaters of man's best friend. The old wagon boss near cried (someone said he'd rather eat his wife than a hoss!).

Well, the belly-filled boys slept real good, but the others couldn't shut an eye till the pack-ponies arrived with grub about four in the morning. They'd got lost somewhere.

But there was a kind of coolness for a few days between the "cannibals" and the righteous group.

6

It was no wonder Red never went hungry when he was in the Fitzroy Crossing country of North Western Australia a few years later. He was white stockman for Emmanuel Brothers, the big cattlemen at Fitzroy Station running 125,000 head south of the Kimberleys. There Red learned from his *abo* stockriders how to catch and cook goannas (big lizards), how to find wild melons, and how to break open old gum trees to dig out the big white grubs, which he said "tasted like ice cream, an' the outer layer like a biscuit cone—darn good eating!"

Today that same Red is ranching way down near Uva Lake on the far llanos of Colombia, South America.

He hated the cold weather, though he could take it as well as any man I ever knew. And he hated spending most of the good summer weather pitching hay when he would rather be riding.

That's why he sold his place in Canada. And that's what took him to the other parts of the world where cowboys and horses still work the range. He went to Australia for a couple of years, and then to New Zealand, and eventually to South America by way of Mexico, in which land he stayed over a year, ramrodding a place in Sonora, owned by an American. Then he heard of the llanos and went to Colombia, still seeking the perfect ranching country where one could start on little.

Down on the Uva his nearest neighbor was a young chap from Montana, who lived about twelve miles away. Their holdings were about one hundred and fifty miles from the nearest town worthy of a name—Villavicencio, east of Bogotá and in the Department of Meta.

It's a big wide prairie country with no roads, no telephones, "no nuthin," as they say.

But in the spring of 1970 there was an uprising of the Juahiba Indians, who came on the prowl from the north, under the leadership of a white Spanish renegade.

Red first heard of the troubles while in Villavicencio. One of the local "tame" Indians told him that this Colombano, Rafael Jaramillo, had become disgruntled when he lost his job as Chief of Police for Meta Department. Furthermore, he was hoping for the governorship, and knew that trouble on the llanos would draw the Federal troops away from the capital, Bogotá, leaving the city (he hoped) so poorly defended that a sudden coup might put the administrative buildings into the hands of his friends.

Red had ridden the 150 miles to Villavicencio for mail and supplies, and from what he heard there he thought the *insurrectos* were still far in the north, for news had just come in of the wrecking of three mobile malaria clinics that had been working among the Indians. Red left Villavicencio for home and had only gone one day's travel when he met some people camped by the roadside. They were starving. They told him the hostile Indians were looting and killing all over Meta territory. They (the travelers) had barely escaped into the monte scrub and had made it so far by traveling at night and hiding by day. They added that many had been killed, and that one Gringo rancher, Don Jaimie, lay naked and mutilated in the yard of his burned-out ranch house.

So Red explained that he was the man called Don Jaimie, and that he was very much alive as they might see; but at once his thoughts went to his neighbor Ted and to the little American Baptist Mission forty miles north of him. He found the mission deserted except for one old *mestizo* who told him that all the whites had been ordered to go to the ranch of one George Sarmiento. Off to Sarmiento's went Red, only to find that Ted had left the day before to ride to the Uva to see if he (Red) was okay. Red set off in that direction.

He found his own place burned to the ground, the stock run off and Tony, his hired man, lying dead in the yard, full of arrows and with his head and limbs cut off by a machete. His only weapon had been a shot gun, a thing easily out-shot by the bows all the Juahibas used. Apparently the palm-leaf thatch of the house had been set alight with burning arrows.

Wasting no time, Red rode hell for leather for Ted's ranch, only to find Ted also butchered and mutilated and his place burned.

The only thing Red could do was get back to Villavicencio with all haste, keeping to cover as much as he could. He reported all he knew. When the Rurales (police) went out he went with them as scout, since he knew the country well. They promptly slashed out an emergency strip in the Monte, and soon some Federal troops arrived by plane. But enough troops were held back all the time to protect Bogotá, and Rafael Jaramillo saw the game was up. He fled with most of his men into the tropical jungles of southern Venezuela and northern Brazil.

The troops did not pursue the Indians with great fervor, because the stink of their massacre of natives a few years before was still remembered in the United Nations. Altogether, about three hundred haciendas were burned, and a good many ranchers and settlers of different kinds were killed. Red sent me *El Tiempo* the chief Bogotá newspaper, which contained full accounts of it all. His loss was great, but he grimly started to rebuild.

When he wrote to me about all this, Red said, "Don't worry—I'll make it yet. After all, Texas was like this just about one hundred years ago. Old Jingle-Bob and others like him who went across the Pecos used to get raided by them Comanchees from the *llano estacado,* and by Mex boys from below the Rio Grande, and *they* made it—plus a lot of *dinero* to boot.

"At least I know what I'm fighting—it's Indians—and I feel better off than you hombres in Canada who have to fight a lot of faceless bureaucrats to hold on to your ranges, plus you get pressured by marketing boards and by the forestry boys, and by oil people who have the government and the Land Alienation Act on their side, till you don't know who in hell to shoot at.

"Here, as long as you can stock your range and defend it, it's yours; and I don't see them making parks and tourist resorts and hot-dog stands in this neck of the woods. Not in my lifetime.

"No cattleman in his senses could leave a good grass range like this. There's good horses here, you bet, and I'll breed up some more. How's the *snowballs* up your way?"

CHAPTER TWENTY

Slim's team

1

Slim Gooding had sold his ranch at the forks of the Pine, and bought the old Flatt place southwest of Fort St. John on the river. There was a big log house on this place, and we often camped there when traveling back and forth to town.

Slim made his move in winter, so as to be able to travel on the ice and avoid the coulees and steep grades of the wagon road; and it was on a darn cold winter's day when his arrival with the first load co-incided with our stopping at his "new" house.

We were expecting him for early supper and had a big feed on the way, when I spotted him approaching. He was just a speck in the distance at first, and a very small speck, too, in contrast to the wide frozen river with its banks so high and steep that at this season the sun no more than gilded the top of the north bank.

As he came closer, however, I could see that he was riding on a big load of mixed household stuff piled high in a hay rack. The bob sleighs were drawn by a most ill-assorted team, consisting of, on the far side, his little mule Jinny, who couldn't have weighed more than seven hundred pounds; and on the nigh side his big Percheron stud, a horse weighing close to a ton!

But funniest of all, the first-class passenger that stood upright at the very apex of the load was—a goat!

This creature, a white Saanan nanny, was not tied or restrained in any way, but stood like a sentinel, looking around with interest at the scenery, while the wind tossed her white beard.

As soon as this cavalcade drew up at the house, I went out to help Slim to unload. The goat at once jumped down from her mountain and ran to the mule's head. Jinny greeted her with a grating bray that echoed back from the hills, and went to nuzzling her friend. By the look of Nanny's bag I guessed she was Slim's milk supply, and so it proved.

"That tarnation worthless goat, she won't part from Jinny," was Slim's greeting, but I could see he felt proud of her.

We busied ourselves for the next half hour unloading beds and bedding, cookstoves and culinary tools, tables and chairs and big old boxes which felt as if they held bricks, plus assorted harness, ropes, saddles, and the miscellaneous junk that all old bachelors seem to accumulate.

For Slim, sixtyish, gray, gaunt, and tall, was a bachelor. Not quite from preference, for he once said to me, "Ever' time I began to cotton to a gal, I got beat out by some city guy with a white collar! Seems I've been so busy all my life I ain't had no time to court!"

And Slim was a tremendous worker. He'd been born in Missouri, but as a young man rode for an outfit in Idaho, coming to Alberta in time to see the settlers coming in. He had a small place on the Rosebud, and rode at the stampedes, but about 1928 he'd shipped his stock by railroad to head-of-steel at Grande Prairie, and trailed in from there to the forks of the Pine.

2

We finally got all the junk unloaded and started to the barn with the team, Nanny leading the way.

"Yep," said Slim, "that dang goat!" He grinned—"The varmint thinks she's Jinny's baby or somethin'. Can't keep 'em apart; and ole Jinny she knows she ain't got no hope of other offspring—so Nanny thar, she kind of takes the place I reckon."

I had already filled the mangers with sweet hay against Slim's arrival, and as we tied up the team I ventured to ask him whether he gave the little mule an advantage on the evener, for surely that big stud must just about pull her back, didn't he?

"Not on your life," said Slim, with that outward gruffness I knew so well. "Ole Jinny, she's old enough to be his maw, and she knows a hell of a lot more'n he ever will!

"I raised a mess of them mules down on the Rosebud. I got most of them yit, and I'll be bringing them up here soon as I git around to it—look out! Don't touch her ears, she don't like it! Say—supper ready?"

"Yes, my wife's been waiting for quite a while."

"Let's eat then," said Slim.

As we left the barn I heard a scrabbling sound and looked back to see Nanny jump in the manger and settle down by the head of her pal.

3

In Slim's words, he did indeed have a "mess" of mules, as well as goats and chickens, with, of course, a few good saddle horses.

Goats have traditionally got on well with horses, and I remembered how, in my boyhood days, a billy goat was a common thing in any English horse stable. Rightly or wrongly they were supposed to keep the air of the stable "healthy" for the benefit of their more fastidious companions—although one wondered what was so "healthy" about that rank goat smell!

Slim finally got his big family and all his "contraptions" to the new quarters. Even I was surprised at all the poultry and the big herd of goats. Every time he went to the barn to feed his horses he would be surrounded by a pack of what he called "the varmints." They would just about climb all over him, trying to get at the sack of oats he'd be carrying from the granary.

He'd kick at them with his heavy boots, which they seemed to enjoy, bleating happily and staring at him with their uncanny yellow eyes which somehow always look evil—quite unlike a sheep's innocent stare. Slim would scowl so grimly, swear so convincingly, and thrust the animals to right and left so angrily, that you would think he hated them.

"I'll cut your throat!" he'd say, and grab a goat by a horn, give a twist and up-end it; or he'd slap one over the eyes with a mitt saying, "Git outta here—or by grab I'll tear the everlasting liver outta you!"

I've gone in his barn to put my horse away, and seen every manger erupt goats of all colors, ages, and sex. They would put a scare into my Monte horse, a high-strung animal, unused to being sniffed at, bleated at, and nearly upset by the mixed nannies and gamin kids running between his legs.

With all his outward sourness, Slim allowed himself to be well-nigh eaten out of house and home by his menagerie. One reason for the large numbers was his reluctance to kill either a goat or a fowl for the table. He'd sometimes give one away—alive, of course—with strict orders that it be *kept* alive!

Slim preferred a vegetable diet, anyway, and tops with him was the southern dish called hominy.

He raised a lot of corn, and through the year he'd make a "mess of hominy grits" about once a week, soaking the corn in lye, and then taking the big black pot out on the doorstep while he rubbed off the husks.

His greatest word of contempt was "trifling." He'd say, "Them boys up the crik, I wouldn't give them an aig—why, they-all are the trifling-est guys I ever seen. Don't have enough savvy to pack sand down a gopher hole. Work?—they forgot it 'fore they was weaned!"

He himself was a terrific worker, to whom weather meant nothing, as you can imagine when he had to put up hay enough for all his "messes" of stock which included over two hundred head of fine Angus cattle. On top of all this, he grew "a mess of garden sass" each year, on a little flat by the river.

As a teamster, two, four, or six up, I never saw his beat. He'd come down that three-mile narrow grade that snaked down the steep hill to his ranch buildings, with a span of mules on a big hay sleigh, when the road was glare ice from a frozen chinook.

He was a good roper and rider, too, and yet, true to his Missouri boyhood, he still preferred a "pancake" saddle to his heavy stock saddle, if he was just "visitin'" and not riding the range.

"My fust riding," he said, "was on the ass end of a big ole mule, with a bag of grist corn in front of me. That's how my paw would send me off to the mill when we lived in Missourah."

He always exchanged y's and i's for a's, so Canada became Canady and Alberta, Alberty, and Idaho, Idiho.

He was a great reader and loved history, and although he had never got beyond the fourth grade he could reel off all the details of the Civil War of 1860. His hero was, of course, that doughty cavalryman, Robert E. Lee, although in general he favored the Northern cause.

Slim is gone now. His horses and mules have been dispersed, and replaced by tractors.

Like so many others, Slim was persuaded by the proponents of mechanics into buying a truck. Scorning to be "taught to drive"—he who had "skinned" mules and hosses over mountain trails and through lashing blizzards—Slim got behind the wheel and "let 'er go," shouting "git up!" for speed and "whoa thar" for stopping; cramming on his squealing brakes at every turn of the road.

The truck killed my old friend one dark night when the trail was slippery with rain. The stink-wagon didn't sense the danger in time, and had no concave hoofs to grip with.

There was nothing "trifling" about old Slim. He spoke the truth from his heart, and there was no deceit in his tongue: he never disappointed a neighbor though it were to his own hindrance; and he was merciful to all beasts, both great and small. Blessed are such men.

Part VII: VAQUERO LAND

Old Mexico Vaquero

CHAPTER TWENTY-ONE

A troop of range mares

1

All good things come to an end; and at sixty-three I sold the Peace River outfit and decided we would take a busman's holiday and ride back over the trail that had brought the cattle and the horsemen into Canada from the south.

We followed the east side of the mountains all the way through Alberta, Montana, Wyoming, Colorado, New Mexico, and south into the land of the Dons through the great cattle state of Chihuahua to the borders of Durango and Coahuila.

We were "at home" throughout our wanderings, for cow folk are alike wherever you travel, and language is no barrier.

At Calgary we visited with Frank Jacobs, the genial editor of *Canadian Cattlemen* magazine, and from him got letters of introduction to various cattlemen's associations down south.

In Great Falls we stopped over at Charlie Russell's old studio, preserved as he left it when he passed on to another range. I was more than ever impressed with the absolute truthfulness of his work, and my thoughts flew back to the memorable meeting in Calgary with this pleasant and modest man.

At Cheyenne I visited the lady archivist and greeted her with, "How is Queen Victoria's Wyoming?"

Whereat the lady said in astonishment, "What do *you* know about that?"

So we got into a discussion on Moreton Frewin that kept us jawing long after quitting time, as I told her I had met Frewin as a boy in Sussex. That had been after his retirement from ranching, and after he had sold up the Powder River ranch and brought the stock to Canada, bringing with them the famous 76 brand, which is still in use at Crane Lake in Saskatchewan.

The phrase, "Queen Victoria's Wyoming," had come about as a consequence of the fact that nearly all the big cow outfits that first used the Wyoming range were sponsored and owned by British cattlemen, of which Frewin was among the first.

We may complain today of American ownership of so many oil companies and so forth in our country of Canada; but we might remember that a century ago (and less) it was British capital and British owners who pretty well controlled the range-cattle business in the western range states, and the Americans suffered no real loss of sovereignty because of it. The same was true of the great beef industry of the Argentine Republic.

The Matador Cattle Company and the Swan Cattle Company are only two of many outfits I could mention that controlled immense acreages; and it was these companies that were largely responsible for the great improvement in quality of both the cattle and the horses that grazed the plains country.

One of these men, by name Anson, was the prime founder of the quarter-horse craze that sweeps on to this day all over North America.

2

In Denver (it was January), we plunged on foot through about two feet of fresh snow to see the museum; for our taximan got stuck three blocks from the building! And we thought we had left deep snow behind us—'way up on the Peace!

However, we later refreshed ourselves in Somebody's Irish bar, where we met up with a couple of Canadian cowmen, one of whom confessed, "I sure oughter have brought my long johns!"

Gradually, as the bus (with its ex-cowboy driver) took us further south, we began to feel the flavor of Spain. Gulches were being referred to as *arroyos,* brush was called *"chaparral,"* and many of the place names were Spanish.

We never traveled farther than seventy-five or a hundred miles a day, usually stopping off in the afternoon at some little town so as to have the rest of the day to explore. Since there were two daily buses, we could then get one in the morning to continue on our southerly way. We got to know several bus drivers, and they were certainly top hosts.

As we would get on, the driver would usually turn to the passengers and say, "Now, folks, we got a couple Britishers from up in Canady where they don't ever see much but snow (!), so I'm giving them the front seat, and you folks jest point out anything they want to see!"

Our fellow passengers were equally helpful and kept up a running commentary about the history of the Southwest, which lost little in the telling. The "trail of hunger" was pointed out, with gruesome details, and the events of the Civil War would be "prettied up" with embellishments that varied according to the "northern" or "southern" point of view held by the commentators.

In New Mexico we realized we were close to the land of the Comanches, those wild people and superb horsemen who were probably the first of the red men to make use of horses.

To our east lay the Trans-Pecos, and from there had come the big-hatted cowmen into the Mesquite desert we were now crossing. It was they who had pushed north to Colorado with their hardy stock; as later comers pushed into Wyoming and so into Montana to flood across the border onto the good grasslands of Alberta and Saskatchewan, naming little towns with the names of their brands, bringing with them Spanish terms for horses and equipment.

A claybank horse they called a *grulla* from their name for a crane (Latin: *grus*), a bird of gray and brown-clay color.

So throughout the cow country a girth became a *cincha* (cinch), the tie straps *latigoes,* leather leggings *chaparejos,* and a catch rope a *reata* (or lariat); while an enclosure was a *corral* and a roundup a *rodeo*—all words which have today become "naturalized Canadiana."

3

It was in Santa Fe, the old capital of Spanish colonial days (which still looks more Mexican than American), that we met Johnny Crowhoppie, a big sheepman from the Peñasco River, half way between Alamogordo (with its white gypsum sand dunes) and the border town of Artesia.

He invited us to his ranch, and met us at Alamogordo (the "big cottonwood tree") with a car to drive us across the Sacramento range (where snow lay deep in the pines) to his ranch on the Mesquite plains below.

Here I fulfilled the wish of a lifetime—to ride with the *vaqueros* over the desert. Johnny had some top quarter horses, but I chose a little sorrel mustang with big eyes, and what a little horse that was! Quick as a cat, game as a rooster and sure-footed as a goat. It was blowing a cold wind as we set out to gather a band of sheep for shearing; and a tumbleweed skittered across the ground as we climbed out of a dry wash. "Chico," my horse, gave a couple of good bucks, which by luck I outrode, and the three *vaqueros* from then on felt I was fit company and *"muy caballero!"* These sheep were not "under herd" but fenced in. Their pasture contained about twenty-five thousand acres, and we had to do some riding, but the sheep knew the drill and all gathered up to head for the home ranch.

We gathered up the biggest bunch of woollies I'd ever seen all together—about seven thousand head, and that was only about one third of the sheep on that range which contained several such pastures! We saw lots of cattle, too, but the sheep were needed at home because the Mexican shearers were expected that night.

Next day the shearing commenced, and it was great to see those itinerant Mexicans, under their *capitan* work at their job and talk and laugh at the same time.

And then a big gray car arrived and a couple Border Crossing guards got out and wanted to know if Johnny had any wet backs on his crew.

Johnny, fed-up with being pestered by so many government men from "sheep sanitary squads" to range-weed inspectors, replied without lifting his head from the lamb he was earmarking.

"Couple in that car over there," he said. Over strode the two border *hombres,* pistol holsters swinging at their hips. My wife and I were snuggled in the car drinking hot coffee, for the desert wind blew cold.

One of the officers opened the car door. *"Buenos días, señor,"* I said, *"Es mucho frío, no? Quiere usted café con leche?"*

"Where youse from?" the fellow said, hearing my gringo accent.

"Canada!" I replied.

He slammed the door shut as if he was disappointed.

4

Within a few days we found ourselves south of the Rio Grande.

Mexico is a land of good horses. Even the little nags that pull the orange carts all over the city of Chihuahua show good conformation, and any one would pass for a good saddle or buggy horse in the North. These humble animals are not too well cared for, I fear, and are usually sadly overloaded. We saw many a light wagon piled six and seven feet high with oranges and carrying up to three or four men to boot, always going at a good jog-trot except on the steepest hills.

We bought oranges off those carts so cheap that I haven't the courage to write the price. They must be a boon to the poorer peons who almost live on them, for they are full of vitamins. The smell of dried orange peel was everywhere and was not the least offensive—far nicer, in fact, than most of our city smells.

It was good to be in a land where a horse was still a necessary possession, and good to be where a rancher or cowman is considered a first-class citizen, rather than being looked upon as a small-time operator walking in the shadow of the big oilmen.

There was, so far at least, little industry to spoil the range land. We saw no oily-boys; neither did we see any tourists in shorts and sun-burned legs wandering around looking for pretty stones and leaving an un-pretty mess, such as we have to put up with in the North. As to the city-bred Mexicans themselves, they preferred to drink their *tequila* and read their papers in some *alameda* or by the bubbling fountain in one of the parks.

5

In Chihuahua, Señor Isquarios, the charming and affable secretary of the *Asociación des Ganaderos* (Cattlemen's Association) was most kind to us, and gave us introductions to many of the big cattlemen of this almost exclusively cattle state, and we saw many *ranchos* and many cattle. Many of these cattle show the old Spanish breeding to a greater or lesser extent, but this was overlaid by obvious crosses of Hereford, Angus, and Shorthorn, not to speak of the Zebu (or Brahma) crossbreeds, which were much in evidence on some *haciendas*.

We had already met one of these ranchers, a Señor Pinoncelli, at the stockyards in El Paso, where we had spent a couple of days. He had arrived with a trainload of his Mexican cattle, destined for the feed lots of New Mexico. He had invited us to his *hacienda,* and there he told us how his father, a Basque of the Pyrenees, had come to the U. S. Southwest as a shepherd but had finally got a spread of his own in Mexico, as many Basques have done. In the old days the American sheepmen got many of their shepherds from the Pyrenees and the hills of Scotland. They were indentured for five years, then they were free to strike out on their own. There are still many Basques in the West, especially in Wyoming and Montana, with a few in Canada. But they are not now all shepherds, for the state educated their children and weaned them away from the old life. They did not like this state interference, for a Basque always thinks that the place for his wife and children is *with* him—even if he is in a humble sheep camp. So, for many years now we no longer have them coming to America.

Heading them

Much the same applied to the Scots. Around the turn of the century hundreds of McCallums and Macleans and Sutherlands and Sinclairs came from Scotland as indentured shepherds. Many of these Scots, like the Basques, saved their wages and obtained sheep spreads of their own. But, again, their families grew up to follow a different road.

Señor Pinoncelli also had a large general store called *"El Buen Trata"* (the "Good Deal") which stocked rancher's supplies from barbed wire to all kinds of horse equipment. At this store I could not resist buying a couple of *jáquimas* (hackamores), a bridle with braided lines ending in a *morel* (a sort of quirt) and a Navajo saddle blanket. I almost bought a *reata,* but really I would have no use for it, and in the meantime my wife wanted a *bolsa* (sort of handbag), so we settled for that.

The *vaqueros* are the best ropers I have ever seen. Where we in the

north use a thirty- or, at best, forty-foot lariat, those fellows will use
a fifty- or sixty-foot one. Their lariats are braided from rawhide, which
is heavier than manilla rope, and to add to that weight they often braid
buckshot into the loop end. This explains how they can throw their
loop farther than we do.

In the North, of course, a rawhide rope does not work so well,
because of extremes of temperature and weather ranging from wet
to dry. A wet rawhide is useless, but it doesn't rain much in Mexico
as far as we could tell, for all through February the sun shone as warm
as in May or June in Saskatchewan.

6

At the cavalry barracks I was lucky enough to meet a major who
invited us to witness a display of horsemanship. My wife and I arrived
and were provided not only with chairs in a shady spot, but even a
strip of carpet to put our feet on, and cool drinks on a side table.

The horses were as good as any cavalry or police mounts I have
seen, and the riding and jumping was good.

The major, who had been to Europe as military observer, took me
to the stables and we looked over all the mounts. My Spanish was
spotty and English he had not; nevertheless, we were both horsemen
and so we understood each other famously.

These cavalrymen were all tall, lean-limbed, northern Mexicans,
reared (you might say) in the saddle. They were smart and straight—
quite a contrast to the squat dark little infantrymen in the next barracks. I was told that they had been recruited from the very poor
villages of the south.

When I expressed surprise that cavalry should still constitute an
important part of the army, the major told me that they often had
to aid the Rurales (Mounted Police), as sometimes a whole gang of
brigands-*cum*-cow thieves would hole up in the Sierra Madre to the
west. He went so far as to criticize our Eighth Army in Italy for not
having had a cavalry brigade for use in the rough country!

A word on Mexican bits and spurs. They are "supposed" to be very
cruel. But the fact of the matter is that while the long curb bits *might*

well be cruel if they were abused, the Mexican rides with such a light
hand and so loose a rein that they are not so. These horses neck-rein
with a mere touch of the rein on their neck. This, together with the
swing of the rider's body, can produce a very sharp turn with no effort.

The huge-rowelled spurs also look barbarous, but are not so. The
long blunt rowels look very smart (to a Mexican, anyway) but can
inflict much less actual pain than can our small-rowelled cavalry spurs.

"Corridas"—the "Running of Bulls," or as we would say, "Bull-
fights"—are another matter. There is no doubt that most *city* Mexicans
really do believe that the matador has some almost occult power over
the bull during the last moments, and that he more or less mesmerizes
the beast into immobility before making the final plunge with the
killing sword. But any cattleman will immediately note the labored
breathing, the out-thrust tongue, and the heaving flanks of the bull,
and will realize that the animal is, as we would say, "played out." Such
men have all seen a played-out animal become—in our parlance—
"hotted up," at which stage he staggers and can only move his head
or take a few short steps. Being "played out" in this sense ends in
death, as we have seen on the range only too often when an animal
has been run overmuch.

The last well-aimed sword thrust simply hastens the end, and I have
seen a matador drive his sword into a bull which was already col-
lapsing, although the spectators might not have been aware of it.

In this, I think, lies the skill of the matador. It is he who must gauge
when—the bull having been "run"; having been forced to expend
tremendous energy in attacking the picador's horses; having lost a great
deal of blood from the picador's lance and from the barbed *banderillas;*
having had his shoulder muscles torn and pierced by the lance to make
a seat for the swordthrust—the exact moment has arrived to drive in
the sword, only seconds (perhaps) before the animal collapses and dies
from its own exertions.

This is not to doubt the bravery and skill of the matador; for
certainly, if he misjudges this "moment of truth," his own life must
be forfeited; but in a general way I think that bullfighting is a "phoney"
sport, no matter how exciting and colorful and dramatic it may appear
to the spectators who are being fooled.

CHAPTER TWENTY-TWO

1

On our way back north we were able to stop at Deming, New Mexico, where I was anxious to meet Rusty Tulk. I knew him only by correspondence as president of the Open Range Cowboy's Association, of which I was a member, together with several hundred other ex-riders of the unfenced range from Canada to the United States and old Mexico.

It was early March, but the wind blew strong and cold on that Chemisa and Mesquite desert that hasn't a hill in miles. So we spent most of three days in Rusty's red-roofed ranch house of 'dobe bricks, all overshadowed by the biggest and tallest mulberry tree I ever hope to see.

In the comfortable living room, in view of the peaks called the Tres Hermanas, Rusty and his side-kick Charlie Beall work for hours on their list of members, while outside the desert winds blow. Here we heard his story, told in the drawl of the Southwest.

Rusty Tulk was born at Weed, New Mexico, a small settlement in the Sacramento Mountains, in 1886, the son of a small settler who ran a few cows in the Piñon country. When he was ten he started to ride. That summer of '96 his father contracted to gather the remnants of the C A Bar cattle. This ranch had sold out on range tally. The year before, the bulk of the cattle had been rounded up. The new owner knew there were still some of the stock on the range and took a chance that this outfit would bring in enough cattle to make it worthwhile. It proved so, as the wagon came in that fall with over nine hundred head of C A Bar stuff.

Five years after that, Rusty's dad got an order for eighty head of horses to be delivered across the Texas line for a freight outfit. They had to go down the state line in south east New Mexico, and they

A tight spot for Charlie

figured to hold the horses that night by the state fence, right near the J A L outfit which grazed in both Texas and New Mexico. The next morning Rusty (fifteen) and his brother (fourteen) were saddling up a big gray that was real snuffy. Spence Howell, who ramrodded the J A L, rode up to visit. Their's was a stag outfit and they didn't see many visitors.

He watched the boys and noticed the ride Rusty made on the gray. The upshot was that he told Rusty: "I can use you, kid. Whenever you get through with the hoss drive, drop back in. I need a man to ride the rough string (the younger horses not yet well broke), and I reckon you'll do." Rusty said he'd see what his father thought. If he wasn't needed too bad at home, he'd hire on.

His dad said, "Okay."

Rusty rode the rough string for two years. In 1903 he was taken off to help trail a herd of 6,100 steers to Portales, where they would be put in cars for the J A L steer ranch in Montana. The distance was two hundred miles and took about a month, as they grazed them along. The herd was cut into two bunches. Rusty rode with the first herd of 3,200 under a wagon boss named Lee Singleton. Three days behind came the other herd of 2,900. There was lots of grass that year, and the herd spread out enough that the second bunch had good grazing, too. There was no trouble on the drive, but a dirty rain-and-dust storm gave them a mean time when they were loading at Portales.

Rusty took his pay and headed for Arizona. He landed up at Pierce, twenty-five miles south of Wilcox. Pierce was a mining town mostly, but boys from the cow outfits used to drift in for a little hellery.

There was a Mexican wanting to sell a big, tall bay horse. Someone said, "That horse is mean. Bet you no one wants to ride him."

Someone else said, "I'll put *my* ten dollars on the horse—anyone covering?"

There was a fellow called Bob Warren stepped up, but Rusty said, "Here's my ten, I'll take him on."

Bob said, "Why, kid, that horse'll plumb murder you!" Rusty didn't like the "kid" stuff.

Bob took on the horse and got thrown. Rusty stepped up again and waved his ten spot. A big fellow there—a rancher—said, "Look, kid, I won't bet for or agin you, but if you ride that horse I'll just *give* you a ten!"

Rusty rode the horse to a standstill. The big man paid. He said, "Well, I didn't bet for you this time, but I'll bet a million on you from now on."

Rusty said to Bob, "Well, are you satisfied to drop that 'kid' stuff? I been doing a man's work long enough now." That was the last time anyone called him "kid."

This Bob Warren had a little spread out in the Mesquite, and also a wife. He said, "Rusty, I can't pay you much wages, but I got a few steers to gather up, and a few horses to gentle down, so you're welcome to beans and coffee till you gets you a job." So Rusty stayed till the fall cattle work. They gathered a few steers and worked out a few ponies, drifted around generally, and raised some hell. Bob was quite a guy, but his wife understood him and asked no questions when the two of them sometimes failed to get back at night. Sometimes they'd spend a night in Pierce without going to bed, but as long as they drifted in with three or four steers, their beans were ready for them on the table and no questions asked.

It was pretty smooth country, and they'd break some of the ponies for buggy teams. One day they had a team of ponies on the gallop. Rusty said, "Say, Bob, I wonder if one of them ponies can outrun t'other'un?"

Bob said, "We'll see!" and laid on the rawhide.

Rusty tells, "That little ole four-wheel outfit did pretty good back to the ranch, but them ponies was neck and neck all the way!"

That fall, Rusty got a job with the Alair outfit—the X Y X—in a roundup that took in the country from Wilcox to Douglas. But this outfit had too many gentle horses to suit Rusty, so he took on with an outfit north of the tracks—the K H—but didn't like that country and dropped back to the Turkey Creek (Smith's) ranch in the Chiricahua Mountains for the calf roundup that next spring.

In the summer he rode the Mesquite, doping calves for screwworms. After working out the fall beef, he was set to riding the mountains to pick up the strays and get them down to the desert before the big snows. Rusty says this is the work he liked best. It was cool up there in the timber and as exciting as hunting big game. The slicks up there were really wild. He had some narrow escapes, such as when he roped a cow and she went one side of a pine and his horse the other. They met face to face. His horse was pulled down, and the old cow's horns were about a foot from him, she with her tongue out straining to get at him. Rusty pulled his gun and shot her between the eyes. He paid for her, too.

Rusty says, "There was real satisfaction in working that scary stuff down to the winter range." Some of them he'd have to rope and tie down. Then he'd come next day with a trained ranch ox to which he'd neck the cow. The old ox would head for the home corral and drag the cow with him.

In the spring of 1907 Rusty entered a riding and roping contest at Douglas. One of the boys there had a letter from the Miller Brothers' 101 Ranch asking him to pick up some good riders for their show (a traveling Wild West show and rodeo)—and they had to be good bronco busters and good ropers as well. Rusty stated his terms—free transportation to Chicago (where the show was) and guaranteed return, plus so much a day. Millers wired back the O.K.

A forty-dollar cow

2

His first day's ride was at the Chicago Colosseum. The horses were real bad, and of course they had no chutes. His first horse pitched clear across the ring and hit the fence, falling on Rusty's leg. Rusty pulled his saddle cinch and broke clear. He tried to get the horse up, but couldn't. Another cowboy started working on the horse, but Rusty said, "That's no use—his neck's broke." Two more cowboys rode up, put their ropes on the horse real quick, and dragged him back into the alley. The outfit had a wagon there for just such emergencies. They loaded up the dead horse and drove off pronto.

While Rusty was saddling his next horse—right in the ring, of course—he saw three fellows talking to Miller. One of them said, "Was that horse hurt real bad?"

Miller said, "Hell, no. That's part of the act."

Rusty had his mouth open to say the horse was dead, when another cowboy wheeled him around and put his hand over his mouth. "Shut up!" he said. "Them's the Humane Society. Don't say a word."

"Well," Rusty says, "I'd never even heard of them Humanes. This was my first lesson. I saw right then why they snaked that bronc out so quick, and what the wagon was for. By gosh! Old Joe (Miller) never overlooked anything!"

Next year Rusty followed the Colonel Fred Cummings Show to England. That lasted a season. The British thoroughly enjoyed these shows and many young men went west as a result. Rusty and his pals all enjoyed themselves. Rusty said he had a fine time and plenty of drinks!

Rusty's next run-in with the Humane Society was at Cincinnati while riding for the Harry Hill Show which was playing the Eastern circuit. The Humanes, Rusty says, were as thick as thieves, and "as snoopy as them ole desert Salamander rats." Rusty was riding a big old black called Powder Keg. In his own words, "I'd raked him a bit a couple of days before, but he'd scabbed over. This night I had on my white angora chaps. I'd kicked outta the stirrups and was raking him pretty high, so I knocked them ole scabs off and he bled a trickle. Soon as I took him back to the hoss tent I seen a coupla them Humanes. They got to asking which boy rode the black. I shucked off them chaps and kicked them into a corner, and lit me a cigarette all innocent.

"A little later they came back again and got talking with the boss. They said, 'You might as well tell us who rode the black, otherwise we'll stop the whole show!' So Harry beckons me, and we both go with the Humanes to a court. When they'd finished their say, the old judge says, 'From what I can tell, you boys got a pretty good show. I ain't going to say nothing till I see for myself.'"

Well, there was a big plate-glass window in the court, looking right out on the street. Rusty spotted a big dray, pulled by one horse. That animal was just naturally a big one, but worn down to hide and skeleton. Again in Rusty's words, "Only fat on him was his legs all swelled up, and him puffing like he was wore out. I beckoned the Humanes. 'Take a look at that,' I says. 'If you fellas would clean up your own backyard you wouldn't have time to worry about a spot of blood on that ole, fat, grain-fed outlaw who's a-doing what he *wants* to do.'

"Well, the upshot was we was turned loose and caught up again when the show was ready to pull out. The old judge says, 'I'm a-turning you boys loose. Went to the show last night and didn't see nothing wrong—only had me a good time. That ole black hoss ain't hurt as bad as when I nick myself a-shaving.' The Humanes was okay. Said it was the first time they'd been beat in a case, is all."

3

In 1913 Rusty met an Indiana girl, Maybelle Dunsker, a cowgirl riding with the show. In her act she was the only girl on the range, and all the cowboys were in love with her. She just naturally liked them all, and couldn't decide which to marry. So it was arranged that she would ride out, and whoever caught up with her and took her off the saddle would be the one she'd take—sealing the bargain with a kiss. A fellow called Fred Cox (who was married, anyway) usually filled the role of lucky man.

Then one night after the show someone shouted that some drunks were molesting the show girls. Fred took the lead: "Come on, we'll scatter them!"

When Fred got on the scene one big drunk sneered at him, "You must be from Texas."

Fred said, "You're Godamn right!" and knocked him cold. But he busted his fist badly, and it swelled up twice normal size.

Fred said, "Gosh, who's going to take Maybelle off tomorrow night?"

Rusty said he'd take on the job. Fred doubted it, but Rusty said, "Hell, Fred, I can throw that little ole gal over the top of my head."

"Well," Rusty tells it now, "I was pretty shy."

He lit another cigarette, and looked long and hard at the purpling Sierra to the east.

"But that was on account I'd been on the range all my life and hadn't never kissed anyone, unless maybe my mother—but I wouldn't remember. And being shy, like I said, I would grab Maybelle off her pony onto my knee; but when it came to sealing the bargain I'd take my hat off at the full gallop and just pretend to kiss her behind it."

Rusty was still looking at the Sierra.

"Well, this day I lost my hat before I picked her up. I kept a-making signs for one of the boys to throw me a hat, but they just grinned, so I picked her up the way I was. When she left her horse she always threw her left arm around my neck, and with my right arm around her waist it was no more than lifting a feather. This time I didn't know what to do, but she just pulled my head down with a laugh and gave me a good smacker. After that someone would always lift my hat as I galloped by; so after a while I'd have been disappointed if they hadn't of.

"The show closed, but I had another contract."

That contract was to ride at the 1913 Stampede at Winnipeg. The main boss of that show seemed to be Ad Day of Culgary. Seems he was a big rancher as well as a show promoter. Rusty rode himself into the finals on the saddle-bronc string. However, he had bad luck and got smashed up in the wild-horse race just before the final bronc ride. This put him out of the running, and Emery La Grande took the championship. When the boys got their prize money, Rusty found he was overpaid fifty dollars. Ad Day said, "Well, Rusty, got enough?"

Rusty said, "Seems to me it's a little more than I got coming."

"That's all right, Rusty," said Ad, "some of you boys come a long ways, and it costs money to get back. You had a bit of bad luck, so we just eased up on you a bit."

Rusty added, "That's the kind of fella Ad was."

Day, a nephew of the Uncle Tony Day who'd lost out in the 1906–07 winter, on his Alberta ranch wanted Rusty to stay in Canada and break horses for him, but Rusty couldn't get Maybelle out of his mind. She was in Carolina with a new show.

Rusty headed back, he says, hardly taking time to eat. "There was Maybelle all right. I didn't want to lose Maybelle, so we got married right there in Camden, Carolina. We stayed with the new show till 1915. That fall we jumped up north and joined the Hill Show again in Ohio.

"After one season our boy was born. He wasn't doing so well on Nestlé's milk, and I didn't think the show business was the right place to bring up a family, so we came back to New Mexico. We had us a little place in the valley and some cows. Later on I bought this setup. There's some good irrigated fields, where we grow some cotton and forage crops with the help of my son across the way. I don't work no more. I've wound up with twelve grandchildren and six or eight great-grands. They all think a heap of their ole Granpa."

Rusty hitched his chair, and started to roll another cigarette. "Them cowgirls was kinda tough, some of them, but not my Maybelle. She was always a little lady, and I really took on when I lost her.

"I remember in one show—I think it was Wyoming Bill's Wild West outfit—there was a cowgirl name of Lulu Parr used to ride a bronco twice a day. This hoss was called Apache. Lulu she always had her hair in rats. After a while her hair would go to poppin', and there'd be rats scattered all over the place.

"Finally Lulu found two shows a day was too hard. So the boss says, 'Rusty, you're pretty small and slim; I guess you're it.'"

They put a big blonde wig on Rusty and a fringed divided skirt. The boss told Rusty to ride a real tough one. One day Rusty had been on a toot and was feeling pretty good. He got all dolled up in Lulu's outfit, and they saddled a horse called Johnny-on-the-Spot.

Usually the girls' horses were saddled up right near the grandstand, but for Rusty they kept back a bit for fear someone might spot the hoax.

Rusty tells it, "Feeling good as I was, I figgered to give the audience something to take home. When Johnny made his first buck I pulled my six-shooter and fired a two-three shots right between his ears. That ole nag just scooped himself 'way back and I went right over his ears like it was the act, and got the best hand I ever had. But Lulu was kinda mad. She says, 'Rusty, how come *you* always ride them, and then get bucked off a-riding for me?'

"'Little gal,' I said, 'you put up a real good ride that time, long as you *were* on top.'"

CHAPTER TWENTY-THREE

Rusty and Maybelle

1

Not many American wagon bosses have had the doubtful privilege of ramrodding an outfit in Old Mexico, but on my visit to Rusty Tulk in Deming, New Mexico, I had the pleasure of meeting such a character.

His name is Charlie Beall, ex-cowboy, ex-Texas Ranger, ex-Border Crossing Officer at Columbus, New Mexico; now retired and living at the Baker Hotel in Deming. However, the hotel does not see much of Charlie, because he spends most of his time with his old friend Rusty on the latter's *rancho* in the shadow of the Las Floridas peaks.

At eighteen, having knocked around the West Texas cow country where he was born, Charlie headed for the river country of south Texas. Here a horse fell on him, breaking his hip. The boys had to go on roundup, and Charlie says, "I just naturally bedded down in an ole shed till my hip healed. There was a nigger boy at the ranch who was mighty good to me. He kept me fed and watered for six weeks, and where he raised the grub from I just don't know. I had about four dollars is all, and soon as I could ride I saddled up to go get a job; so I gave the four bucks to this boy. The kid said, 'Mister Charlie, I didn't figure on money.' 'That's all right, *amigo*,' I said. Never saw him again, on account I got me a job with an outfit at Van Horn.

"That was a stag outfit, and kind of rough—but I liked it, and by time I was twenty-two I got to be wagon boss. The company had made a deal with the Mex Government to run a big bunch of cattle on the other side of the Rio Grande, on the side-oat desert between the river and Moctezuma in Chihuahua.

"Quite a lot of our cattle had drifted across there, and the Mex Government didn't like it—us going across with a white crew and all. So somehow an arrangement was made to pay twelve *pesos* ($1.00 U. S.) a head for the grazing, and we could let the stuff run. We'd naturally need to have a roundup each year, and the Dons said that on their side we could have an American boss, but we'd have to hire Mexican help.

"Well, I'd been across some, and spoke pretty good Mex, so the boss says, 'Charlie, you get on well with those *vaqueros*. Go to Moctezuma and hire yourself a crew and have them report here at such-and-such a date. I want you to ramrod a wagon on the other side. You can run her all summer and bring back whatever of a beef-cut you can find up to El Paso in the fall. Then you pay off the men till next year. I'll meet you at El Paso. In the meantime, run in about a hundred or a hundred and fifty head of horses from the North Tank, and some of the boys can help you fit 'em up to have ready. I'll see to freighting in stores from Van Horn.'"

So Charlie got his men lined up—fourteen top *vaqueros*, most from the Sierra Madres, but some that were raised on that desert, plus a *cocinero* who had run an eating place in Chihuahua.

They had plenty of Mexican beans and chiles, and the cook made *tortillas* every evening. When they wanted meat, Charlie would send out a couple of *vaqueros,* and they'd shoot a beast and there'd be a good feed all around.

Charlie ran the wagon for four years.

"The first years were good," Charlie said. "We had good weather and usually found water enough, although sometimes we had a dry drive. There wasn't so much chaparral in them days and the work wasn't hard. We branded a lot of calves and always came back with some beef. I said to myself—this is a good country."

But it was not to last.

About 1914 Pancho Villa, the revolutionary, began to be pretty active along the border, especially from El Paso west. He raided some stock ranches so hard they folded up. Now, Charlie got on really well with the Mexican help, but from time to time some of Villa's men would come riding along, and these fellows began to stir up trouble. Charlie had instructed his *cocinero* to kill a beef and put on a big spread any time the *bandidos* paid the camp a visit. This way he figured he'd save having cattle run off. He knew other outfits were robbed unmercifully, and his policy was to feed everybody, say nothing, keep out of politics, and do a good job for the company.

However, things got bad and then worse. In 1916 some of his top hands joined Villa's men, and he was running shorthanded. Soon a bunch of Villa's men raided over into Texas and stole a bunch of horses.

Charlie ran into this bunch grazing between the Rio Grande and Moctezuma. They were all hobbled and looked tired and hungry. By the tracks, Charlie reckoned that the bandits had gone into town for a spree. He recognized the Texas brands, so he cut the hobbles and headed the horses for the river. He chased them five or six miles and they were running fast, so he pulled up and jogged back to camp.

After a couple of *tortillas* and some coffee, he saddled a fresh horse and loped up to give the nags another boost; but before he caught up with them he ran into half-a-dozen of Villa's men. They were armed to the teeth, and there was nothing he could do but talk mighty polite.

They surrounded him, and while a couple galloped off to bring the horses back, the others took Charlie's six-shooter, told him to dismount, and then began to make camp and get some coffee going.

"Well," Charlie said, "they brought them nags back at the high lope, and then I noticed a horse I hadn't seen with them before. It belonged to a *vaquero* by name of Diego. This Diego was a top hand, but against my arguing he'd taken off to join Villa's men two or three weeks before. I reckoned quick that this hoss had got away from Diego and somehow got with this bunch of nags. I didn't say anything then, but pretty soon these fellows began to argue about what they'd do with me. Seems like the general opinion was that dead men tell no tales, and they got to discussing which one would have to shoot me.

"So I thought fast, and then I talked fast. I said, '*Amigos*, did I ever fail to feed you boys when you hit my camp? You all know Diego, and I know (I didn't, though) that Villa thinks the world of him. You know he's a good man and *muy caballero*—and a real good friend of mine. Well, that's his hoss right there. That hoss of Diego's got mixed up with those *estrangeros* and I was going to rope him out. I know Diego will be coming to look for him; but now, I'm warning you, if anything happens to me you'll have to answer to Diego. That's all. Just think it over.'"

The upshot was that the bandits finally gave Charlie back his six-shooter and turned him loose.

Finally, the last year, things got so bad that Charlie told the company, "I can't work cattle and fight bandits both." So he quit.

The next wagon boss didn't last long. He got too free with the rope and took to branding Mex stock. One by one he lost his crew, and the boss finally decided to pull the wagon out of Old Mexico. The company then got Charlie, who knew the *vaqueros* and was liked by them, to get some Mexicans, and gather what was left of the stock and deliver them at the Rio Grande at so much per head. That finally cleared up the deal.

2

After that Charlie joined on with the Texas Rangers for eighteen months. All this time Charlie had been supporting his widowed mother in San Antonio, sending along money every month (or as often as he could) by any freight outfits pulling north.

At San Lazario he got in a running gun fight with a bootlegger who had a 'dobe house on the Texas side of the river. This fellow dodged for the house. Charlie shot and missed. The bootlegger got to the house door, and his wife (like the pioneer wives you see in the movies) handed him a 30-30. He shot at Charlie and broke his left arm below the elbow. Charlie went down. He figured he was a good man with a six-gun, and he kept shooting, but couldn't hit his man. Anyway, Charlie ran him off below the border.

This was about 1926. As Charlie said, "I could have shot this rascal in the back as he went to the 'dobe, but I wanted my man alive. That cost me my left arm." (It subsequently got gangrenous and had to be amputated.)

The man was picked up in 1943, but had to be turned loose, because the courts could not prove U. S. citizenship, although everybody knew he was born north of the river.

For many years after that Charlie was Customs Officer on the Border at Columbus, New Mexico. He and Rusty showed us the bullet holes in the buildings from the Villa raid of 1916. Charlie said, "I was here for the cleanup. We used mules to dig a big grave for all the Mexican boys. I remember one *muchacho*—about sixteen he was—lying dead under his dead hoss. That boy had three new suits of clothes on him, and three more tied behind the saddle. He had all the pockets stuffed full of cigars. They sure had raided those stores, and my guess is this boy was going to have him some good smoking in Old Mex—only he never got there. Villa had come north by Casas Grandes while Pershing was heading south from El Paso to catch him at Chihuahua, and the old *bandido* sure caught the troops at Deming napping!"

Rusty and Charlie and I paid a visit to Las Palómas just below the border, and made the rounds of the *cantinas*. There was plenty of good music, as there was a bunch of *mariachis* at every joint. There are only about twenty homes in Las Palómas, and twelve of these are saloons. Everybody in New Mexico and Chihuahua knows Tilly's Place, so we went to see her. She runs a souvenir store, and she'll sell you anything from a Siamese elephant to a bottle of *tequila*.

It was good to see Americanos and Mejicanos all being happy together. Charlie, especially, seemed to be everyone's friend, and his quick changes from Spanish to English were astonishing.

Villa—self-styled General Francisco Villa—*Commandante del Division del Norte*—was finally ambushed a few years later and shot in his own car.

We called at the Villa home in Chihuahua and met Señora Villa—the bandit's widow—who showed us the car, which stands rusting in the front yard as a sort of show piece. It is as full of holes as a colander.

According to the Señora, Pancho's great weakness was women, in which connection he was *"muy malo hombre."* She even showed us a lot of old photos of these girl friends, but added, "I was not jealous—I was his legal wife and could afford to ignore the others."

From other Mexican friends we heard of some of his atrocities, and saw the rows of cottonwoods on which, as one said, "Corpses used to hang like meat in a butcher shop."

Our landlady's father had been a postal employee. When Villa captured the Post Office in Chihuahua he ordered all the *Federalistas* shot. Our landlady's father was out of the building, and as the bandits whooped through the streets, some friends stuffed him into an empty wine barrel and sat on it, which saved his life.

"*Dios Mia,*" said our landlady, "*that one* was *diablo-lobo.* Only by the Grace of God did my poor *Padrecito* escape!"

We heard of much worse than that. Enough to realize how many parts go to make up a man like Charlie Beall—big enough to help keep the peace of the Border, and big enough to let bygones be bygones now that all is quiet and friendly.

English and Spanish are the common languages of the Southwest; Canada might learn something from the border country, where two languages are used without embarrassment, legal safeguards, or coercion.

And so, within the year we said, *adios,* and came back to Canada.

EPILOGUE

1

Thinking and smoking in the twilight, I look out across the prairie and my mind goes again to all the great changes wrought by a technocratic society.

I think of old Tom Whitney of the Circle Diamond who said one day, "You know, we hadn't ought to use a grub wagon on roundup like we do. We oughter pack our stuff on pack horses. That way we could spread out when we move camp and leave no tracks."

Somebody said, "Why?"

Tom replied, " 'Cos you know dang well any granger who sees a wagon track is just natcherly bound to foller it, and then first time he strikes a nice place with a spring, he'll file a homestead on it. Them pack rats are nosy as hell, and they'll beat us out yet."

And I thought of a much later man, George Ross of the Lost Creek Ranch, the third of that name to ramrod that spread, who'd said at a meeting of the Western Stock Growers, "Boys! Any time you do just opposite to what the government men say, you'll have a chance to win." But he died in 1971, a young man at forty eight.

Only one man I knew was more grass-wise than George, and that was the late Rube Gilchrist of Maple Creek who never abused a range or hurt nature's delicate balance. There was even one government guy who could see farther than most, though his own Department of Agriculture paid him little heed, and that was the late Archie Budd of Swift Current Experimental Station. It was he who once said, "There is no substitute for native range. Only on natural and unspoilt prairie is there a succession of growth to fit every season of the year."

But the boys with the bulldozers thought otherwise, and the ranchers were pressured to help keep industry booming by breaking up range land and seeding to foreign grasses, as if they knew better than the One who created our great natural grassland from Red River to the mountains—grasslands that once supported bison in their millions. Man can never put it back as it was.

The dwindling ranges of the West still support a lot of cattle, it's true, but who can say what changes are to come? Oil, coal, potash, and other uneatables are considered more important today than food.

The range today is fenced and cross-fenced. The roundup wagon works only such places as the Cypress Hills, and cowboys are few and far between. I mean real working cowboys. There are certainly many good ropers and bronc-riders, but that is because today those activities have been commercialized into "sport," and outside the rodeo "season" many of these boys are working for industry on assembly lines.

Rides are not long today. On the largest spreads cattle are located by plane, and as often as not cowboys and their horses are taken by truck to where the work is. Only in isolated mountain areas and in a few parts of the foothills' country is a horse a real necessity, as it used to be. Four-wheel drives may cut up the land and lead to erosion, but they work fast—and today everybody has to speed up to rope that dollar before somebody else does.

2

The passing of the horse as a working partner has certainly changed the Canadian and American rural culture for the worse.

The motor car has proved itself not only a source of pollution, but a deadly enemy to isolation, and therefore to wild life. In just the same way, the tractor has altered for the worse not only the uses to which land has been put, but the way of life for farmers themselves, with no compensatory rise in production per acre. The only rise has been in production per *man;* and thus the tractor has encouraged larger and larger farms, which may prove as fatal to our rural economy as were the *latifundia* to the Roman state.

The first farmer to buy a stink-wagon unfortunately set a pattern that was followed by thousands, until at last every farmer was forced out of horses on the doubtful but highly advertized precept of: "Less work and a higher (!) standard of living"; as well as by the fact that the industrialists no longer made horse machinery.

Actually, the farmer found that he worked *longer* hours; for while ten hours a day was enough for horses, he found that machinery didn't need a rest and "ate on the run," so to speak, and so he could operate 'round the clock.

There is also a great deal of wasted land because the big machinery cannot work in small, confined areas. This brings about the bulldozing of bluffs and the filling of sloughs, a real death blow to wild life.

There is waste of power because a tractor is often used for a task that one horse would do, for who would hitch up four horses to haul a barrel of water to the garden? And when a tractor breaks down, the whole unit is immobilized, yet it would be an unheard of thing for two, four, or six horses to be all put out of action at once.

It is really bad that the farmer has lost that intimate contact with the soil so well understood in the old saw: "The farmer's foot is the best manure."

Few tractor operators care to stop their machines to leave the seat, as a teamster so often has to do; for he has to rest his horses and go to their heads to lift collars from sweaty necks, make adjustments to harness, or alter the draft to suit a particular horse; or perhaps to scrape his moldboard if his plow is not "cleaning," or to see that his seed drill has not a plugged spout. Also there may be a root or stone to move, and none of this is "wasted" time, for he may take up a handful of soil to find out what seeds are germinating, what "heart" the soil is in, and does it need manure or lime or special tillage; and while doing all this he can stretch his limbs, breathe pure air, and listen to a meadowlark before he remounts the implement seat.

This is part of that "tending of the garden" which Adam was set to do—a very different thing to traveling back and forth in a cloud of dust while the tractor radio pours out the latest rubbish cooked up by people with nothing better to do.

3

The farmer's health has undoubtedly suffered in several ways from mechanization. Many have become hard of hearing from the noise to which they are subjected to hour after hour; many suffer from headaches and nervous ills from the combination of a sedentary posture, unceasing noise, and noxious fumes.

The horseman learned a lot from his beasts. He learned the virtue of patience, he learned that violence (as distinct from discipline) got him nowhere. And he learned to study and adjust himself to the differing temperaments of individual horses. He acquired a tolerance of different ways, and so knew when to coax and when to drive; all of which stood him in good stead when dealing with his fellow man.

Forking hay to the calves

It was by no accident that even after horses became outdated for patrol work, the Royal Canadian Mounted Police still took training in equitation; or that Air Force trainees during Hitler's war had to undergo a certain amount of the same to learn co-ordination, initiative and self-control.

Women, too, are missing something, for they have a natural affinity for animals. Perhaps it is a manifestation of the maternal instinct that brings out their love and understanding of all weaker things. Be that as it may, it was often the farmer's wife that could walk up to and catch the horse that evaded her husband's best efforts, or who could milk a cranky cow or set a flighty hen.

As to the children, they learned responsibility early in the horse days, for at the end of a ride they could not abandon a pony as they now abandon a tricycle or a Skidoo.

In riding or driving to school they learned far more than by sitting in a bus. They learned initiative, they learned to take care of each other, they learned the secrets of nature. And when Dobbin brought them safely home in, perhaps, a blizzard, they had to unharness him, feed him, and bed him down before they themselves had supper.

Above all, the children had contact with, and knew as a friend, a living thing, a fellow being who breathed and ate and rested as they did. In short, the countryman has traded a good way of living for a very doubtful "standard of living." As a result, the rural vote is now of little consequence, and the whole structure of society has become weakened. From now on the thinning ranks of rural dwellers will find themselves powerless to stand up to the pressures of industry.

4

But the very worst feature of all in the passing of the horse—in the long view—is the matter of pollution.

There is no doubt that from oil exploration right through the processes of seismographing, surveying, drilling, transporting (by land or sea), refining, to its final use as a source of power, it is oil that is the greatest curse. Oil that has done far more harm in the world than good. Oil that has *not* increased food production. Oil that has taken thousands off the land to be its servants.

For its sake, the farmer gave up his freedom, spread pollution on his precious land, lost the manure which would give life to his soil, and put himself at the mercy of the machine companies, because power he must have; and he no longer raises his own.

He has a constant struggle to keep up with the new styles, for obsolescence of what he has is a foregone thing. This is what has turned the farm into the firm, this is what has made a mere rat race of man's oldest and most satisfying activity.

And he *must* have cash, and more cash, for he must pay for fuel for his monster. Only a horse can find his feed in the sloughs or in the bluffs.

One wonders how many would recognize a form of power advertised as "of low initial cost, self-feeding, unrustable, unfreezable, with no batteries, no need for spare parts, self-perpetuating, can be operated in units from one to six or more, each unit operating independently if required. Guaranteed for a minimum of twelve working years with proper care, guaranteed not to change models for indefinite time. Will not get stuck in mud or snow unless overloaded. Will pass through water up to four feet when in use. All waste automatically turned into most up-to-date fertilizer at no extra cost. Worn out units make excellent pig and poultry food."

And that is old Dobbin, folks!

Old Dobbin who can pull a load or be ridden. Old Dobbin who can be put to use at any time, alone or with any number of his kind. Old Dobbin who can find his own way home, or if a vehicle breaks down can be ridden home. Old Dobbin who needs no service station or repair shop or insurance, Old Dobbin who can make little Dobbins to replace him. Old Dobbin who causes no air, water, or land pollution.

5

Today the last laugh is with Bill Greathouse, for after thousands of lively, big-hearted animals have been rounded up and sold to the canneries to make more land available to pay for tractors, to tear up more land and grow more wheat to pay for newer tractors and machinery . . . now, quite suddenly, people want horses.

Not country people. *They* are still ashamed of unprogressive Dobbin, the "hay burner"; but city professional people, status-conscious people want horses. The same people who buy the old wooden beds, and the wash basins and oil lamps that the country people sell at auction because they don't look nice in farm houses heated by natural gas.

So the trudging servants of the farmers, the trusty partners of the cowboy, are bringing good prices, and Bill Greathouse would be well-fixed today! Even if these animals are only used as "hobby horses"; just as useful border collies and other sheep dogs have become "pets," and dang useless and frustrated ones, too.

Men who could afford it began some years ago to concentrate on the newer "breeds" of horses (which are more colors than breeds). Anything spotted became an apaloosie, anything of pale color with a silver mane became a palomino, anything square-rumped and stoutly built became a quarter horse.

And most of them, even at that, are too good for the work they do. And many must bear the indignity of a pancake saddle and the incongruity (for the West) of a young rider with the jockey cap and jodhpurs and short stirrups of the Pony Clubs.

But it is still good. Good that the bridles jingle once more, that saddle leather creaks again under the weight of the children and grand-children of those who betrayed the useful beast that had served man well since long before history was recorded.

It is good that on the trail rides in our mountain parks you can again hear talk of saddle trees and cinchas, hackamores and hocks, and that fifteen-inch tapederos swing above the oiled tourist trail, where once the wild bunch coughed in the dust.

Today, we old men of an almost forgotten life still thrill in thought to those wild rides, when we threw our hearts ahead into the dust of galloping hooves, forcing those wild ones by our will and the strength of our mounts to turn this way or that; and so with an even fiercer will we thundered down the hillside, splashed through the ford and up into the corral.

Fear we knew not, for we rode in a sort of exultation, little heeding the sharp snags, the crumbling banks, the tide of dark water, or the badger holes that pockmarked the ridges. Little heeding the check, the crouch of muscled haunches, the dizzy leap that followed.

Because our eyes were with our hearts, watching that foxy, long-maned gray or that striped buckskin.

When we raised a gloved hand to brush away the tears forced from our eyes by the mad pace, that glove brought the pungent smell of horse to our nostrils, the smell of sweat and hay.

The days draw in for us. What matter? We have seen and felt the best the West could offer, and I feel sure that when all things are made new, there will be horses for our delight in the New Jerusalem; for is it not written that into that city shall enter no evil thing?

And was there ever evil in a horse?

The horse trough

GLOSSARY

GLOSSARY OF WESTERN TERMS ETC.
USED IN THIS BOOK

Abo. Australian aborigine. Many are stock riders on cattle stations.

Antelope. Pronghorn. A prairie ruminant. Not a true antelope.

Anzac. Member of the Australian-New Zealand Army Corps, 1914-18.

Battle Creek. A creek cutting through Cypress Hills. Not Battle River at Battleford.

Bench. Not a thing of wood, but a plateau.

Bluff. Not a hill, but a grove of small trees, usually poplar.

"Bottom." Slang for "staying power" (in a horse).

Box elder. Coll. name for Manitoba Maple. Common along creeks. Hence "Maple Creek" and "Box Elder Creek"—two different streams named after the same tree.

Broke. (Of a horse.) Broken in to ride and/or drive.

Bronco. (Sp.) Untamed horse.

Brouse. Small twigs and brush fed on by stock or deer.

Buckboard. A kind of buggy without springs.

Buckbrush. Coll. for various species of small shrubs. Snowberry, shrubby cinquefoil, etc.

Bull Durham. A kind of fine tobacco sold in small bags, favored by cowboys.

"Cavvy." (From Sp.) Herd of loose extra saddle horses on roundup.

Cayuse. An Indian (or native) pony. A mustang (from tribe of Indians).

Chaps. (From Sp.) *Chaparejos.* Leather or fur leggings to protect a rider's legs.

Cheyenne Club. Old-time Cattlemen's Association. Once virtually the Government of Wyoming.

China eyes. Eyes of pale, opaque blue. Seen on horses with a wide blaze, or pintos.

Chinook. A warm wind from the Pacific that enters the plains from the southwest in winter. (From tribe of Indians.)

"Chouse." (to). To chase or drive out an animal from some place.

Cinch. (From Sp.) *Cincha.* A saddle girth.

Cocinero. (From Sp.) A cook.

Corral. (From Sp.) An enclosure (usually of poles) for holding stock.

Coulee. (From Fr.) *Couloire.* A steep-sided gully or water course.

"Cow hospital."   Cowboy slang for dairy farm, where cattle are stabled.

Cricket bit.   A curb bit with small wheel in the *port* to distract a horse.

Cutter.   A small driving sled with narrow upturned runners.

Digger.   Soldier's slang for Australian (1914–18). From the "diggings" (gold mines).

Dogie.   Slang for yearling cattle raised on farms and brought to the range.

Draw.   A shallow valley or winding depression on the prairies.

Draw pin.   A steel (bolt-like) pin fastening the eveners to the drawbar of a wagon or other vehicle. It can be pulled up and out to release the horses and eveners.

Dude.   (Pr. "Dood.") Any greenhorn from the East, especially applied to tourists and hunters. Hence "Dood Ranch," which caters for them.

Fetlock.   The joint of a horse's leg. Just above the hoof.

Fiddle-headed.   Of a horse. A big ungainly head.

Fistula.   A running sore, such as a saddle sore, on a horse's withers which does not drain properly.

Five Roses.   A well-known brand of flour sold in hundred-pound bags of white or colored cotton.

Freeze-up.   Late fall. When the ground first freezes for winter.

Ganadero.   (From Sp.) A cattleman.

"Gimp."   Cowboy slang for lots of fire and action (in a horse).

Granger.   Member of an association of farmers (U. S.). See nester and homesteader.

Greasewood.   A semi-evergreen, somewhat prickly and oily shrub. Grows on alkali land.

Hackamore.   (From Sp.) *Jaquima.* A kind of light halter with braided nose band.

Haver.   Havre, a cow town in Montana, on the Milk River.

Hay burner.   Farmer slang for a horse.

High lope.   A fast canter—almost a gallop.

High tail.   A slang verb to indicate making off in a hurry. Fleeing.

Hollow-gut.   An imaginary disease of cattle. A tactful way of saying starvation.

Homesteader.   A settler who came West to take free land for farming (see nester).

Honda.   (Sp.) Often called Hondoo. A leather or metal ring in a lariat to make a loop.

Keewadin.   (Cree) The north-west wind that brings winter to the prairies.

Kincaid Act.   An act passed by Theodore Roosevelt (U. S.) to enlarge the size of homesteads.

Lariat. (Sp. Reata.) A throwing rope or lasso, for catching horses and cattle.

Latigo. (Sp.) Leather thong to lace to cinch (on a saddle).

Lobo. (Sp.) A timber (or buffalo) wolf. Sometimes loper or loafer.

Loco. (Sp.) Mad or crazy. Range horses become so from eating locoweed.

Made it. A person has accomplished his task or desire.

Make a dally. (Sp. from *da la vuelta*) give a turn of a rope around the saddle horn.

Makin's. Tobacco and papers—the "makings" of a cigarette.

Matador. (Sp.) Bullfighter. Or, the Matador Cattle Co. of Texas and Saskatchewan. (Up to 1924.)

Maverick. An unbranded animal, named for Colonel Maverick, old-time Texan.

"Medicine Line." Slang for Canada-U. S. boundary line.

"Mossy horn." Slang for aging steer with horns scabby and rough at base.

"Nester." Slang for homesteader. In U. S., "Granger" has the same meaning.

Neverslips. Horse shoes made in different sizes for cold shoeing. Equipped with screw-in calks.

Nez Percé. (Fr.) Indian tribe from Idaho. Chased onto the plains by General Miles (U. S. Army) 1877. In the West the Z is pronounced and there is no final accent.

Night-hawk. The wrangler who herds the cavvy by night.

Old stager. Steady, reliable old horse. Applied originally to stage horse.

Outfit. Slang for many things. Equipment, a ranch, a vehicle, a camp, a "setup."

"Pancake" saddle. Cowboy slang for European flat-seated saddle.

P.F.R.A. Prairie Farm Rehabilitation Act. Set up in drought years.

Pin bone. A horse's hip bone.

"Pine Tree" brand. Brand of the late Vern Maclean, thus:

Pinto. (Sp.) A skewbald or piebald horse of two solid colors. (Sp. "painted.")

"Prairie wool." Upland hay that clings together like wool. Mostly rough fescue.

"Queen Victoria's Wyoming." The present state of Wyoming, so-called in early days due to the presence of many British ranchers in the 1880s.

Quirt. (From Sp.) A type of braided, flexible, leather riding whip.

Ramrod. Slang for foreman or overseer.

"Rep." A cowboy representing a brand at a roundup. Hence "repping."

"Rig." Almost any kind of vehicle, machine, or equipment.

Road allowance. Strips of land running north and south or east and west, surveyed for roads.

Romel. (Sp.) Sort of quirt made by braiding end of reins together.

Russian thistle.   Not a true thistle. A prickly, fleshy weed thriving on dry land. Accidentally imported to Canada by Russian settlers.

Rustle.   To help oneself. Hence, cattle stealing, or cattle finding their own feed in winter.

Saddle horn.   The high pummel on a cowboy's saddle to which he dallys or ties his lariat when catching an animal.

Salt sage.   A type of sage brush.

Sawhorse.   Pack saddle that looks like one.

"Scary."   Frightening, spooky. Of a situation or thing.

School Section.   Sections 11 and 29 (640 acres each) in each township in the Torren's Survey. Set aside for sale with proceeds for education.

Sidewinder.   A rattlesnake.

Skiff.   Not a boat, but a light fall of snow.

"Slick."   Or "slickskin." An unbranded horse or cow. See maverick.

Slough.   Not a bog. A grassy prairie pond. When they dry, hay smelling of mint can be cut.

"Spooky."   Frightening. See "scary" with a touch of something supernatural, not understood.

Stone ram.   Stone sheep are a form of Rocky Mountain Bighorn. Found in North East British Columbia.

"String."   The horses a cowboy rides. Three to six to a rider. Hence, "one of his string."

Sulky.   Not a mood, but a two-wheeled cart. A plow with seat, called a sulky plow.

Tackerberry.   A buckle. Device to join latigo and cinch (on saddle). Easily disengaged.

Tapaderos.   (Sp.) Stirrup covers of heavy leather to protect cowboy's feet in brush.

Tie fast.   To tie a lariat fast to saddle horn, instead of dallying, where the rope is passed around the horn with the end held by hand.

Trail.   Not a made road. A "track" or "pad" made by the passing of wagons (two ruts) or by pack horses or game (one rut).

Troto Sereno.   (Sp.) Jog trot.

Turkey.   Cowboy slang for bag of extra clothes, tobacco, etc., with his blankets. Hence, to "pack one's turkey" is to tie this behind the saddle or on a lead horse, ready for departure.

Wagon.   Four-wheeled springless vehicle drawn by two or four horses. Used for freighting, etc. When used to carry supplies for roundup usually called "chuck," or "grub" wagon; or just "the wagon."

Wagon boss.   The "captain" or foreman of a roundup crew.

Walleyed. See *China eye.* Off-colored eye on a horse.

"Wash." A gully on the prairie caused by water erosion. Usually dry except after heavy rain; hence, "dry wash."

Whang leather. Oil tanned rawhide or "latigo leather." Used for variety of purposes and very strong.

Whitemud. A white clay. Sometimes used in pottery. Hence, Whitemud River.

Wrangle. To herd, watch, take care of. Hence, wrangle field means saddle-horse pasture; wrangle horse is horse kept up for herding. Horse wrangler is one who herds the cavvy (g.v.) of horses on a round up. The cowboy who takes care of or guides "doods" (g.v.) is called a dude wrangler.

Night herd